Mechademia : Second Arc

T0338089

Mechademia (ISSN 1934–2489) is published twice a year in the summer and winter by the University of Minnesota Press, 111 Third Avenue South, Suite 290, Minneapolis, MN 55401–2520. http://www.upress.umn.edu

Postmaster: Send address changes to *Mechademia,* University of Minnesota Press, 111 Third Avenue South, Suite 290, Minneapolis, MN 55401–2520.

All submissions must be between 5000–7000 words. Essays that are substantially longer cannot be accepted. Citations should be given in *Chicago Manual of Style* 17th ed. using bibliographic endnotes rather than footnotes or in-text citations. Please see the Mechademia Style Guide (see PDF on mechademia.net) for more details on citation style and essay formatting. Submissions and editorial queries should be sent to submissions@mechademia.net.

Books for review should be addressed to

Forrest Greenwood
Indiana University Innovation Center
2719 E 10th St
Bloomington, IN 47408

Brian White
#101 Etosu O2, 26–14
Edogawa-ku, Shinozaki-machi 4-chome
Tokyo
Japan

Address subscription orders, changes of address, and business correspondence (including requests for permission and advertising orders) to *Mechademia,* University of Minnesota Press, 111 Third Avenue South, Suite 290, Minneapolis, MN 55401–2520.

Subscriptions: For our current subscription rates please see our website: http://www.upress.umn.edu. Digital Subscriptions for *Mechademia* are now available through the Project MUSE Journals Collections at https://muse.jhu.edu.

Mechademia : Second Arc

VOLUME 16, NO. 2
SUMMER 2024

MEDIA INDUSTRIES AND PLATFORMS

....

Transnational Frictions

• • • Introduction

Media Industries and Platforms

BRYAN HIKARI HARTZHEIM

If there is one constant in the anime industry, it is a sense of crisis. In his industrial history of anime, Jonathan Clements documents how the industry careens from one crisis to another in the financing, production, and distribution of anime, concluding: "Responses to various previous crises have created 'anime' as we know it."[1] While the theme of this special *Mechademia* issue is "Media Industries and Platforms," each of the essays here has chosen to focus on the many overlapping industries and platforms of anime. This was not by design, though perhaps reflects a sense of crisis within contemporary anime production in Japan that can be broadly organized along two axes. On the one hand is the industry's race to the bottom in terms of employee working conditions, particularly for younger, early-career animators. In the wake of the Tōei Dōga strikes in the 1960s, it has long been established practice that animators and artists are employed via contracted labor.[2] In-between animators are paid by the drawing—industry averages range from two to four hundred yen—thus necessitating workers produce acceptable work at a constant clip to make a living wage. On the other hand is the industry's propensity for overwork due to poor scheduling and management. Though animators must subsist on poverty-level wages early in their careers, even experienced animation staff find themselves overworked by studios taking on too many projects and sponsors refusing to increase production budgets.

How these companies, studios, and workers respond to these tense labor and management issues will dictate, to paraphrase Clements, how anime is shaped going forward. Already we are seeing one short-term solution to mismanagement and overproduction that is often categorized as a "labor shortage": desperate production coordinators taking to social media to recruit animators.[3] An increasing number who respond to the calls are international art school students who don't necessarily need the income but appreciate the experience and notch on their CVs. This online help can uncover hidden talents (the innovative "webgen" animators) but more often results in additional problems for on-site staff who must correct drawings for being too

1

unpolished or showy. Some companies have incorporated in-between animating software programs like CACANi to plug animation gaps, while others have used generative art programs to create background images for entire short films.[4] Such tactics are indicative of a general trend where studio heads now openly pin their hopes on generative AI to solve production bottlenecks and "make anime with small teams."[5] Companies are so utterly focused on taking on as much work as possible that they are willing to resort to stopgap "solutions" that will decimate the industry's strongest asset: the informal system of mentorship that exists through experienced veterans passing down their accumulated craftsmanship and technical knowledge to passionate but inexperienced novices.

Some of this worker stress and precarity is particular to the anime industry, while some of it is symptomatic of broader issues in the Japanese economy and creative industries. There is a sense that many in the Western media who express their dismay at the depravity of anime worker conditions would be equally shocked at the compensation in Japan (exacerbated by decades of deflation and fluctuating currency exchange rates) of early career game developers, advertising producers, and university faculty. Still, the most exploited of anime's workers are particularly vulnerable even when compared to these other creative fields, resulting in various efforts to improve circumstances on their behalf from crowdfunding animator housing to creating skill certification tests to ensure quality control.[6] Calls to form unions are complicated by a variety of factors, with wage dumping and preying on precarious animators chief among them.[7] The Writer's and Actor's Guilds' successful 2023 negotiations with Hollywood film and tech studios for more favorable compensation and working conditions was not built overnight, but was the product of a long history of collective bargaining, worker solidarity, and a more recent supportive media, political, and public environment toward union efforts. With worker strikes and unions among non-company workers still a rarity in Japan, such clashes will take considerable time that current workers do not have the wherewithal for. The issues have not gone unnoticed by legacy media, which, when not resorting to sensationalism, can occasionally report responsibly through extended news features.[8] A July 2023 segment of the NHK documentary program *100 Cameras* on animation studio MAPPA plays like a subdued episode out of *Shirobako*: a production manager dramatically attempts to track down the drawings from an AWOL animator; a touch-up artist spends nine hours enhancing over 2500 scenes; various animators try in vain to please the demands of the detail-oriented director.

Within this managed chaos, a young key animator confesses to his sempai: "I always think I'm fine. And then, disaster." To which the veteran animation director replies: "That's normal for the first 10 years."

While fans have historically been ignorant to such conditions, heightened awareness has been created in recent years primarily through critical media exposés, white papers from industry associations, and, most importantly, animators taking to social media to vent about their working lives and frustrations. As anime production has exploded, moreover, so has fan media, which also draws attention to the creators themselves. But for every smart blog discussing production issues with subtlety, there are a dozen "influencers" downplaying problems or spreading misinformation. In an age where there are more anime "critics" than ever before, how can scholars of anime (and the cultural industries more broadly) cut through the clutter to provide nuance, lucidity, and insight on industry? With the exception of researchers based in Japan who have conducted ethnographic work on animator working lives, academia might seem to be fairly quiet on these recent labor issues. This is not necessarily evidence of scholars' lack of attention to anime's media industries and platforms; while legacy and social media is focused on the present, academics have worked relentlessly to shed light on what made such conditions possible,[9] how workers make sense of and negotiate such conditions,[10] and how these conditions are characteristic of broader sociopolitical changes in a neoliberal—and potential post-neoliberal—world.[11] As such, the articles in this issue build off of this existing research to illuminate the anime industry's newest crisis by focusing on three key areas: its historical past, production past/present, and transnational present/future. Each of the articles offers original case studies for studying the creation, production, distribution, or adaptation of anime in and outside Japan.

Industrial Histories

The three articles in this first section focus on examining anime's industry through its history. Opening this section is a chapter from Nishimura Tomohiro's groundbreaking revisionist history of Japanese animation. The abridged chapter featured here, translated by Jason Cody Douglass, is from Nishimura's 2018 award-winning book *Nihon no animēshon wa ika ni shite seiritsu shita no ka: Orutanatibu no Nihon dōgashi* (How did Japanese animation come about? An alternative history of *dōga*). In the book, Nishimura interrogates the concept of the word "animation" in Japan, tracing its ontology to debates about the moving image among theorists and practitioners primarily in the postwar period, while arguing that the new terminology also gave birth to "dormant concepts" behind it. The chapter Douglass translates for this issue focuses on the influence of ephemeral animation—shorts, commercials, self-produced animation—produced in the 1950s. Through their reception in festivals and festival-adjacent spaces, Nishimura argues these avant-garde works were instrumental in helping to create the conditions for the stylistic diversity that animation in Japan would experience in the coming decades.

Marie Pruvost-Delaspre's article moves us from the 1950s into the 1960s through an extensive examination of how the animation director position was first created. Drawing upon her comprehensive account of the formation and growth of the Tōei Dōga animation studio,[12] Pruvost-Delaspre examines a pivotal moment in the history of not only the studio, but the broader structure of animation labor in Japan. The role of the animation director was anything but ordained, as competing animation styles within the studio existed between the precision of Mori Yasuji and the idiosyncrasy of Daikuhara Akira. The "Mori model" eventually won out, Pruvost-Delaspre argues, in a kind of compromise between the agency of the artist and the management of the studio. Engaging with production memoirs and ékonté (storyboards), Delaspre-Pruvost shows how the initiation of the animation director role in the 1960s "inaugurates a conception of animation that profoundly modifies artistic relationships and the distribution of creative tasks."

Rounding out the historical focus, Nagata Daisuke and Matsunaga Shintarō take us into anime's production spaces of the 1970s and 1980s. Both Nagata and Matsunaga have authored books in Japanese on the perspectives of animation workers through extensive "ethnomethodological" approaches.[13] This article, translated by Kendall Heitzman, focuses on traces of animator discourse via anime magazines. By analyzing interviews and roundtable discussions in the anime magazine Animage, the authors show how industrial changes in the 1970s and 1980s to the types and audiences of anime led to stylistic distinctions between generations of animators. Specifically, Nagata and Matsunaga highlight animators who discuss their position as either "artists" or "craftworkers," highlighting how animators came to be valued not through striking originality, but through completing quality work within established character designs and storytelling parameters. Together, these three studies definitively show how anime studies is ripe for a "historical turn" that empirically unmasks and explains anime's stylistic diversity through focused studies of organizations, institutions, and individuals responsible for introducing techniques and practices into the production workspace.

Critical Production Platforms

Where historical accounts of the industry mobilize the archive, this section investigates the perspectives, behaviors, and relations of the anime industry's various creative producers. The articles in the next section focus on anime platforms of three kinds: in-person writing spaces, new media formats, and user-generated online databases. Collectively, the articles in this section combine approaches from production studies and platform studies by examining not only the architecture of structures or systems but how they form and are formed by complex sociocultural, institutional, and technological frameworks. Bryan Hikari Hartzheim's article begins this section with a focus on the industry's "above the line" staff involved in script development. Hartzheim maps anime's "writer's room" through participant observation of *uchiawase*, or "consultations," where various stakeholders engage in committee-based scriptwriting for two separate commercial anime franchises at Tōei Animation Studios. Though technically above the line in their collective ownership of the scripts, the participants of script development are far from uniform in their authority and precarity. Writing by committee, in fact, is a process of consensus that involves various negotiations representing distinct interests: the corporate office, the production floor, and the self-authored reputation all come together in service of creating compelling stories. But though these roles within script development might be tightly controlled, the practice of idea generation itself can be spontaneous, showing why franchise writing paradoxically holds potential to subvert established narrative conventions.

Brian Lanahan Milthrope tackles the rise and fall of the OVA (Original Video Animation) studio Kaname Production. Unlike studios like Studio Ghibli or Kyoto Animation, which have cultivated and promoted a consistent style that audiences have become familiar with, Kaname Pro is characteristic of startup studios that surfaced in the 1980s and folded only after a few disjointed years of small hits and failures. Rather than look at Kaname Pro from a lens of inadequacy, however, Lanahan productively uses the studio as an opportunity to examine how media platforms like the OVA—and the studios that use them—functioned as sites for creators to experiment with new forms of animated techniques and expressions. As "studio-platforms" like OVAs and "platform-studios" like Kaname display fan-creator relations that do not fit neatly into the hyperconsumer model commonly associated with the otaku, Lanahan identifies the "amateur" as a way out of current teleological histories of anime fan knowledge formation

Moving from the studio to the individual animator, Alex Tai's article focuses on the animation curation site known as "sakugabooru." Sakugabooru is devoted to making superstars out of the industry's "below-the-line" animator craftsmen and craftswomen through its obsessive cataloguing of their short sequences of exceptional animation. Tai argues there is a value in this selective viewing that engenders a heightened appreciation of the animated form itself. Using the animation of Yoshiyama Yū and her work on the franchise *Pretty Cure* as an example, Tai shows how fans gain a viewing perspective from the "animator's desk" by identifying and then tracing the animator's signature linework, timing, and other authorial touches over a corpus of works. As a collective practice, however, *sakuga* appreciation does not exist in isolation, but is a shared activity with communities of fans across the world. The result is a collective awareness and advocacy for better pay and working conditions for the industry's most precarious and vulnerable.

Transnational Frictions

The third section looks at the influence of anime production beyond Japan's borders. In the wake of Marc Steinberg's *Mechademia*, vol. 16.1 issue that introduced a new wave of media mix scholarship,[14] the two articles featured here ostensibly examine how transmedia characters or worlds are transformed through media mix models. Both authors, however, are really interested in the complex political discourses that are facilitated by such transnational moves. Ai-Ting Chung centers her study on the Taiwan Bar Studio and its series of educational animated short films. Using cute *iyashi* (healing) characters to tell alternative colonial histories of Taiwan, Taiwan Bar helps to rearticulate a sense of "Taiwanese-ness" distinct from those taught in traditional school curriculums sympathetic to Chinese and Japanese colonizers. Animated characters become spokescreatures for political advocacy, opening a "debate on how to rearticulate the colonial history of Taiwan." Chung also adroitly points to the English subtitling of the shorts as complicating the position of the Taiwan Bar activists, evincing a desire to appeal to English-language audiences "in order to earn respect and support from the West for their national sovereignty as a bulwark against political pressure from China."

The final article in the issue by Muyang Zhuang investigates the live-action Chinese adaptation of the anime and manga franchise *Hikaru no Go*. Referring to scholarly discussions on anime culture, mediatized memory, and media mix, as well as theories of mediatization, Zhuang examines the suspension of the memory of *Hikaru no Go* in China over the last two decades. Titled *Qihun*, the adaptation was initially boycotted by fans of the original work before attracting a local audience in China through its realistic period settings and costumes. This created a "regional intimacy" that appealed to viewers' nostalgia over the turn-of-the-century period in which the adaptation was set. This nostalgic waxing was also accompanied by memories of major political events, such as the handover of Hong Kong to China in 1997, which is also directly addressed in the adaptation. *Qihun* thus became a "vehicle carrying numerous newly shaped memories" that changed depending on if the viewer was from Hong Kong, Taiwan, or the PRC. Zhuang argues that the cultural memory that originally motivated *Hikaru no Go* was thus reactivated and extended by transnational fandom, regional intimacy, and productive distribution networks. His article, as well as several of the other articles in the issue, point toward unexplored sociopolitical tensions and territories when studying anime's creative media industries. Cumulatively, the articles collected here show a way forward for scholars of not only anime but East Asian media industries and platforms more broadly to present critical reframings and question existing definitions within discourses of industrial crisis.

....

Bryan Hikari Hartzheim is Associate Professor of New Media at Waseda University's School of International Liberal Studies and Graduate School of International Culture and Communication Studies. His research specializes in the style, histories, and industries of video games and animation in and around Japan. He is the author of *Hideo Kojima: Progressive Game Design from Metal Gear to Death Stranding* (2023) and the co-editor of *The Franchise Era: Managing Media in the Digital Economy* (2019).

....

Notes

1. Jonathan Clements, *Anime: A History* (London: BFI, 2013), 213.
2. Funamoto Susumu, *Anime no mirai wo shiru: Posuto-Japanimation kiiwaado wa sekaikan + degitaru* (Understanding the future of anime: The keyword for Post-Japanimation is "worldview and digital") (Tokyo: Ten Books, 1998), 38.
3. Kuroda Kenro, "Group Founded to Improve Work Conditions in Anime Industry," *The Asahi Shimbun*, June 17, 2023, https://www.asahi.com/ajw/articles /14919481.
4. Petrana Radulovic, "Netflix and Wit Studio Face Pushback for AI-assisted Short Film," *Polygon*, February 1, 2023, https://www.polygon.com/23581376/netflix -wit-studio-short-film-ai-controversy.
5. Kotajima Daisuke, "Anime *Chainsaw Man* irei to naru '100% shusshi' no riyu wa?" (The reason for the exceptional "100% investment" in the anime *Chainsaw Man*), *Real Sound*, October 5, 2022, https://realsound.jp/tech/2022/10/post -1141127.html.
6. Matteo Watzky, "Anime's Present and Future—Interview with Terumi Ishii and Ayano Fukumiya," *Full Frontal*, November 10, 2023, https://fullfrontal.moe /animes-present-and-future-interview-with-terumi-nishii-and-ayano -fukumiya/.
7. Alex Dudok de Wit, "Why the Anime Industry Lacks Unions and How That Could Change: A Veteran Producer Speaks," *Cartoon Brew*, January 3, 2022, https://www.cartoonbrew.com/artist-rights/why-the-anime-industry-lacks -unions-and-how-that-could-change-a-veteran-producer-speaks-212042.html.
8. Takahashi Katsunori, "NHK *Close-up Gendai+* 6gatsu7ka no tokushu wa 'anime-sangyo teishikin mondai ni semaru" (NHK *Close-up Gendai+* Special on June 7 tackles the anime industry's low wage problem), *Anime! Anime!*, June 7, 2017, https://animeanime.jp/article/2017/06/07/34165.html.
9. Marc Steinberg, *Anime's Media Mix: Franchising Toys and Characters in Japan* (Minneapolis: University of Minnesota Press, 2012).
10. Ian Condry, *The Soul of Anime: Collaborative Creativity and Japan's Media Success Story* (Durham: Duke University Press, 2013).
11. Stevie Suan, *Anime's Identity: Performativity and Form Beyond Japan* (Minneapolis: University of Minnesota Press, 2021).
12. Marie Pruvost-Delaspre, *Aux sources de l'animation japonaise—Le studio Tōei Dōga (1956–1972)* (The Origins of Anime: Tōei Dōga Studio [1956–1972]) (Paris: The Presses Universitaires de Rennes, 2021).
13. Nagata Daisuke and Matsunaga Shintarō, *Sangyōhendō no rōdōshakaigaku—animeetaa no keikenshi* (Labor sociology of industrial change—An experiential history of animators) (Kyoto: Koyo Shōbō, 2022).
14. *Mechademia Second Arc: Media Mix* 16, no. 1 (2023).

Industrial Histories

How Did the Concept of Animation Come About?

A Focus on the Reception of Norman McLaren

NISHIMURA TOMOHIRO, TRANS. JASON CODY DOUGLASS

Translator's Introduction

When scholars craft histories of Japanese animation, or of the global webs and transnational threads of cultural productions tied up in animation industries based in Japan, what exactly do they mean by "animation?" Variations of this question are stitched through the six chapters of Nishimura Tomohiro's 2018 book *Nihon no animēshon wa ika ni shite seiritsu shita no ka: Orutanatibu no Nihon dōgashi* (How did Japanese animation come about? An alternative history of *dōga*), which weaves a revisionist history of a century of animation in Japan while stringing together methodological and terminological interventions that garnered the academic achievement award of the Japanese Society for Animation Studies in 2019. Two worries are patterned on the book's patchwork of case studies: that too often a present-day understanding of "animation" is projected back upon the past in ways that overshadow how creators and audiences understood, categorized, and discussed audiovisual media in distinct eras; and, that the tendency within anime studies to collapse the distinction between "anime" and "animation" writ large has pigeonholed Japan-related (and Japanese-language) studies of animated media as pertinent only to those with an interest in anime or manga and not to those theorizing animation or moving image arts on a broad scale. In his dyed-in-the-wool approach Nishimura believes that interrogating the apparentness (*jimeisei*) of the animation concept is best achieved by turning toward creations on the fringes (*shūenteki*) or at the outer limits (*kyōkaiteki*), and that conceptual transitions or upheavals of industrial convention most often occur when works at the margins redefine what constitutes the center.

Translated for this issue of *Mechademia: Second Arc* is an abridged version (six of eleven sections) of the book's fourth chapter, entitled "How Did the Concept of Animation Come About? A Focus on the Reception of Norman McLaren." The reasons for this selection are many-fold. Positioned at the halfway point, the chapter sews together the book's discrete halves, which are divided not only between the prewar/wartime and postwar but also by the "before" and "after" the emergence of animation as a unified concept, which Nishimura presents as having occurred during the latter half of the 1950s. Grasping this bifurcation is crucial to reading Nishimura, as his periodization hinges upon the idea that genre divisions before the mid-1950s, such as puppet films or silhouette films, were drawn from what the viewer saw on screen, whereas those proliferating after that period were rooted in filmic process rather than representation. In relation to this issue's focus on industries and platforms, this chapter constructs a narrative of interplay between large-scale/commercial and small-scale/self-produced media, as well as the aesthetic affordances of both independent and commissioned projects. Though Nishimura does not write in terms of platforms, the film festival and festival-adjacent screenings (such as the Asahi Culture Film Assembly) are framed for his purposes as the privileged sites of distribution, discussion, and networking, and his concluding gesture toward animation in the digital age should dovetail with other articles in this issue focused on case studies drawn from decades well after those discussed here.

The chapter's opening section summarizes the terminological argument laid out in preceding chapters, after which point Nishimura launches into a detailed account of the exhibition and reception of experimentally animated shorts in the mid-1950s and the ripple effects those works generated across the film and television industries, through the press and trade journals, and even within common parlance. Nishimura's extreme focus upon the works of Norman McLaren, and particularly the impact and legacy of *Blinkity Blank* (1955) within Japan, is perhaps at once the chapter's greatest strength and deepest weakness. Nishimura excels at attending to the inherently enmeshed histories of "domestic" and "foreign" animation within Japan (including Chinese and Soviet animation), but he also demonstrates a tendency of occasionally stretching single sources into overly broad conclusions, and his positioning of works by McLaren and others made individually (i.e., through the erasure of Evelyn Lambart, Claude Jutra, etc.) echoes strains of auteur and great man theories at odds with other aspects of the book. In the interest of emphasizing more of the former than the latter, and in adherence with a strict word limit, some sections in the middle of the chapter that deal at even greater lengths with the reception of *Blinkity Blank* as avant-garde film have been excised. Even in an abridged format, the chapter's novel proposal—that a conceptualization of animation as a diversity of styles and techniques united by frame-by-frame production processes emerged within Japan in large part through the reception of avant-garde works, particularly film festival darlings—should continue to shine through.

The aim of this translation is to introduce some of Nishimura's most compelling ideas to an English-language readership; thus, every effort has been made to translate even tricky terms into English. This includes culture film (*bunka eiga*), educational film (*kyōiku eiga*), puppet film (*ningyō eiga*), line film (*senga eiga*), silhouette film (*kage-e eiga*), live-action (*jissha*), avant-garde (*zen'ei*), frame-by-frame photography (*komadori*), and the like, each of which loses some richness and specificity during the process of translation. However, two terms have been borrowed from Japanese in order to preserve the precision of Nishimura's prose: *manga eiga* and *dōga*. Manga eiga, referring to certain kinds of drawn animation and occasionally translated as "cartoon film" (despite the cultural-historical baggage of "cartoon"), is believed by Nishimura to have served in opposition to the loanword *animēshon* throughout the 1950s and much of the 1960s. Dōga, literally "moving pictures" and another term used to refer to cel-based or hand-drawn works, is crucial within this chapter not only because it had long been treated by many as a Japanese translational equivalent of the English word "animation" but also because of confusion in the 1950s between that term and the homonym *dōga* (referring to illustrations for children's books). Conversely, Japanese film and book titles are retained in Romanized forms for clarity and accompanied by translations. All endnotes are taken from the original, whereas only one of thirteen figures were retained for reasons of copyright. Where necessary, brief clarifications appear in brackets within the text. After reading this translation, those interested in engaging with other sections of the book can consult pages 15–20 of the preface for detailed chapter summaries.

How Did the Concept of Animation Come About?
A Focus on the Reception of Norman McLaren

NISHIMURA TOMOHIRO

ANIMATION IN POSTWAR JAPAN

Today, animation has become an exceedingly popular word, familiar even to children. However, if we look back historically, it was by no measure a common term. In prewar Japan, "animation" was hardly ever used. It is not that there are no instances of its use, but it was not widely known as a word nor as a concept.

Common instead in prewar Japan were discrete terms such as *manga eiga,* silhouette film, and puppet film, and a peculiarity of these genre divisions was a blurred distinction between animated and non-animated works. For example, "puppet film" referred not only to puppet animation filmed frame-by-frame, but also to puppet plays shot straight through. "Silhouette film" similarly incorporated live-action works. In this way the confusion between live-action and animation resulted not from a lack of awareness toward animation but as a result of differing criterion between the genre divisions used then and those used today.

The question "what does the work look like," that is, what was the spectator seeing, served as the basis for prewar genre divisions. Regardless of whether the puppet was filmed frame-by-frame or in a single shot, projected on the screen was a puppet. Thus, "puppet film" signified no more than the fact that the spectator was watching a puppet. Similarly, audiences of *manga eiga* viewed manga, and those watching silhouette film saw silhouettes. Whether or not the work was made frame-by-frame, its generic distinction followed from how it appeared. For a while into Japan's postwar era, these same terms, rather than animation, continued to be used, inherited from prewar parlance. "What does the work look like" continued to operate as the criteria for evaluation.

This conceptual continuity with the prewar era continued for around ten years from 1945. To verify this, consider *Eiga hyakka jiten* (1954, Encyclopedia of cinema),[1] the most comprehensive film reference book of its time, with entries penned by established critics and authors. Examining the terminology corresponding to animation in the book affords us a better understanding of how the concept was understood at the time.

In terms of animation-related genres, *manga eiga,* line film, silhouette film, puppet film, and *dōga eiga* appear as entries in *Eiga hyakka jiten.* The historical account of *manga eiga* reads, "films on the subject of manga, a type of *dōga eiga.*" Line film was explained as "films in which lines move, a type of *dōga eiga,*" "used for educational film, scientific film, etc." The practice of calling [drawn] works made for educational purposes "line film" was popularized much earlier in the prewar period. On the other hand, *dōga eiga* is glossed, "including *manga eiga* and line film, a general term for moving drawings." Silhouette film, introduced simply as "a type of *dōga eiga,*" corresponds, like *manga eiga* and line film, to works of "moving drawings," with *dōga eiga* acting as an umbrella term for the three.

However, what must be noted here is that *dōga eiga* in this context cannot be treated as a translational equivalent of animation. First of all, animation does not appear anywhere as a heading, or even as a word, in *Eiga hyakka jiten*. In 1954, the term was not popular enough to merit an encyclopedic entry. The book's authors, who had been active as prewar critics and filmmakers, followed existing conceptual precedent.

This point is evident in the puppet film section written by Tanaka Yoshitsugu, who had worked on *manga eiga* at J.O. Studios [in the mid-1930s]. Tanaka's explanation of puppet film—"divided into both those films in which the puppet's neck, torso, and limbs are detachable and moved little by little one frame at a time, and those string- or hand-manipulated puppet plays filmed as is"—includes not just puppet animation but also recordings of puppetry. "A type of *dōga eiga*" is not written in this entry, as it was with *manga eiga* or silhouette film. Puppet plays shot straight through are indeed not "moving drawings," so puppet film could not be called *dōga eiga*. *Dōga eiga* may have encapsulated drawn animation, but the term did not refer to animation as a whole.

In postwar Japan, animation as a word began to be used by authors and critics in the mid-1950s within certain technical settings. And as a concept, animation was entirely unlike the ideas underlying prewar genre divisions such as *manga eiga*. That is because the word asked not "what is seen on screen," but rather "in what way is the work being made," a question of process [rather than representation]. The basis for genre distinction became one concerned with stop-motion means of production. Furthermore, with a basis for distinction grounded in the production process, animation developed the ability to refer generally to works made from all sorts of materials and techniques. In other words, if made via individual frames, then ultimately, regardless of style, a work would be viewed as belonging to the same genre. It was at this time that animation became a superordinate concept inclusive of not only drawn animation but also puppet animation, abstract animation, pixilation (living objects moved and filmed frame-by-frame), and the like.

The emergence of a new term gives rise to the dormant concepts behind that term. The appearance of the term "animation" signaled the formation of a new animation concept that would come to replace genre divisions carried from prewar into postwar discourse, such as *manga eiga*, puppet film, and silhouette film. But the 1950s were a transitional period. Enduring prewar ways of thinking were not merely swept away, and this new idea did not immediately take root. Within these transitional circumstances, how did the concept of animation come about? Investigating this question is the goal of the present essay.

THE WORKS OF NORMAN McLAREN

The focus of this essay concerns the conditions of animation in mid-1950s Japan. I emphasize this period because it was around this time when the term came into use and the concept is thought to have been established. I begin by calling attention to the reception of works by Norman McLaren.

Nowadays, McLaren is well-recognized as an animator, although his creations, rather unlike ordinary *manga eiga*, possessed a strong tendency toward the experimental. They occupy a position at the outer limits of animation, and elude conventional genre divisions. By thinking about how these fringe works were received, we might manage to better understand how those at the time came to grasp animation.

Born in Scotland, McLaren started making animation in the early 1930s. Initially engaged in work at the GPO Film Unit in London, McLaren relocated to the United States before being invited in 1941 to join the animation division of the National Film Board of Canada (NFB). Based in Canada, until his death in 1987, he created many animated shorts while simultaneously endeavoring to train the generations that succeeded him. He left behind approximately seventy works, which collectively garnered more than two hundred accolades.

The theatrical release of McLaren's *Blinkity Blank* (1955) in Japan in 1956 has become a topic of discussion, but it was not actually the first work by McLaren to have been screened in Japan. Art critic Takiguchi Shūzō attests to having seen *Fiddle-De-Dee* (1947) and *Pen Point Percussion* (1951) at the American Cultural Center in 1955.[2] However, as an inconspicuously held screening, it did not attract much attention.

As an artist, McLaren employed a wide range of techniques. One such technique, known as "cameraless animation," involved forgoing a camera and drawing directly onto film, a practice sometimes referred to as "direct painting" when particularly transparent film stock is used. *Fiddle-De-Dee*, a purely abstract work created by means of this method, was painted with lines that disregarded individual frames and occasionally meandered onto the parts of the film strip devoted to music and synchronized sound.

McLaren is also known for his practice of etching soundtracks directly onto films. Sound and music are encoded onto the audio track of a filmstrip in the form of engravings, and when that portion of the film passes through a projector, the projector discerns those encodings and emits a corresponding noise. The documentary *Pen Point Percussion* explains the mechanics of McLaren's hand-drawn soundtracks.

Though some of McLaren's works were exhibited at the American Cultural Center, they were seen by only a small number of spectators. His name suddenly began to be known in Japan with the 1956 theatrical release of his representative work *Blinkity Blank*. Only five minutes in length, the film was screened alongside Julien Duvivier's feature *Marianne of My Youth* (1955) and billed with the Japanese-language title *Sen to iro no sokkyōshi* (Improvised poem of line and color). To this day, that is still how *Blinkity Blank* is referred to in Japanese: with a title that has survived since 1956.

Blinkity Blank, a work of cameraless animation, was made with a technique known as "cine-calligraphy." Cine-calligraphy involves use of a sharp, needle-like tool to scratch off the black outer layer of film, resulting in white lines. In *Blinkity Blank*, some of those white sections are painted in with colors such as red and green. The soundtrack is also partially drawn on, as McLaren scratched over an initial layer of a recorded Maurice Blackburn composition. The drawn-in soundtrack elements sound like the dull beats of a percussion instrument.

In a 1965 edition of his serialized column "The World of Animation" (*Animēshon no sekai*) in the newspaper *Asahi Shinbun*, Kuri Yōji drew explanatory diagrams introducing some of the techniques employed by McLaren (Figure 1).[3] As a participant at the Annecy International Animation Film Festival during the same year, Kuri had been taught by McLaren the methods for drawing directly onto filmstock. The first panel of Kuri's diagram explains cine-calligraphy, the second panel introduces direct painting, and the third concerns drawn-on soundtracks. The man operating the projector in the final panel is sketched in the likeness of McLaren.

McLaren did not originate direct painting and drawn-on sound techniques. For instance, it is said that Oskar Fischinger's experiments with hand-drawn sound and direct painting predate McLaren's, and Len Lye's *A Colour Box* (1935) is also a famous pioneering work of direct painting. Having worked at the GPO Film Unit, Lye was actually a predecessor of McLaren. McLaren's achievement lay in his further development of these preexisting techniques.

At this point I ask again, how were McLaren's uniquely produced works understood in terms of filmic genres? In the case of Japan, his creations were not initially recognized as animation. Noted first as avant-garde (or experimental) film, only later did they come to be appraised as animation. Yet, those two interpretations did not exist separately, but coexisted without contradiction. Understanding this is essential when thinking about the concept of animation in the 1950s: one aspect of its development was that it occurred alongside avant-garde film.

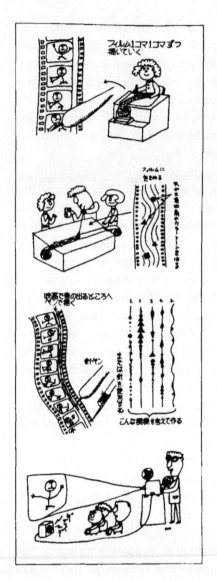

Figure 1. Kuri Yōji's "The Making of Cameraless Films." *Asahi Shinbun*, August 22, 1965.

EDUCATIONAL FILM AND ANIMATION

Before discussing the relationship between avant-garde film and animation, I wish to first touch on the relationship between educational film and animation. When considering animation in the 1950s, the issue of educational film cannot be ignored, and it also cannot be said that this topic is unrelated to McLaren. At that time, animation could be classified within educational film in a broad sense; in particular, there was a deep connection between educational film and art animation not framed as entertainment (*goraku sakuhin*), a relational trend that had continued from the prewar period.

Before the war and during wartime, educational film was referred to as "culture film" (*bunka eiga*). In accordance with the 1939 Film Law, which enacted compulsory screenings of culture film in movie theaters, business guarantees were extended to suppliers of culture film. But with the repeal of the Film Law following the conclusion of the war, culture film ended up being shut out of the realm of entertainment. The main production companies of culture film vanished and production rates plummeted, falling for a time to catastrophically low levels. But from the early 1950s, educational film rose again to prominence.

In the early postwar period, the term "culture film" was still being used. At the level of content, gradually returning educational film followed in the same vein as prewar and wartime culture film. Educational film was primarily intended to enlighten or instruct, with documentaries constituting the category's core. This included various short films in addition to theatrical features. For example, tourism film, scientific film, PR film, and other kinds of shorts were all considered educational film, and *manga eiga* or puppet film could also be classified as such. Artistic works were also included; that was because artistic forms of expression were thought to possess educational value. Thus, certain kinds of avant-garde film were treated as educational film. In the prewar period, Oskar Fischinger's *Study* series was screened as culture film, a designation authorized by the Ministry of Education. Though that may have been an exceptional incident, the postwar avant-garde works were also screened under the guise of educational film.

The rise to prominence of educational film at the start of the 1950s stemmed from the proliferation of societal and school-based educational programs, as well as from an increased abundance of PR film. The inaugural Educational Film Festival, an expressly promotional event, took place in 1954. Though that festival featured domestic productions, an affiliated event launched in the same year—the World Short Film Festival (held in Yamaha Hall)—gathered films recommended by foreign embassies. Likewise, the newspaper company *Asahi Shinbun*, a supporter of the Educational Film Festival, founded the Asahi Culture Film Assembly in 1955 and held periodic screening events at venues such as Yamaha Hall. The trend of both the World Short Film Festival and the Asahi Culture Film Assembly was focusing on documentaries while also showcasing a diversity of innovative works.

At the time, winners in the shorts categories at the Cannes International Film Festival and other critically acclaimed shorts were exhibited alongside feature-length films. As with the case of 1955 screenings of Karel Zeman's *Inspirace* (1948), even shorts would sometimes become popular topics of conversation. Zeman's work is a puppet film unusually made from glasswork. Screenings of *Blinkity Blank* also occurred because it had been awarded the Short Film Palme d'Or at Cannes in 1955.

The Asahi Culture Film Assembly regularly screened selections of such animated shorts. For instance, the 4th Asahi Culture Film Assembly, held on October 11, 1955, under the theme "Into the World of Illusion" (*gensō no sekai e*), incorporated *Inspirace*, Maruyama Shoji's *Muku no ki no hanashi* (1947, Tale of the muku tree) from Tōhō Educational Film Unit, Pat Griffin's *The Thames* (1948), *Animated Genesis* (1952) by Joan and Peter Foldes, Ōfuji Noburō's 1952 version of *Kujira* (The whale), as well as a French cinepoem. Live-action works were included therein, but artistically oriented animation accounted for the majority of the program.

Muku no ki no hanashi is a poetic work that portrays an old tree throughout the passage of the four seasons, with music composed by Hayasaka Fumio, and visuals which aimed to blend linework and sculpture. *Animated Genesis* offers a surrealistic depiction of the history of humanity since the dawn of the universe. The maiden work of Foldes, who would later create the pioneering masterpiece of CG animation *Hunger* (1974), *Animated Genesis* was awarded the *prix pour la couleur* at Cannes. *Kujira* is a remake of a film by the same name that Ōfuji Noburō created in 1927. A vivid silhouette film employing colored cellophane, it was awarded second place in the short film competition at Cannes. *The Thames*, part of the *Musical Paintbox* series, was drawn to look like sketches.

Including *Inspirace*, such foreign animation was distinctive in comparison with conventional *manga eiga*, which is why those works were deliberately selected to be screened by the Asahi Culture Film Assembly. Of this unprecedented endeavor of the 1950s, animation scholar Okada Emiko, who attended the "Into the World of Illusion" screening, later recollected, "the first postwar screening of non-commercial animation in Japan happened then, in that venue, in front of a great many spectators."[4] Was it not precisely because of the framework of culture film (and educational film) that such a special program was made possible?

The World Short Film Festival, held in association with the Educational Film Festival, screened McLaren's newest works on an almost annual basis.

Beginning with a screening of *Rythmetic* (1956), each of the following films were screened at the festival during their initial year of release: *A Chairy Tale* (1957), *Le Merle* (1958), *Serenal* (1959), *Lines Vertical* (1960), *Canon* (1964), and *Mosaic* (1965). McLaren's works occupied a distinctive place at a festival primarily featuring documentaries. Yet the films were highly popular, as evidenced by Hani Susumu's remark that "at events such as the World Short Film Festival, always from Canada came works by Norman McLaren, who has since become a famous figure."[5] At a time when there were not yet animated film festivals in Japan, screenings and festivals linked to educational film afforded art animation an opportunity to be presented.

BLINKITY BLANK AS ANIMATION

The latter half of the 1950s was a period in which animated shorts—rather unlike conventional *manga eiga*—appeared from within Japan as well. In terms of artists performing essential roles at the time, Ōfuji Noburō and Mochinaga Tadahito can be put forward.

Ōfuji, whose film *Kujira* took second place in the Short Film competition at Cannes, made another silhouette film using colored cellophane, *Yūreisen* (1956, The phantom ship), which received a special honorable mention at the Venice International Documentary and Short Film Festival. Though Ōfuji had not yet enjoyed much critical acclaim within Japan, he had become Japan's most recognized animator abroad. Meanwhile, Mochinaga, a puppet animator who had worked in Shanghai, returned to Japan in 1953 and later established Puppet Film Studio (*Ningyō Eiga Seisakusho*). In 1956 the studio presented *Urikohime to amanojyaku* (1955, Princess Uriko and the demon boy), *Gohiki no kozarutachi* (1956, Five little monkeys), and *Chibikuro Sanbo no tora taiji* (1956, Little Black Sambo subdues the tiger), the last of which won top honors in the Children's Film category of the Vancouver International Film Festival. Through Mochinaga, puppet animation in Japan began in earnest.

As a connection between Ōfuji and Mochinaga, I wish to touch upon Iizawa Tadasu. Having founded Puppet Art Productions (*Ningyō Geijutsu Purodakushon*), Iizawa entered into puppet animation with a focus on commercials. The beer PR film *Bīru mukashi mukashi* (1956, Beer long, long ago) received particularly high critical acclaim, with puppets made by Kawamoto Kihachirō and manipulated by Mochinaga, and a silhouette scene overseen by Ōfuji.

Yūreisen, *Chibikuro Sanbo no tora taiji*, and *Bīru mukashi mukashi*—celebrated within and outside of Japan—were all made in 1956, the same year in which *Blinkity Blank* became the subject of popular discourse. With the exhibition of alternative animation from abroad, and as similar works produced domestically began to draw more attention, an opportunity emerged for the appreciation of *Blinkity Blank* as animation.

But in light of the continued prevalence of prewar concepts, the recognition of McLaren's work as animation was no simple matter. This was because the film was not bound by the genre divisions of *manga eiga*, puppet film, and silhouette film inherited from prewar texts. How could one possibly speak of the avant-garde work of McLaren and a typical *manga eiga* as belonging to the same category? The possibility of such a categorization required the replacement of prewar concepts. In other words, it became necessary to accept the idea that works shot frame-by-frame could be classed as members of the same group regardless of their particular style. McLaren's work, upon being understood in terms of this idea, was the first to be positioned as animation.

In 1957, Iizawa wrote an essay entitled "The Magic of Cinema: An Outlook on Animated Film" (*Eiga no majutsu—animēshon eiga no tenbō*). The essay begins with the sentence, "animated film, at least in Japan, is a word not often heard." He then introduces *Bīru mukashi mukashi* as he was someone who was present at the site of its production. Yet from that position, even Iizawa calls animation "a word not often heard." Iizawa raises the critical acclaim of Ōfuji's *Kujira* and *Yūreisen* and the invitation Ōfuji received to contribute to *International Animated Film Weekly* when he writes, "animated film, in the context of global cinema, can be understood as drawing a great amount of interest." He then touches upon the subject of McLaren's *Blinkity Blank* winning an accolade at Cannes and subsequently being introduced in Japan, suggesting that "animated film is something which enables extraordinarily broad and varied experimentation." He continues:

> However, even though [the word] animation has a kind of experimental ring to it, "*manga eiga*" like the films of Disney can, as a matter of course, also be considered animation. We have been calling such films [in Japanese] "*manga eiga*." But animation is not only manga; in fact, its domain is vast. [6]

The way in which Iizawa's argument proceeds in these passages is profoundly interesting. After using McLaren's film to explain animation's diverse forms of expression, he only then notes how Disney *manga eiga* are also animation, as if the idea had suddenly struck him.

Together with the exhibition of a variety of styles of animation, the concept of animation had propagated. *Blinkity Blank* served as a representative work for the diversity of animated expression. Or conversely, through the reception of the diversity and experimentality of the forms of expression in McLaren's work, it might be said that the concept of animation was established [in Japan]. At that time, the word "animation" came to incorporate a variety of stylistic expressions and had an "experimental ring to it" as described by Iizawa. Through the proliferation of such works, what had until then been *manga eiga* was rediscovered as animation. That is to say, the concept of *manga eiga* did not expand to incorporate various styles of animation, but what spread instead was a way of thinking about a stylistically diverse array of works as animation, and *manga eiga* was included as one part of that equation.

FROM *MANGA EIGA* TO ANIMATION

In 1956 a wide variety of animated shorts, domestic and foreign, received public attention within Japan. Viewed from a different angle, 1956 also marked the embryonic rumblings of commercial *manga eiga*. Tōei Dōga (now Tōei Animation) was formed in 1956, and the following year saw the release of the studio's first short, *Koneko no rakugaki* (1957, Kitty's graffiti), a production helmed by Yabushita Taiji. Concurrently, Otogi Puro, the studio spearheaded by Yokoyama Ryūichi, made a stir with the release of *Fukusuke* (1957) [a film named after its frog-like protagonist]. From there, Tōei's Yabushita oversaw the completion of the studio's debut full-color feature, *Hakujaden* (1958, The tale of the white serpent), and Yokoyama also completed a feature on 35mm in the form of *Hyōtan suzume* (1959, The gourd sparrow).

The late March 1958 issue of film journal *Kinema junpō* included a special focus entitled "*Manga Eiga*: The Attraction of 1958." Covering the founding of Tōei Dōga and the release of *Fukusuke*, the issue concerned commercial *manga eiga* in Japan coming into full bloom (though at the time of publication, *Hakujaden* had not yet screened in theaters). As stated in the foreword, "at last, *manga eiga* in Japan appears to be stirring anew . . . this will necessitate the consideration of viewpoints held by both creators and viewers."[7] It is possible to read the aim of this issue as the reconsideration of *manga eiga* as animation. It is particularly interesting that the issue's contributions were authored by the likes of Hanada Kiyoteru, Takiguchi Shūzō, and Okada Susumu. Hanada and Takiguchi were leading critics of avant-garde art, and Okada was known for his positions on avant-garde film. All three had reviewed *Blinkity Blank*, and in this issue both Hanada and Takiguchi referenced McLaren. The new "stirrings" of *manga eiga* were being theorized by critics of the avant-garde.

As someone with a profound interest in moving images, Takiguchi wrote frequently on animation. His essay for the special issue of *Kinema junpō*, entitled "Manga, Dōga: On 'Spatial Shyness'" (*manga, dōga—kūkan kyōfu*) opened: "Recently, *manga eiga* has generally come to be referred to as *dōga*. When speaking with someone unfamiliar with this, they might mistake *dōga* for the homonym *dōga* [illustrations for children]—as in, 'the *dōga* of *manga eiga*, no wait I mean the *other dōga*'—so this sort of usage has become confusing."[8]

This use of the word *dōga* [in reference to *manga eiga*] had actually existed before the war and continued during and after wartime. Yet Takiguchi, despite being active as a critic since the prewar period, surmised that references to *manga eiga* as *dōga* were a recent development. What this meant was that the meaning of the long-established word *dōga*, and the meaning of the same word as it was being used by Takiguchi in 1958, were not necessarily the same. Along with the appearance of the loanword "animation" in postwar Japan, the Japanese term *dōga* had come to be used as something of a translational equivalent. Though the word *dōga* had previously existed, new light was shed upon it by the emergence of the word "animation."

Takiguchi was using "*dōga*" as a translation equivalent of "animation." This usage is different from the notion of *dōga* as *manga eiga*, puppet film, and silhouette film that originated in the prewar period and continued into the postwar era. After transitioning through the concept of animation, *dōga* also became a superordinate concept encompassing various styles of animation. When Takiguchi called attention to a recent change in what is identified as *dōga*, he was actually picking up on the word's shifting meaning and usage. In turn, Takiguchi's essay notes a usage of the term *dōga* that still would have been unfamiliar to many people. He writes, "when one says *dōga*, this is most often in reference to run-of-the-mill *manga eiga*, so when used in an abstract sense *dōga* still doesn't quite click." Indeed, at the time *dōga* still didn't quite click.

This sense of misunderstood meaning is expressed in Takiguchi's previous reference to mix-ups between *dōga* and its homonym. This misunderstanding would also be faced by the Animation Association of Three (*Animēshon sannin no kai*), formed in 1960. Manabe Hiroshi, one of the group's members, used the word *dōga* in response to a reporter's request for his definition of animation, but printed in the finished article was instead its homonym.[9] This terminological confusion was thought to have resulted from the common belief that *manga eiga* were for children, but it was perhaps also the result of unfamiliarity with the word *dōga*.

Nevertheless, after that point, the practice of referring to *manga eiga* as *dōga* caught on. Through the release of many styles of shorts from the mid-1950s in Japan, the word "animation" propagated and diverse forms of animation increased in number, but this did not change the fact that the majority of such productions continued to be *manga eiga*. As a result, it became common practice to refer to *manga eiga* as *dōga*.

Incidentally, Okada Susumu's contribution to the same issue, "*Manga eiga* are not films," is an essay that discusses how *manga eiga* meaningfully differ from ordinary [read: live-action] theatrical films. Okada writes of how pre-cinematic "moving pictures" (*ugoku e*) led to the birth of *dōga*, which contributed in turn to the birth of films. When considered from the present day in which animation's turn from analog film to digital resulted in a state of affairs in which some consider "animation to not be film," this essay seems prescient.

THE GAP BETWEEN ANIMATION (OR *DŌGA*) AND *MANGA EIGA*

The 1950s were a transitional era for the formation of the concept of animation. Genre divisions held over from prewar discourse remained in use, but propagating at the same time were ways of thinking about animation that differed from prior convention. Hence the emergence during this period of much confusion concerning the term animation. That confusion would be carried over into the 1960s.

From the standpoint of those involved with the production of *manga eiga*, a notion of animation permissive of diverse forms of expression was a rather difficult one to accept. Nagai Yasuji, a producer at Japan Animation Film Company (*Nihon Animēshon Eigasha*), wrote an essay in 1962 on the topic of "Trends in Global Animation." Following his claim that only very recently had the technical term animation become popularized, Nagai continues:

> Though common wisdom up until now tells us that films made from manga, lines, puppets, and silhouettes can be said to be animation, with the ever-increasing complexity of film techniques the technical term 'animation' has also had to expand considerably. Be that as it may, as for experimental films appearing anime-like and therefore being deemed animated films, where would such a scope begin and end? Such an ambiguous and vague interpretation of the term would be worrying.[10]

What Nagai questions is the gap between "common wisdom up until now" and the word "animation." As "common wisdom up until now," Nagai offers *manga eiga*, line film, puppet film, and silhouette film—all terms persisting from prewar usage. Though he agrees with the recognition of these preexisting genres as animation, he feels resistance toward the inclusion of experimental works into animation. How those involved in the production of *manga eiga* grasped animation did not differ much from Nagai's way of thinking. From the perspective of those working in commercial settings, experimental films were unrelated and there was no need for the concept of animation to expand far enough for the inclusion of such films. They understood animation as an extension of preexisting genre divisions, and expressed discomfort with the thought of a categorization of animation that incorporated experimental films. A gap arose between this attitude and the way of thinking about animation promulgating concurrently.

Bear in mind that when Nagai discusses experimental films, he is referring to not only foreign works of experimental animation such as McLaren's but also the much-discussed creations of the Animation Association of Three. Trailblazers of independently produced animation in the postwar period, the group's three members actively introduced graphical styles and experimental techniques. That is, they put into practice the diversity of animation opened up by works such as McLaren's. But from the perspective of those engaged in commercial animation, such an experimental praxis seemed unrelated. A gap formed between the two parties' interpretations of the word "animation," creating an opposition between commercial animation and independently produced animation.

On the other hand, it was also not the case that *dōga* could be unproblematically used as a translational equivalent of animation. A Japanese version of *The Techniques of Film Animation* (1959), authored by John Halas and Roger Manvell, was published in 1963 as *Animēshon—riron, jissai, ōyō* (Animation: Theory, practice, application), becoming the first book in Japan to use the word "animation" in its title. In the postscript, translator Itō Ippei writes:

> Though it appears that *dōga* is becoming something of a translational equivalent of animation in Japanese, I believe it is incorrect to render "animation" as "*dōga*" . . . this usage of *dōga* would end up delimiting only that involving *ga* [drawings or pictures], whereas there are many types of animation such as puppet animation, silhouette animation, still animation, animation with three-dimensional objects, and many beyond these, so rendering animation as *dōga* is probably not suitable.[11]

Itō's position included the recognition of various types of animation, yet from that very position he resisted the use of *dōga* as a translational equivalent of animation. His reasoning was based in a consideration of the existence of styles such as puppet animation or pixilation, which go beyond the confines of works involving moving drawings [implied by the *ga* of *dōga*].

Mori Takuya makes a similar argument in his 1966 publication *Animēshon nyūmon* (An introduction to animation): "Unfortunately, in Japanese there is no suitable word for animation," he says, continuing, "in our country animation is for convenience rendered as *dōga* or called *manga eiga*, yet these terms represent but a subset of animation, rather than its entirety."[12] In the 1960s, there were a considerable number of skeptics when it came to the use of *dōga* as the translational equivalent of animation. Yet this usage of *dōga* for animation, with all its ambiguity, would eventually take root.

Animation gradually became a common term in the 1960s, but that did not mean that the term *manga eiga* would ease to exist. The expression *manga eiga* may be falling out of use nowadays, but the convention of calling manga-like animation "manga" continued into the 1980s.

Animation and *manga eiga* coexisted, and the former did not supplant the latter. The gap between the two could not simply be eliminated. The use of the term "*manga eiga*" ended following the popularization of the term "anime" to refer to the same films. For example, the annual Tōei Manga Festival (*Tōei manga matsuri*) started in 1967—preceded by the Big Manga Parade (*Manga ōkōshin*) in 1964—would change its name in 1990 to the Tōei Anime Festival (*Tōei anime matsuri*), and was changed again later to the Tōei Anime Fair (*Tōei anime fea*).

Incidentally, in the present age *dōga* is used in a manner that goes beyond the meaning of animation. For instance, sites for the posting of videos such as YouTube are called "video sharing services" (*dōga kyōyō sābisu*), including the Japanese site *Nico Nico Dōga*. These video sharing sites began appearing in the 2000s and proliferated in the blink of an eye. Here *dōga* is used to refer to all moving images, including but not exclusively animation. The emergence of a new moving image environment in the form of the internet afforded yet another novel meaning for the word *dōga*.

When used as a translational equivalent of animation, *dōga* referenced the movement of pictures or drawings. With video sharing services, *dōga* refers to the movement of images on screen. The latter usage offers no strict distinction between live-action and animation. Perhaps this is in response to the weakened differences between live-action and animation resulting from the development of digital technologies.

Terms and the meanings they possess change along with eras. Further, when the meaning of a word changes, the conceptual rules imparting meaning upon those words also change. The many Japanese terms relating to animation have changed along with their meanings through the long course of history, and in the present day remain in the process of change. Recent advances in digital technologies in particular have destabilized the conceptual rules of animation. We in turn are faced with the need to respond flexibly to animation.

....

James Cody Douglass earned his PhD in Film and Media Studies and East Asian Languages and Literatures from Yale University. His research focuses on histories and theories of animation in East Asia. His dissertation, "Animation Before Anime," asserts that animated media circulating into, within, and away from Japan during the mid-twentieth century stand to tell us much about how such texts shaped, and were shaped by, the cultural forces of class, gender, age, and race. His publications can be found in *Film Quarterly*, *Animation Studies*, *Women Film Pioneers Project*, *Transcommunication*, *Animation and Advertising* (Palgrave, 2019), *Gurōbaru animeron* (Seikyusha, 2022), and *The Intersection of Animation, Video Games, and Music* (Routledge, 2023). He has served as Guest Faculty at Sarah Lawrence College, Part-Time Acting Instructor at Yale University, Japan Foundation Fellow, and Visiting Research Fellow at Waseda University.

....

Notes

1. Iwasaki Akira et al., eds., *Eiga hyakka jiten* (Encyclopedia of cinema) (Tokyo: Hakuyōsha, 1954).
2. Takiguchi Shūzō, "Bijutsu eiga zakki" (Notes on art film), *Bijutsu hihyō* 48 (December 1955): 48–49.
3. Kuri Yōji, "Animēshon no sekai 5 kamera nashi no eiga no tsukurikata" (The world of animation 5 the making of camera-less film), *Asahi Shinbun*, August 22, 1965, 21.
4. Okada Emiko, "Būmu ga kuru made, soshite . . .—Showa 20 nendai kara ima made anime ni deatta toki to basho" (Until the arrival of the boom, and then . . . : Times and places I've encountered anime from the decade after 1945 until today), in *Gekijō anime 70 nenshi* (70-year history of theatrical anime), ed. Animēju henshūbu (Tokyo: Tokuma Shoten, 1989), 148.
5. Hani Susumu, *Kamera to maiku—gendai geijutsu no hōhō* (A camera and a mic: Methods of contemporary art) (Tokyo: Chūō Kōronsha, 1960), 111.

6. Iizawa Tadasu, "Eiga no majutsu—animēshon eiga no tenbō" (The magic of cinema: An outlook on animated film), *Geijutsu shinchō* 8, no. 5 (May 1957): 228.

7. "Manga eiga—1958 nen no miryoku" (*Manga eiga:* The attraction of 1958), *Kinema junpō* 199 (March 1958): 38.

8. Takiguchi Shūzō, "Manga, dōga—kūkan kyōfu" (Manga, *dōga:* A space of dismay), *Kinema junpō* 199 (March 1958): 40.

9. Manabe Hiroshi, "Animēshon no kanōsei—sannin no kai o tōshite kangaeru koto" (The possibilities of animation: Thinking through the animation association of three), *Hon no techō* 4, no. 10 (December 1964): 58.

10. Nagai Yasuji, "Sekai no animēshon no keikō" (Trends in global animation), *Kiroku eiga* 5, no. 7 (July 1962): 7.

11. John Halas and Roger Manvell, *The Techniques of Film Animation* (New York: Hastings House, 1959), translated by Itō Ippei as *Animēshon—riron, jissai, ōyō* (Animation: Theory, practice, application) (Tokyo: Tōkyō Chūnichi Shinbun Shuppankyoku, 1963), 375–76.

12. Mori Takuya, *Animēshon nyūmon* (An introduction to animation) (Tokyo: Bijutsu Shuppansha, 1966), 9–10.

Production Models, Technological Innovations, and Animation Practices

The "Invention" of the Animation Director's Position at the Tōei Dōga Studio

MARIE PRUVOST-DELASPRE

This article investigates changing production models within the Japanese animation industry of the early 1960s through the lens of Tōei Dōga studio's history. More specifically, I analyze the creation of the new position of animation director during the production of the film *The Little Prince and the Eight-Headed Dragon* (1963, *Wanpaku ōji no orochi taiji*). The creation of the animation studio Tōei Dōga (now Tōei Animation) was through the will of its producer Ōkawa Hiroshi, president of the Tōei Film Company, which Ōkawa had saved from bankruptcy a few years earlier. As he was interested in the rise of cultural industries, Ōkawa's vision was to build a structure capable of producing animated theatrical feature films at an annual rate, something that had never been done in Japan at that time. To achieve this ambitious program, it was necessary to transition from the fragmented and disparate industry of the postwar period to a model of animation production that was sustainable over time and financially viable. Building upon the experience of second-generation pioneers who founded the first commercial animation studios in the 1920s and 1930s, such as Masaoka Kenzō and Yamamoto Zenjirō, Tōei Dōga's executive team furnished a working space with brand new equipment close to Tōei's studio in Ōizumi, an area in northwestern Tokyo. Their goal was to organize an efficient production line in a context of global labor shortage, meaning they would have to recruit and train numerous unexperienced workers. The production system that was established in 1956 at Tōei Dōga has continued to have a lasting impact on Japanese animation: the studio was sometimes jokingly referred to by professionals as "Tōei University" because of its importance in the training of a whole generation, gradually institutionalizing a certain organization of work, conception of animation and staging, and distribution of creative roles.

The observations of various sources make it possible not only to trace back the gestures of the animators at work but also to shed light on what collaborators and studio leaders said about this production model. The analysis of production documents is particularly valuable in these circumstances, since it allows for the precise observation of when and how animation practices or techniques were changed, appropriated, or institutionalized in the production model. Though many tangible elements have been dispersed or destroyed and thus cannot be considered as proper archives, it seems necessary to give importance to these material aspects of the work done by Tōei Dōga's employees. Investigating the remaining production documents (preserved and accessible through exhibits, private collections, auction catalogs, etc.) was a key element to this study, although it was done with the awareness that a preliminary sorting has been applied to them and they cannot be considered exhaustive. Along with the studio's films, this non-film documentation constitutes the main primary source of this study, supported by secondary resources such as memoirs and interviews from the studio's employees, comments made on the films by journalists and experts, or existing academic studies. The main purpose here is to create a corpus of documents to carry out an essay on production history, in a perspective close to that of production studies with a stress on the history of techniques and the social conditions of technical innovation. Inspired by the sociology of artistic professions, I argue that a case study such as this one could be useful to further analyze the division of labor in animation studios and the emergence of the "artist as a worker" figure defined by Pierre-Michel Menger,[1] as well as power-based professional relationships.

The aim here is to read the Tōei Dōga production model not only through official speeches and testimonies but also by taking into account the collaborative dynamics visible in the films, based on details introduced into the final product by the animators. As Howard Becker reminds us:

> Art worlds consist of all the people whose activities are necessary to the production of the characteristic works which that world, and perhaps others as well, define as art. Members of art worlds coordinate the activities by which work is produced by referring to a body of conventional understandings embodied in common practice and in frequently used artifacts. The same people often cooperate repeatedly, even routinely, in similar ways to produce similar works, so that we can think of an art world as an established network of cooperative links among participants.[2]

How are these art worlds organized and how do they function? How can we study them and highlight the "cooperative links" that are built between the actors of the production? Looking closely at the end of the assistant system and the establishment of the position of animation director around 1961–62 shows how the analysis of works and production documents can lead to a better understanding of production structures. In the case of Tōei Dōga, these evolutions grew from the tension between animators and management to preserve or limit their artistic freedom.

From "Production Units" to the Animation Director Method: An Ever-Evolving Production System

Tōei Dōga has adopted different production systems for short and feature films according to principles linked to the studio's economic and historical context but also to the vision of the studio's management team. Originally, animation work was conducted in small groups, each composed by a veteran animator, a couple of well-trained new recruits, and a bunch of inexperienced trainees. I call this early model, used for Tōei Dōga's short films and first feature length, the "production units system" because every group functions independently, as a kind of miniature for the whole team. It is worth noting that such a model is not surprising in the context of the transition from short to feature film production, and that a description of a relatively similar organization is given of the making of *Snow White and the Dwarfs* (1937) at Walt Disney Studios.[3] After a few months, the organization of production was gradually transformed at the end of the 1950s into a seconding system, consisting of a hierarchical division of creative tasks between a key animator and his assistants, partially inspired by the Disney Studios, lasting until 1963, when the creation of the position of animation director took place.

The influence of the animation director position remains visible in the strongly hierarchical conception of professional relationships, which has led to the specialization and division of activities within the studio. A similar movement occurred in the Hollywood cinema of the 1910s, where, according to Janet Staiger, a logic of "departmentalization" developed in the studios, tending toward an increasingly important compartmentalization of creative tasks.[4] Without necessarily concurring with the usual Taylorist interpretation, this departmentalization is also at work in animated production, which is organized around a powerful control of creation. These logics of compartmentalization and control forged Tōei Dōga's upper management approach to the planned and hierarchical organization of work. However, this preestablished conception of the division of tasks requires nuance. If we can easily understand how Taylor's principles of rationalization of work organization are perfectly suited to the production of cartoons, as they seem to describe the stages of planning and control of its production, we should not mix up official discourses with the study of institutions. As Donald Crafton reminds us, the adaptation of the concepts of scientific management to American animation is a conscious, voluntary, and ideological process, linked to the dependence of this nascent industry on military orders for propaganda and educational films.[5]

Nevertheless, even if they remain deeply hierarchical and hindered by the constraints imposed by management, the production models set up in the first years of the studio's existence are far from being fixed and show complex power relations at play. For example, Kimura Tomoya suggests in his work on the history of the studio that it was not until the end of the 1960s that the predominant role of animators in the production process was challenged by the rise of directorial figures such as Ikeda Hiroshi or Takahata Isao.[6] Indeed, at the end of the 1950s, in the framework of Tōei Dōga's short film production, which served as a training ground for new recruits, small groups of animators worked around a supervisor. Depending on their level of experience, they would draw the same scene from key poses to in-betweens and do their own cleaning, which signifies their responsibility for several stages of fabrication from the layout (setting the characters in the frame and on the background) to the creation of the complete and on-model animation. The supervisors who distributed the tasks and corrected the shots were veteran animators Mori Yasuji and Daikuhara Akira. This production system was indeed "animator-centered" and based on a relative decompartmentalization of the usual logic of specialization and distribution of tasks, diverted into different criteria of specialization. Specialization is almost always at play in the distribution of work among animators. In this instance, the division of work is made according to the degree of competence of the workers (for example a dialogue scene for a novice, an action scene for an experienced animator). Later in the studio's evolution, these criteria were transformed from the degree of skill (more or less advanced) to the range of talents of the animators (scenes involving water, delicate acting, etc.). This evolution can be linked to the long history of the essentialization of work hierarchies in animation—in postwar France, for example, director Paul Grimault claimed to divide the work among his collaborators according to the human qualities he attributed to them. But even if such a logic takes full advantage of the specific talents of each animator and limits the consequences of the lack of training for newcomers, it does not offer any guarantee of maintaining a graphic coherence and a consistent vision of the film's staging. This is why Tōei Dōga tried in its initial years to remodel this first organization of work, leading to various socio-technical innovations, among which was the subject of this essay: the position of animation direction.

A Japanese Version of the Seconding System?

The history of Tōei Dōga perfectly illustrates to what extent production and work organization models change over time. After the various experiments carried out on short film production between 1956 and 1958, the studio progressively abandons production in small groups to move to an organizational principle closer to the seconding system used in American animation, but which is still informal. We can find traces of this work organization in the credits of the first Tōei Dōga feature films. For example, if we see how certain animators were credited under *genga*, or "in-between animation" in earlier works, we can then see how the same animators take on the role of *dōga*, or "key animation," in later films, indicating the dynamics of promotion to positions of greater responsibility. This is also corroborated by the accounts of several employees of the studio at the time. In his chapter in the book *Zusetsu telebi anime zensho* (*The Complete Illustrated TV Anime Book*) (1999), the historian and former Tōei Dōga animator Sugiyama Taku mentions a "second key animation system [*daini genga seidō*]," involving corrections and clarifications brought to the first layouts (*daiichi genga*), which is quite close to the logics of division of labor in the seconding system.[7] Another source that corroborates the development of this labor structure is the description given by Ōtsuka Yasuo in his memoirs. In a chapter entitled "Sekando," an abbreviation for seconding system, he precisely describes the process set up for the production of the studio's first feature film.[8] A team of about thirty employees worked on the first scenes of *The White Snake Enchantress* (1958, *Hakujaden*) in December 1957. Ōtsuka describes how the animators were divided into two groups led by the two main animators: Mori Yasuji was assisted by Sakamoto Yūsaku, Kita Masamu and Konno Shūji, while Daikuhara Akira was assisted by new recruits Nakamura Kazuko and Ōtsuka Yasuo, as well as by Katsui Chikao, who had already worked at the animation studio Nichidō, created in 1948 by Masaoka Kenzō and Yamamoto Zenjirō under the name Nihon Dōgasha and acquired, after it changed names in 1952, by Tōei as an investment to build its own animation department.[9]

This first division of labor was doubled by a second one, in which assistants distributed the scenes to animate between their own assistants according to a stylistic and technical logic. For example, from the beginning, Ōtsuka Yasuo stood out for his great qualities in the rendering of action scenes, which allowed him to animate very dynamic shots, such as the final storm of *The White Snake Enchantress*, while Nakamura Kazuko was in charge of the dialogue scenes between the two heroes. This division of labor was innovative in that it mixed an American-style system, in which the experienced animator gives his assistant subsidiary work, such as cleaning up the drawings, with a much more embodied conception of the animator's practice by which one seeks to make the nature of the artist coincide with the scene he draws. Given the workload represented by a feature film, the supervisors spent much of their time checking and correcting the shots of their assistants. We can say that this model prefigured the animation direction model even though the position itself was implemented a few years later, officializing an informal practice with all that it implies in terms of reorganization of teams, credits, and salary scales.

The assistants themselves counted on and distributed work among a few in-betweeners who formed groups of five or six people around each assistant but were not quoted in the credits. This back-and-forth system ensured the quality control of each shot and a supervision by one of the two main animators on each image of the film. The system changed slightly for the studio's second feature film, *Magic Boy* (1959, *Shōnen Sarutobi Sasuke*), since there were five main animators credited: Mori and Daikuhara, as well as Ōtsuka Yasuo and two former animators of Nichidō, Kumakawa Masao and Furusawa Hideo. The assistants did not change, Ōtsuka being simply replaced by Kusube Daikichirō and Ōkuyama Reiko for *Alakazam the Great* (1960, *Saiyūki*). The following year, for *The Littlest Warrior* (1961, *Anju to Zushiōmaru*), Kusube became key animator and Ōkuyama took his place as an assistant. Ōkuyama then moved with Kita and Katsui to key animation for *Arabian Nights: The Adventures of Sinbad* (1962, *Arabian naito: Shindobaddo no bōken*). These successive and rapid promotions are probably justified as much by the talent of the animators as the need for the studio to have a sufficient number of people in charge of key animation, which allows a stable and homogeneous production. Though supervision is more and more present, creative freedom is still on the agenda. Indeed, in this model, key animators have the possibility to modify the storyboard of their scenes by adding certain details, gags, or visual effects. Ōtsuka also calls this work organization the "dangō skewer" model, referring to the Japanese dumpling composed of several glutinous rice balls on a stick, suggesting that each small team was quite independent, though linked to the other teams by the grouped effort of film production.[10] We can thus understand why this first production model, in which a whole group of animators was trained, was later a reason for nostalgia and regret, when the distribution of tasks became more and more controlled.

It is also important to underline here the role of the *ékonté* (a production document similar to a storyboard) in the distribution of tasks: the *ékonté* was used as a means of communication for the director and his team, since it indicated the duration of the shots, the intentions of the characters, and other details on the rhythm and tone of each scene. Depending on the director, the *ékonté* could be relatively rough and fast, as in *Jack and the Witch* (1967, *Shōnen Jakku to mahōtsukai*), or on the contrary extremely detailed and precise, as in the work of Ōtsuka Yasuo and Takahata Isao for *The Great Adventures of Horus, Prince of the Sun* (1968, *Taiyō no ōji Horusu no daibōken*), for which there was more than four hundred pages produced for its edited version.[11] Under its diversity, the *ékonté* process hides a rather free vision of the work required from the animators and allows the appearance of almost improvised scenes, drawn from the imagination of the animator in charge. This is particularly true of the studio's first feature films under the technical direction of Yabushita Taiji, and in the practice of Daikuhara, who was known for leaving a great deal of autonomy to the animators working under his supervision. Some examples of this artistic autonomy include the scene of the witch's undressing in *Alakazam the Great* imagined by Tsukioka Sadao, or a scene in the same film attributed to Ōtsuka Yasuo in which an oriental dancer is transformed into a circle of fire that is crossed by a series of monsters of all shapes.

A Blurred Line Between Creativity and Control

The Adventures of Sinbad by Yabushita Taiji and Kuroda Yoshio was the last Tōei feature film created within this initial model of production organization that emphasized the seconding system. A certain number of signs indicate that its blurred visual identity accelerated the studio's transition to a more modern approach to characters and staging. Sugiyama points out that the film was a breaking point in the studio's history: upon its completion, Tōei

stopped recruiting full-time animators and started employing freelance artists, inducing a "stylistic degeneration" which he calls "shedding,"[12] meaning
the studio was undergoing such changes that it was literally shedding its skin
and changing its identity as a whole. Sugiyama stresses the importance of
this period in Tōei's gradual transition from what Ōtsuka called a "one-crop
culture"—in reference to the main role given to animated feature films, which
consumed most of the time and energy of the teams to such an extent that it
amounted to a monoculture (with all the economic risks underlying the model)—to a studio culture with multiple production departments that conducted
theatrical feature and television serial production at the same time.

Criticized for its lack of clarity, *The Adventures of Sinbad* bears traces of the
disappearance of the seconding system. The segmentation of scenes, which
each developing their own style, contradicts the homogeneity of style and
tone usually sought in animation films. On the other hand, animation direction represents a slow but inexorable process of implementation of a strong
control on the artistic freedom of animators and production teams at large. It
can thus also be understood as a means to change the local studio culture, to
affect in a way that benefits work management, or in other words to control
what Mathieu Mallard has described as the "sense of animation."[13] That is to
say, a knowledge and understanding of animation as a technical apparatus
and a means of expression—according to the time and cultural context—
shared by the production teams. According to Mori himself, the artistic intermediation specific to his conception of the role of animation director as a
spokesman for the animators gradually faded with time and became more
of a supervisory role.[14] This indicates that though animation direction was
a compromise between the animators and the creative team at first, it could
have gradually become a tool for production management.

It seems that in the early 1960s, the progress in the training of young animators was complete enough for the seconding system to cease. The studio's
new project offered a reversal of perspective, as Mori Yasuji himself suggests:

> *The Little Prince*, based on Japanese mythology, was a turning point
> in many respects. Mr. Serikawa Yugo, a newcomer, was appointed to
> replace Mr. Yabushita, who had directed all Tōei's films until then. In
> addition, at a staff meeting, we discussed the creation of an animation
> director position. Tōei Dōga was now in its sixth year, the number
> of people able to draw key animations had increased, and a lack of
> unity was beginning to appear in the work as a whole, with different

people taking charge of different characters on the screen. I also had an opinion about character design. It seemed to me that in the context of an animated film, where the characters move on screen, it would be acceptable to change the drawing style to make it simpler.[15]

In the new model that emerged, the decision-making power was shared between the figure of the executive producer, who monitors the budget and the schedule, and a duo composed by the film's director and animation director, who distribute scenes to the animators according to the script and supervise their work. The films of the 1960s thus present a tension and a back-and-forth movement between a strict conception of artistic hierarchies and the search for a more fluid model where creative freedom dominates. This quest may find its temporary resolution in the innovation of Mori Yasuji, whose production position as the first animation director combines freedom and control in a way that questions the creative management at stakes in the studio.

The central purpose of animation supervision is to achieve a certain graphic unity, as director Ikeda Hiroshi points out: "We can say the way of making animation has really changed with *The Little Prince and the Eight-Headed Dragon*. In terms of character design, this is when the position of animation director was created, which made it possible to homogenize the style of the feature film. Before that, each animator drew in his own way, and it was fine to just gather the drawings, quite different, at the end."[16] In the early days of Tōei, most of the preliminary tasks, such as character creation or the monitoring and controlling tasks, were done for the animation department by Daikuhara Akira and Mori Yasuji because of their experience. In this sense, an entity of quality control of the work was already in place at the end of the 1950s, since the two supervisors had to revise most of the drawings. However, as Ikeda suggests, this "revision" consisted in correction and improvement of the shots concerned but did not include any intervention on the homogeneity of the scenes, each bearing the signs of the direction taken by the animators involved. This difference of styles between the animators is inevitable, insofar as Daikuhara and Mori each developed their own conception of animation.

In his memoirs, Mori Yasuji indicated that to compensate for the variations in style from one scene to another, he recommended entrusting the main characters of *The Little Prince and the Eight-Headed Dragon* to specific animators so that their difference in style made sense in the diegesis. This transformation of the production model involved a strengthening of animation supervision, which can be seen as a "vernacularization,"[17] a local transformation-variation of the American studio system. In a sense, through Mori's introduction of the position of animation director, the reinforcement of animation supervision alludes to one of the techniques advocated by the founding engineer of the Toyota production model, Ōno Taiichi: the "go and see" principle (*genchi genbutsu*), a device evoking craft workshop habits that consists in exercising visual control over any action at any time. The introduction of supervisors allows the quality of animation to be controlled and an organizational hierarchy to be maintained, while at the same time assuring the freedom and creativity of the artists to limit discontent. The innovation of its implementation does not directly harm the classical division of labor in the studio; it proposes a soft break from, and formalization of, a position tacitly occupied by Mori and Daikuhara in the early organizational models. This control and release of artistic constraints thus comes as a recurrent element of the studio's history, with the implementation of animation supervision serving as an anchor point that represents the studio's choice of innovation rather than revolution.

The "Invention" of Animation Direction: An Innovation Institutionalized?

Thus, the position of animation director is only formalized by the studio after it is necessitated by the production process. However, there is no determinism in its creation; as Ōtsuka points out in an interview, the final predominance of the "Mori model's" stylistic uniformity does not mean that another model, inspired by Daikuhara's more idiosyncratic practice, could not have existed: "Daikuhara's work on *The Adventures of Sinbad* was very similar to the duties of a modern animation director, though he is not credited as such in the film. However, Daikuhara's proto-animation director approach fell more into the camp of preserving the individuality of each animator, so it didn't bring about much uniformity."[18] We can conclude that these two visions competed against each other before the "Mori model's" supervision and stylistic uniformity won out over the expression of the animators' touch. Thus, the creation of the role of animation director may have been motivated by the need to have an additional intermediation between the animators, the director, and the art director. The predominance of the "Mori model," defined as a vision favoring stylistic unity and a close supervision of the individual animator's work, can be understood in this context as more in line with Tōei's type of management.

This leads us to reconsider the creation of the position of animation director as a strong tension within the studio between a syncretic and open tradition of animation on one hand and a more homogenous and controlled vision of the practice of animation on the other. Indeed, Ōtsuka reports in the same interview that Mori was very demanding with his animators and asked for a lot of retakes, correcting almost every shot where the character of Rosa appears in *Puss in Boots* (1969, *Nagagutsu o haita neko*) for example, whereas Ōtsuka himself, when he was entrusted with the task of director of animation for *Horus, Prince of the Sun*, followed the model of his master Daikuhara and corrected the animators very little, emphasizing the variation of expression between scenes.

The Little Prince and the Eight-Headed Dragon is a good illustration of the tension between control and creation, insofar as Mori's work as director of animation allowed him to introduce an unprecedented number of formal inventions, while at the same time he reinforced his control over the work of his collaborators. Thanks to these stylistic and technical innovations, the film introduced a real break in the conventions of representation. *The Little Prince and the Eight-Headed Dragon* is inspired by the *haniwa* of the Kofun period and adapted from the thirteenth-century story *Kojiki*, or *Chronicle of Ancient Things*, in a totally modernist graphic style.[19] The film is about the mythological character of Susanoo, a young boy overcome by the pain of the death of his mother, whom he wishes to see in the underworld. This wish brings him the wrath of his father, his sister Amaterasu, the sun goddess, and his brother Tsukuyomi, the moon god. Chased from heaven and exiled by his family, Susanoo meets in his wanderings the young princess Kushinada, whose eight sisters were eaten by the eight-headed dragon Yamata no Orochi. He then devises a plan to slay the dragon, thus winning Kushinada's love and the magic sword that allows him to obtain forgiveness from his family. The script turns the myth into a learning story, focusing on Susanoo's transition from the pain of grief to the joy of shared love.

The direction is entrusted to Serikawa Yūgo, a former assistant director of Shin Tōhō recruited by the studio in 1961. Like Yabushita Taiji, whom he assisted on *The Littlest Warrior*, Serikawa comes from live action cinema. The production begins under the same auspices as the previous films: the production documents show graphic research that experiments with very diverse options, in a particularly striking heterogeneity of styles. Among the character proposals formulated by the animators, very few are kept, and it is finally Mori Yasuji himself who composes the *settei* (graphic elements), introducing an original orientation to the characters. If the settings refer to a rather classical pictorial heritage, the graphic elements display a choice of rupture by replacing the traditional curved and soft lines of the previous films by angular, hard, and geometrical forms.

A myth surrounds *The Little Prince and the Eight-Headed Dragon*, often presented as the place where the invention of the animation director appeared. Hikone Norio, in the introduction to an illustrated sum of Mori's work, glorifies the primacy of the animator in this matter:

> Mori-san was the first animation director ever. For Tōei's feature, *The Little Prince and the Eight-Headed Dragon* (1963), Mori-san, as the first animation director, unified the look of the whole film with the unique set of characters he created. Nowadays, the animation-director system has become the norm, but in those days no clear-cut system existed to unify the animation style of the whole picture. It is due to the success of this film that the system, since then, has become indispensable.[20]

Here, Hikone conjures a romantic evocation of Mori's unique inspiration as an author caught in a system of mass production, but it is precisely the success of the film that serves as a teleological element to the posterity of the model established by Mori. Yet, this interpretation hides another important feature of the animation direction system. Indeed, if this system currently holds a hegemonic place in the Japanese production model, it is thanks to its efficiency as a tool to manage or even reduce the amount of workforce necessary to produce animation of satisfactory quality. In this sense, the animation direction system extends the research initiated by Ōkawa Hiroshi at the end of the 1950s of a quest for a rational and profitable logic of production organization. Beyond the image of Mori as an inspired inventor, we must also consider the sometimes-conflicting relationships between animators, as well as their vertical creative and managerial relations within the hierarchy. It is therefore a question of *innovation*: animation direction can be said to be an institutionalized innovation. A collective, progressive, and negotiated response to a problem fed by a large number of players, some of whom remain unknown in historical accounts. This shift from invention to innovation makes it possible to reintroduce two important factors: plurality and progressiveness, moving away from the myth of Mori's solitary invention to consider that the animation director position is a group response formulated within the system to the problem raised by the supervision and control of creative work. Another response can indeed be to leave the studio, in hopes to find better working conditions elsewhere. We can see here that Tōei Dōga's workers are, in the 1960s, still trying to maintain or gain agency within the organization of labor in the studio, a strategy that will be abandoned by some of them in the 1970s. By then, the "voice" option, defined by Albert Hirschman as activating a loyalist behavior motivated by a strict initiation and high penalties for exit,[21] will give in to "exit," and many longtime workers such as Ōtsuka Yasuo or Takahata Isao will leave the studio.

Tracing Work Organization in Production Documents: A Case-study

From a practical point of view, the position of animation director is based, like the seconding system, on the distinction between *genga* and *dōga;* the novelty is introduced in the reorganization of the production implied by this additional stage. Indeed, much back and forth is necessary between the animator, his assistant, and the director to reach the final state of how a shot will be animated. The presence of the animation director considerably limits this effect, since he works directly on the drawings of the animator, which simplifies the back-and-forth process. Thus, the animation director corrects the *genga* of the key animators, either directly on the animation sheet, or by drawing the retakes on a different color sheet (typically yellow). The animator does not always receive corrections, since the animation director can directly rework the shot before passing it on to the next stage of production, where the animator's drawings and the animation director's corrections will be combined to establish the final version of the shot. Not having to completely redo certain drawings by correcting them on layers is a clear advantage and considerably reduces the time spent on corrections, since the animation director can touch up the shots himself. In fact, the animation director assumes a role of technical director, and his style is recognizable in the finished product. Kimura underlines this predominant place in Tōei's production system by recalling that the animation director was first appointed at the beginning of a project, and that he had the possibility to choose the director:

> The planner would first appoint an animation director, and then the
> director would be decided upon after discussions between the two
> parties. For example, Takahata Isao was asked to direct the feature film

The Great Adventure of Horus, Prince of the Sun, at the request of Ōtsuka Yasuo, who had been asked by the company to be the animation director. In *Animal Treasure Island*, also released in the spring of 1971, Ikeda Hiroshi stated that he had received an invitation from Mori Yasuji, the animation director, to work on a project based on Stevenson's *Treasure Island*. In Tōei Dōga's feature film planning system, even in the early 1970s, the main animators were ahead of the directors.[22]

This account reminds us of the intricate links between the strategies pursued by the studio's management, the practices and approaches implemented and negotiated over the years, and the implication of these different elements on the effective division of labor. The study of the facsimile of *The Little Prince's ékonté* provides a great deal of information and fuels various questions central to the investigation in this regard. The following paragraph is based on the reprinted version of the *ékonté* available in the Blu-ray edition of the film published by Tōei Company in 2020. Although the exact provenance of this document is not specified, it is likely to be a later version used during production. Indeed, it is printed on carbon paper and contains scenes that differ from the original drawings that can be consulted elsewhere. For example, the final scene is not the same as the one that appears on the *ékonté* page reproduced in the book based on Takahata's personal archives.[23] As pointed out in the introduction, these documents are fragmentary and often partly reconstructed *a posteriori*, so the conclusions they inspire must remain hypothetical. First of all, this document clearly shows an evolution of the working methods within the studio: whereas the *ékonté* of *The White Snake Enchantress*, as shown in the reprinted version, appears stylistically very homogeneous (which can lead us to attribute it to a handful of artists) and not very detailed in its form (it does not include any scene timing, for example), *The Little Prince's ékonté* proves to be graphically very diverse at first sight. The graphics of the texts and the panels vary strongly from one page to another, and we can easily see the traces of how these different creations were assembled, since there are often empty pages or crossed-out panels between two sequences drawn by different people. More precisely, these differences might reveal divergences in the very practice of animation and storyboarding: some animators include numerous graphic details about the characters or the setting, others indicate very precisely the planned camera movements, while others annotate at great length. The fact that some sequences are timed to the half-second, whereas others do not include any reference to rhythm and timing, suggests that this is perhaps as much a matter of a diversity of approach to animation as of differences in supervision: the recurrence of comments or corrections on the pages of the storyboard suggests that specific supervisors were constraining in the use of certain tools.

The division of work between animators, that is, the attribution of sequences to be animated to a particular person, also seems to follow divergent logics depending on the parts of the story concerned. Thus, the beginning of the film includes very few stylistic changes, and rather long takes. On the other hand, Susanoo's fight against the dragon is extremely fragmented, with a total of about fifty-five sequences; some sequences are very short, averaging ten shots, and the longest is twenty-seven shots, whereas elsewhere in the film there are sequences of more than forty shots. This battle scene is typically credited to Ōtsuka Yasuo and Tsukioka Sadao, an essential part of the story and the climax of the film, but what the facsimile shows is that many more employees were involved and that each animator seems to have storyboarded his or her shots. It is difficult, from these elements alone, to count exactly how many people contributed to the staging and making of the fight, at what point in the production process and to what extent they became involved, but it is obvious that there was a highly collaborative work at play. Therefore, it is noteworthy that the logic of assigning a specific sequence with narrative unity to one animator, a traditional practice in Japanese animation, does not hold in this case. The presence of annotations added to the existing text, and of what can be interpreted as corrections or external interventions (mostly removal of shots, such as page 169 or page 174 of the facsimile) is also particularly interesting. This is consistent with the association between animation direction and supervision: the organization of work for this film seeks a pragmatic method of delegating tasks while maintaining a high level of control over the final result.

The facsimile includes, after the end scene, what is described as a series of unnumbered pages and duplicate scenes. Upon examination, it turns out that these are not duplicates per se, but rather alternate versions that were set aside during production. It concerns a sequence belonging to the opening of the film, and eight sequences from the fight against the dragon. These sequences—165 to 173—are central to the story as they describe the moment when Susanoo throws spikes at the dragon to finish it off. This suggests that there was much at stake during production in the validation of these *ékonté* pages, and that a high degree of rivalry probably prevailed between animators not only to gain responsibility for certain scenes but also to have their interpretation included in the final version. The highly divided character of this part of the *ékonté* could thus be understood in light of several hypotheses concerning the quest for balance between the supervision of the production team and the desire for creative input by the animators: obviously the fact that the sequences were divided upon many workers is meant to be more efficient in the manufacturing process, as they are mostly complex action shots, but it also ensures that the most important or technical parts of the scene are entrusted to experienced staff, while at the same time attempting to accommodate the wishes of the animators, who are eager to contribute to the sections of the film that seem most interesting to them, as Mori would later recall about the production of *Puss in Boots* (1969).

To measure the stylistic and technical change operated by Mori, it is instructive to refer to the work of Howard Becker on the "cooperative links" and the constraints inherent to collective creation activities. Becker describes how cooperation, as it is always present in the field of artistic creation, influences the production and consumption of works. He defines a "bundle of tasks" that each player must perform to create a work of art, from the raw materials to the activities of exhibiting, distributing, or even reviewing the productions. In doing so, he notes that changing an existing system can be difficult: "Each kind of person who participates in the making of art works has a specific bundle of tasks to do. Though the allocation of tasks to people is, in an important sense, arbitrary—it could have been done differently and is supported only by the agreement of all or most of the other participants—it is not therefore easy to change. The people involved typically regard the division of tasks as quasi-sacred, as 'natural' and inherent in the equipment and the medium."[24] Such an essentialization is reminiscent of the one that presided over the hierarchy of production positions at the creation of Tōei Dōga. This remark allows us to underline to what extent, even if it is considered today as a key position in the organization of animation production in Japan, the introduction of the position of animation director has disrupted the set of rules that governed the relationships between animators, technicians, and supervisors. By imposing a unified graphic style, Mori broke one of the conventions that guided the work of the animators: their belonging to a subgroup developing a specific style, a logic that presided over the organization of films like *The White Snake Enchantress*. It also modifies the place of supervision in the hierarchy of creative positions, associating in the same role graphic creation, a valued and noticed form of expression, and the control of animation, a much more invisible and less rewarding practice.

To Conclude: The Animator as an Artist as a Worker under Supervision

Becker also points out that, beyond the practical and institutional constraints, there exists a set of conventions that facilitate collaboration and the understanding of collective work. These conventions allow for collaborative work to take place in an orderly fashion. In this sense, the position of animation director compensates for the loss of reference points brought about by the modification of the conventions surrounding the creation of the graphic bible and the rising power of the director. Thus, it would seem more accurate to speak of the creation of the position of animation director as an evolution, in the sense in which film economist Laurent Creton understands "configurative innovation,"[25] as opposed to fundamental and all-encompassing paradigmatic innovations. Indeed, innovating inside the system, by bringing perpetual improvements to it, makes it possible to avoid true revolutions that might disturb it. These adjustments are in line with a vision that runs through the cinema industry as a whole, insofar as, in Creton's words, "the historical perspective of the evolution of the cinematographic sector shows that the performance of a production system is characterized by its capacity to integrate elements of divergence and differentiation, while mastering a productive efficiency based on standardization."[26]

If transformation and adaptation are necessary for the preservation of the production system, the question of the consequences of these transformations remains. Mori's desire to develop a unified graphic style is based, at least in his discourse, on the rejection of what he viewed as the defect of stylistic heterogeneity of the previous films. However, this simple consideration alone could not justify the change of the production habits of an entire studio, and other elements must be considered to explain this evolution of the model. The first point to consider is the protest movements among the studio's animators: the introduction of the director of animation and then of television production provoked important upheavals in the organization of work, and thus the discontent of certain collaborators, dispossessed of their usual "ways of doing things" and forced to work faster and faster. Indeed, Tōei Dōga's workers union has been created a few months before, and Kimura insists on the links between the production of the film and the ongoing discussions on working conditions between unionized employees.[27] The second point of interest directly involves the collaborative processes of collective creation, which are modified and challenged by these changes. As Becker argues, the essentialist reading that the players of an art world have of its functioning prevents them from considering the possible transformation to the "bundles of tasks" entrusted to them; any evolution carries its share of compromise and modification of the existing models. This framework can explain the emergence of the position of director of animation, insofar as it responds to a new historical-economic but also structural situation.

Indeed, how can creative spaces be preserved within a model that is increasingly tightened and controlled? According to certain modalities, the position of animation director makes it possible to reestablish a space of freedom under control for the animators, who find themselves protected, so to speak, by this first filter of supervision and correction. This context and the presence of the intermediation of the animation director, can therefore encourage graphic and technical innovation, as it seems to have been the case during the production of The Little Prince and the Eight-Headed Dragon. Takahata Isao puts it this way: "A new generation of animators was emerging. The previous generation had started working long before Tōei was founded. The Little Prince allowed Mori to launch a team of young animators who then began to develop their own style. It was a very ambitious project, trying to develop a new style of animation. Ōtsuka and Tsukioka animated the dragon fight sequence together, but the studio left them free to do it as they wished. It was a good opportunity for each of them to develop their abilities."[28] Due to its inheritance of methods from prewar studios, the production model set up at Tōei is based on a hierarchical and hegemonic approach to production. One can therefore imagine that the intermediary position introduced by Mori, who had difficulty in taking his place in this hierarchy, tried to find a compromise in this system. At the same time, the position of animation director might be seen as an additional level in the infinite range of responsibilities of an animator, a logic on which Tōei's management relied to control possible unrest among employees whose salaries were sometimes very different in a period of strong union activity. In the testimonies of the animators, the supervisor is in fact often the one who echoes the expectations or even the pressures of management in terms of productivity. In all cases, the "Mori model" inaugurates a conception of animation that profoundly modifies artistic relationships and the distribution of creative tasks.

The elements described here document a system of production that is not a model fixed in an immutable practice but, on the contrary, a form in movement, bound to adapt to the material constraints as well as to the aesthetic research. Such a system would thus be more than a production model; it would be the setting up of what Edgar Schein understands as an "organizational culture," or "the pattern of basic assumptions that a given group has invented, discovered, or developed in learning to cope with its problems of external adaptation and internal integration, and that have worked well enough to be considered valid, and, therefore, to be taught to new members as the correct way to perceive, think and feel in relation to those problems."[29] This definition perfectly fits the progressive evolution of Tōei's production system, which went from an exogenous training system (school, short films) to an endogenous training system (assistant), to end up with an integration of these different methods within a third model, that of the animation director. It would be interesting to question what the new cultural organization at Tōei Dōga owes to the practice of creative work in Japanese film studios which are deeply marked by internal negotiations between well-established hierarchical structures and local practices. What is indeed at stake is the emergence of a studio culture, a question I believe is quite central to the understanding of the contemporary Japanese animation industry.

....

Marie Pruvost-Delaspre is Senior Lecturer in Cinema Studies at Paris 8 Vincennes–Saint Denis University since 2017. Her PhD dissertation, conducted at Sorbonne Nouvelle University, focused on the history of animation techniques at Tōei Dōga studio and the evolution of its production system from 1956 to 1972. She published several articles on anime, the history of animation techniques as well as work organization in animation studios, and edited a number of collective publications in French, including *Japanese Animation in France* (2014) and *Grendizer the Never-Ending Story* (2018). Her first monograph is entitled *The Origins of Anime: Tōei Dōga Studio* (PUR, 2021).

....

Notes

1. Pierre-Michel Menger, *Portrait de l'artiste en travailleur: Métamorphoses du capitalisme* (*Artists as Workers : Theoretical and Methodological Challenges*) (Paris: Seuil, 2002).

2. Howard S. Becker, *Art Worlds* (Berkeley: University of California Press, 2012), 34–35.

3. J. B. Kaufman, *Snow White and the Seven Dwarfs: The Art and Creation of Walt Disney's Classic Animated Film* (San Francisco: Walt Disney Family Foundation Press, 2012), 36.

4. Janet Staiger, "The Director-unit System: Management of Multiple-unit Companies after 1909," in *The Classical Hollywood Cinema: Film Style and Mode of Production to 1960*, ed. David Bordwell, Kristin Thompson, and Janet Staiger (New York: Columbia University Press, 1985), 124.

5. Donald Crafton, *Before Mickey: The Animated Film, 1898–1928* (Cambridge, MA: MIT Press, 1982), 162.

6. Kimura Tomoya, *Tōei Dōga shiron: Keiei to sōzō no teiryū* (Tōei animation history: Management and creativity's bottom line) (Tokyo: Nihon Hyōronsha, 2020), 128–29.

7. Sugiyama Taku, "Telebi anime zenshi: Tōei chōhen anime no jidai" (History of television animation: The era of Tōei's feature films), in *Zusetsu terebi anime zensho* (The complete illustrated TV anime book), ed. Misono Makoto (Tokyo: Harashobō, 1999), 109.

8. Ōtsuka Yasuo, *Sakuga asé mamiré* (Drawings covered in sweat) (Tokyo: Tokuma Shoten, 2001), 48–50.

9. Laura Montero Plata and Marie Pruvost-Delaspre, "Shaping the Anime Industry: Second Generation Pioneers and the Emergence of the Studio System," in *A Companion to Japanese Cinema*, ed. David Desser (Hoboken, NJ: John Wiley & Sons Inc., 2022), 229–32.

10. Ōtsuka Yasuo, in *Sutajio Jiburi reiauto-ten* (Studio Ghibli layout designs), ed. Kanō Seiji (Tokyo: Museum of Contemporary Art Tokyo / Japan TV Broadcast Network, 2008), 14.

11. Ōtsuka Yasuo and Takahata Isao, *Taiyō no ōji horusu no daibōken: Tōei animēshon sakuhin* (The adventures of Horus, Prince of the Sun: Tōei's animation film) (Tokyo: Tokuma Shoten, 2003).

12. Sugiyama Taku, "Telebi anime zenshi," 113.

13. Mathieu Mallard, "L'émergence de postures d'autorité dans l'âge d'or de l'animation japonaise. Le cas de la Tōei Dōga et de Mushi Pro (1958–1973)" (The Emergence of of authorial positions in the Golden Age of Japanese Animation. The case of Tōei Dōga and Mushi Pro [1958–1973]), Master's Thesis, Université Paris 8, 2022.

14. Interview with Ōtsuka Yasuo and Mori Yasuji.

15. Mori Yasuji, *Mogura no uta—animētā no jiden* (The mole's song—My time as an animator) (Tokyo: Tokuma Shoten, 1984), 133.

16. Interview with Ikeda Hiroshi by Robin Gatto and trans. Emi Yuki, *Dōbutsu Takarajima*, dir. Ikeda Hiroshi (1971); translated as *Les Joyeux Pirates de l'île au trésor* (Wild Side Films, 2004).

17. Arjun Appadurai, *Modernity At Large: Cultural Dimensions of Globalization* (Minneapolis: University of Minnesota Press, 2010).

18. Interview with Ōtsuka Yasuo and Mori Yasuji, "Nagagutsu wo haita neko," *Animage Bunko*, 1984: 86–106; trans. Benjamin Ettinger (May 2001), http://www.pelleas.net/int/int2.shtml (accessed August 16, 2022).

19. Mori, *Mogura no uta*, 133.

20. Hikone Norio, "Foreword," in *Yasuji Mori: Master Animator—His Animated Drawings*, ed. Namiki Takashi (Tokyo: Pulp Co. Ltd., 1991), 2.

21. Albert Hirschman, *Exit, Voice and Loyalty: Responses to Decline in Firms, Organizations, and States* (Cambridge, MA: Harvard University Press, 1970).

22. Kimura, *Tōei Dōga shiron*, 129.

23. *Nihon no animêshon ni nokoshita mono Takahata Isao* (Takahata Isao: A legend in Japanese animation), ed. Saito Chikashi and Tsutsui Ryoko (Tokyo: NHK Promotion Inc., 2019), 26.

24. Becker, *Art Worlds*, 13.

25. Laurent Creton, *Économie du cinéma: perspectives stratégiques* (Film economics: Strategical perspectives) (Paris: Armand Colin, 2005), 40.

26. Creton, *Économie du cinéma*, 40.

27. Kimura, *Tōei Dōga shiron*, 80.

28. Interview with Otsuka Yasuo, in *Ōtsuka Yasuo no ugokasu yorokobi* (Ōtsuka's Joy in Motion), dir. Uratani Toshiro (Buena Vista Home Entertainment, 2004).

29. Edgar Schein, "Coming to a New Awareness of Organizational Culture," *Sloan Management Review* 25, no. 2 (1984): 3.

A New Labor Model for a New Era of Anime

A Case Study of Anime Production in the 1970s and 1980s

NAGATA DAISUKE AND MATSUNAGA SHINTARŌ, TRANS. KENDALL HEITZMAN,
INTRODUCTION BY BRYAN HIKARI HARTZHEIM

Editor's Introduction

Nagata Daisuke and Matsunaga Shintarō represent a new generation of scholarship on anime industry, production, and labor. Their co-authored book, *Sangyōhendō no rōdōshakaigaku—animeetaa no keikenshi* (Labor sociology of industrial change—An experiential history of animators) (Kyoto: Koyo Shōbō, 2022), was awarded the academic achievement prize of the Japanese Society for Animation Studies in 2023. Both Nagata and Matsunaga are interested in animation as a system of labor from a sociological perspective. Nagata's individual work has focused on disruptions in the industry due to the emergence of otaku culture, looking at how new distribution formats and fan viewing habits led to different production and consumption "logics" in the 1970s and 1980s. Matsunaga's approach is firmly ethnographic, interviewing and observing animators working in the industry about their professional values and motivations despite precarious or exploitative conditions. The following article is a good example of their combined work, which uses labor process theory to analyze anime magazines and the professional animator voices therein.

Originally published in *Mass Communication Research* (Masu komyunikeeshon kenkyū), volume 95 in 2019, the article points a way forward for those interested in understanding not only changes in labor structures during periods of industrial expansion but also how those changes are absorbed and processed by workers in the field. Among the many methodological contributions, there are two key points to take away from the article that will be valuable to scholars of anime in particular and animation industries more generally.

First, in collecting and analyzing interviews and roundtables of animators working in the 1970s and 1980s, Nagata and Matsunaga describe how a new value system came into place through mass television and video production within anime. This value system is of the *shokunin*, or "craftworker," who is prized for dedication in perfecting a trade, rather than the *geijutsuka*, or "artist," who is valued for originality. Such "craft" animators came into focus through the technically sophisticated movements they produced of characters or properties they neither designed nor created. This shift in perspective echoes the "sakuga" fans who emerged in the 1980s and celebrated animators less for a singular vision, but more for their technical skill in shaping or interpreting an existing character or property. Similarly, animators within commercial anime came to be respected for their workmanlike versatility under limited constraints rather than an artistic uniqueness. Of course, this type of refined technique also requires innovation and imagination, but of a different *kind* akin to the iterative process of animation that Stevie Suan describes in his book *Anime's Identity*. It is a perspective, moreover, not shared by all; older directors decry such "craft" animators as machine-like, whereas younger animators find the parameters liberating. While the authors do not have the space to examine the meaning or larger social implications of this shift in labor orientation, it is worth continuing to explore how anime can be viewed as a "skill" or "craft" versus an artform, and what that signifies with regards to creative identity and agency in a commercial production environment.

Second, in their detailed exploration of the pages of *Animage*, the authors reveal the untapped potential that anime's fan magazines contain for understanding how industry and style are shaped over time. More than a promotional device for studios or a simple collection of blurbs and anecdotes, magazines during this period provided a space that connected readers and producers through dialogues on the state of the industry. Scholars can do well to continue to mine these archives for insights into how animation trends, techniques, and labor structures developed through the queries of readers and the real-time responses of those on the production floor.

A New Labor Model for a New Era of Anime: A Case Study of Anime Production in the 1970s and 1980s

NAGATA DAISUKE AND MATSUNAGA SHINTARŌ

ESTABLISHING THE LINE OF INQUIRY

In the 1980s, changes in the Japanese domestic market for anime accompanied the rise of a new kind of consumer, a moment known as the "anime boom." In this article, we hope to shed some light on the evolution of the labor model for the anime creators that made such a transformation possible.

When we think about anime, it is not enough to simply look at the consumers—we need to consider the producers as well. Thomas Lamarre has examined anime as a function of its industrial conditions and the professional status of animators.[1] Lamarre focuses on major transformations in the industry during the development of anime as a mode of expression.

There have been several of these turning points in the history of anime. One was the rise of the consumer during the anime boom of the 1970s and 1980s. Together with this came a dramatic rise in anime produced for television[2], and a corresponding change in the quality of the product. From the end of the 1970s, anime also began to dominate the box office for domestically produced fare, and here again the production values changed accordingly. Together with this, a new image of the consumer was perceived. Among anime that started at this time, there were those that were popular among readers of anime magazines, such as *Space Battleship Yamato*,[3] and those popular with the more general public, such as *Doraemon*. But in the ranking of most popular anime published in the June 1980 issue of *Animage*, *Doraemon* did not crack the top twenty, a development that stunned even the editors of the magazine. A qualitative gap began to develop between what the general public was watching and what anime fans were watching.

Changing market forces and the appearance of a new kind of consumerism gave rise to a new form of anime production: the OVA (Original Video Animation), or direct-to-video anime. OVA companies aimed to sell 5,000–10,000 copies of a work. After a single OVA work, *Dallos*, appeared in 1983, the industry saw exponential growth: 5 works in 1984, 28 works in 1985, and as many as 171 works in 1989.[4] As the market continued to fragment, OVA became a prime venue for exploring a range of artistic possibilities.[5] These qualitative and quantitative market changes also affected how people in the field worked. To survive these market upheavals required having workers who could respond to changes in the amount of anime being produced and the quality expected of it. This article attempts to clarify the various conditions under which the new labor model that supported these market shifts was established.

SITUATING THIS STUDY

The purpose of this article is to look at how this transformation in anime consumption and the shifts in industry were experienced by the workers. Claiming that "collaborative creativity, which operates across media industries and connects official producers to unofficial fan production, is what led to anime's global success," Ian Condry conducted ethnographic research into the relationship between producer and consumer.[6] Condry conducted field work with various creators and interviews with fan communities, discovering two kinds of connections at play. The first was between the creators themselves, and the second was between creators on the one hand and consumers or various other media creators on the other. Both of these connections are called the "soul" of anime, but it is not clear in either case what constitutes these connections. In the latter category, it is assumed even among the various actors involved that there is an unshakable connection between creators and consumers, but it is not clear on either side what this connection actually is.

There is other research out there, however, that examines these connections. One example is a work by Kimura Tomoya, which analyzes the relationship of the market and labor conditions in the anime industry, starting with an analysis of the relationship between management and labor at Tōei Dōga from the mid-1960s, after the company had begun producing anime for television, through the beginning of the 1970s.[7] Tōei Dōga had played a key role in the development of Japanese anime, starting with the golden age of the 1950s. In 1963, however, Mushi Production's *Astro Boy* heralded a new age, in which the main market for anime shifted to television. Kimura focuses on the position of Tōei Dōga, which inevitably entered the television market. Kimura points to how an increase in work and an uneven schedule for new commissions led to a new model for contracts for full-time, salaried creators. The practice of paying according to the number of hours worked, common at the time, shifted to a model in which creators were paid by the project.

And yet, it is not clear from Kimura's analysis how the supply of labor could have been maintained into the era of OVA, when consumer demand diversified. If we know that consumer expectations rose in terms of volume and quality, then it follows that production also expanded and diversified. If that is the case, then a labor force of a size that could accommodate consumer demand was also necessary. This article considers how labor models that made such market changes possible around 1980 manifested themselves.

Initally, we present an outline of the various duties of animators in different roles, then lay out our framework of analysis and situate the data we employ. Further, we give an overview of our previous research of the labor situation in 1980s Japanese anime production with an emphasis on those aspects that pertain to this new study. Finally, we examine a series of discussions that appeared in a magazine at the time, with an eye toward understanding how the anime boom was experienced by animators who were already in the business before the labor model changed. In conclusion, we explore the significance of this project and suggest where future research might lead.

THE WORK OF ANIMATORS

Here we give a brief overview of the work of animators, focusing on the aspects pertinent to our argument. The work of animators can be divided into two categories: the project-management work, performed with one eye always on the external forces of the market; and the work that goes on inside the studio, the drawing, background art, computer graphics, etc. Animators, needless to say, are in the business of drawing; these positions and their work responsibilities are laid out in Table 1. This article is primarily concerned with three categories: animation supervisors,[8] key animators, and inbetween animators. Of course, it is never the case that studio work is completely removed from market realities, and in this article we analyze the relationship of studio and market.

Table 1. Animator positions and their respective responsibilities.

POSITION	JOB RESPONSIBILITIES
Director	Ultimate responsibility for all aspects of work
Character Designer	Designs characters that appear in an animated work
Unit Director	Organizes the work according to director's plan, tasked with continuity of performance of the characters. Generally placed in charge of certain number of episodes or scenes
Storyboard Artist	Creates the series of drawings, or storyboards, that serve as a guide to the various scenes of the work
Animation Supervisor	Corrects the series of drawings, or storyboards, makes sure that movements and drawings adhere to the level of quality that has been set
Key Animator	Determines visual layout following storyboard, creates images of key points in scenes following unit director's plan for performance. Revises layout after it has been checked by the animation supervisor
Inbetween Animator	Creates the intermediate frames (inbetweens) that go between the keyframes created by the key animator

The jobs outlined in Table 1 all have a certain amount of independence. In general, the director gives orders to the storyboard artist, the storyboard artist gives orders to the key animator, and so on—there is a hierarchy based on the chain of command, and remuneration follows those same lines. At the same time, there are veterans who spend their entire careers as key animators but who are deeply respected for the work they do. It is very common for key animators and inbetween animators to be paid by the scene or by the number of drawings they produce.

Many in the industry rely on personal connections or contacts at production companies where jobs are abundant to pick up work.[9] The farther down the chain of command one goes, the more common this is. According to the Japanese Animation Creators Association (JAniCA), the majority of animators are not employed by a single production company, but rather work as freelancers, signing work-for-hire contracts with multiple companies.[10]

FRAMEWORK OF ANALYSIS

As we stated in the first section, this article is mainly concerned with the relationship of the business environment, including market changes, faced by the animation workplace and the actual experience of working in the studio. The study of the relationship between labor models and actual conditions on the ground in the workplace developed into the field of labor process theory. From work in this field we have come to understand how the labor model has an effect on the way laborers work, and how it thus shapes their experiences of labor. Michael Burawoy refers to the labor model used in the workplace as the ideological domain of the labor process.[11] According to Burawoy, this domain determines what sort of experience laborers will have in the workplace. For example, although management-worker relationships will vary by workplace, it is the labor model of any given workplace that will determine whether workers will feel it is a coercive relationship or a collegial one. It is important to note here that, in order to analyze a labor model, it is necessary to ascertain how workers experience their workplace. Even when we look at management-worker relations, we cannot say anything about the labor model used in the workplace without knowing how the workers are experiencing that workplace.

Labor process theory has also considered the connection between the workplace and the larger business environment. Burawoy, resisting theories that saw working conditions as a function of the market environment, treated the workplace as an enclosed community. P. K. Edwards pushed beyond this to examine the relationship of the market and labor conditions.[12] Edwards explained how changes in environmental conditions were experienced by individual workers, and how these changes influenced the labor process. In this conception, the labor model for workers influences how they work, and their experience of labor is constructed from there.

As is clear from the above, even when we are looking at transformations of working models and the related changes in the business environment, we need to set out by describing the experience of the workplace. First, then, this article looks at how individual animators experienced changes in their work patterns. To do so, in the next section we examine what it means to present changes in the labor model to consumers in the form of a new image of workers as portrayed in a magazine.

SITUATING OUR ANALYSIS OF *ANIMAGE*

Our argument here relies mainly on the archive—namely, the monthly anime magazine *Animage*, started in 1978 and published by Tokuma Shoten. *Animage* was designed for mass appeal; at its peak, it set a longstanding circulation record among anime magazines, printing 250,000 copies every month.

The magazine was most famous for its reader column and introduction of animated works. In introducing these works, and for special issues on various themes, the magazine often conducted interviews and roundtable discussions with animators. The articles offer a wealth of information that we can analyze to discover what issues animators faced in creating new works.

In analyzing these interviews and roundtables, we are building on the work of Carolyn D. Baker and Ōsawa Satoshi. Baker explores the nature of interview data from the perspective of ethnomethodology. She proposes treating interview transcripts as data in which interviewers place their interviewees into categories and interviewees describe themselves as representatives of that category.[13] Because of this, the explanation that emerges from their responses reflects the working model of their category. In other words, when interviewees are describing their experiences from a certain position, they are constructing their narrative in a way that their listener can understand it, but at the same time adhering to the model that has been established for them.

In Baker's research, the model is revealed in responses to interview questions, and it is even more clearly applicable in the case of the *Animage* discussions: specialists in a field talking to other specialists in a public forum, where a specified topic yields specified answers. Mass-audience magazines before the first anime boom had never published animator profiles, so the early anime magazines published any number of articles in which animators were asked to discuss major trends in the world of anime production. Roundtable discussions would never have become a regular feature of the magazine were it not for two conditions: readers had quite a bit of interest in the people who were making anime, and editors could envision that desire among their readership to see major topics in anime discussed by a panel. The special discussion themes that the magazine promoted were made possible by having people thought of as "appropriate panelists" assigned to "topics that would be appropriate for them."[14] In the discussions, animators who were a good fit for a particular topic presented themselves to their public and then presented labor models from the standpoint of the individual positions that had been staked out for them in the discussions.[15] What made these magazine conversations so unique is the fact that they were speaking directly not only to their fellow panelists and interviewers but also to readers of the magazine. For that reason, it is important to determine what kind of readership the magazine staff was imagining. In order to understand the readership of *Animage*, we should point out that while in its early days it was indeed a magazine for fans, it was at the same time a general-interest magazine that had expanded to a scale never before seen.[16] On top of that, it performed the function of an industry magazine for anime creators who wanted to continue learning their craft.[17] With all of these aspects in mind, we try to delineate a history of making anime in the 1970s and 1980s by looking at some of these narratives as related in interviews and roundtable discussions for magazines.

We focus on *Animage*, the largest of its kind by circulation, because anime magazines of this period were actively reaching out to aspiring animators. One symbol of this is a small special feature in the February 1985 issue, inspired by a letter to the editor published in the December 1984 issue. In response to a reader's comment, "I want to become an animator," readers sent "suggestions regarding books on animation and other reference materials, letters expressing the same desire, and words of encouragement" (*Animage*, February 1985, 128–29). There was a message from someone saying that he himself had given up but wanted the letter writer to keep at it, and another introducing a professional-training school, as well as a description of coursework at Yoyogi Animation Academy and multiple messages from working animators sharing stories and expressing support. We can read this passionate response to indicate that the readers of anime magazines were not only considered to be consumers of anime, but also a possible talent pool that could help with some of the labor shortages the industry was feeling. We want to keep in mind these circumstances of reception of anime magazines even as we position the discourses in these magazines.

In the next section, as a prelude to our analysis of *Animage* and with an eye toward working to understand the relationship of creators and consumers, we take a systematic look at the ways our previous scholarship has touched on labor during the anime boom.

THE ANIME BOOM AND LABOR SHORTAGES

What is most important in thinking about the anime boom and its relationship to ways of working is the rise of OVA ("Original Video Animation," or direct-to-video), which Nagata focuses on.[18] To animation studios working on anime for television, the relationship with their sponsors is of primary importance. They must produce animation that is on-brand for the sponsors, which naturally limits what they can do artistically. Some creators started to express dissatisfaction with these constraints on their freedom of expression.[19]

A discriminating audience of anime fans, divided into different interest groups, led the way for these creators toward new avenues of expression. As a response to the demands of these varying fan subcultures, the market fragmented into anime created for theatrical releases, OVA releases, and so on. OVA in particular was viewed by creators as a medium that lent itself to freedom of expression. For fans, OVA appeared to be an answer to their demand for anime that did not need to cater to children.[20]

This was the origin of a split between production of works aimed at anime fans and production of works aimed at children. For the anime studios, the rise in workload also meant a proliferation of genres and illustration styles in their work. As a result, the studios were plagued by staffing shortages, which placed a limit on what they could produce.[21] What was needed was a supply of animators to fill the lowest ranks. Next, we take a look at some of the arguments surrounding these considerations.

TALENT AMONG ANIME CREATORS

According to the labor sociologist Harry Braverman, as new projects are conceived one after another, the labor required to put them into practice increasingly becomes standardized.[22] But Braverman's image of workers performing unskilled, repetitive tasks does not appear at first glance to have anything near the charm of the work of the animator, engaged in making creative work. Nor does it explain how such labor is supplied in large quantities.

Matsunaga proposes a localized argument, somewhat at odds with Braverman's, based on the animators' own understanding of their work.[23] The problem of animators working long hours for low pay is well established, but Matsunaga begins to explain the way that workers accept unfavorable working conditions by looking at what he calls the "rationality of the workers themselves."[24] It is only out of a union of different notions that the animators have about themselves that their shared working model appears. Matsunaga demonstrates how the display of individualism that puts animators into the creative category (the "creator model") and the ability to competently follow superiors' instructions that puts animators in the journeyman category (the "craftsperson model") combine conceptually.[25] This allows him to explore the tension between the demonstration of authorship and the limits that are placed on individual style by superiors, in terms of what the illustrations should look like in the end.

According to Matsunaga, the craftsperson model of thinking (what Braverman would call a decline in skills among the labor force) supercedes the creator model, and whichever an individual artist imagines himself to be, instructions from superiors will always take precedence over individual ambitions. Moreover, there is a labor model that stands above this binary opposition: the need to maintain high artistic standards. Although animators must always suppress creator-model behavior, when it is the case that they possess "a high level of skill that is acknowledged by those around them," various things can be forgiven.[26] In the creator model, this registers simply as a meritocracy, but from a craftsperson's perspective, various standards for talent exist, such as when people say someone "can look at a person or a thing and imagine how it might move, and has the talent to draw it quickly and accurately."[27] According to this labor model, whether they are craftspeople or creators, animators have a deep-rooted shared respect for talent, and someone of unusual technical skill will be the object of praise regardless of rank.[28]

But what does it really mean for a laborer to be valued for their talent? When we consider how animators actually work, questions inevitably arise about this shared respect for talent. As we pointed out in our description of the division of labor, the majority of animators are freelancers not bound to any one organization, who bounce from studio to studio any number of times over the course of their careers. Despite this, the respect that animators have for one another's talent is something that transcends any given workplace.

This leads us to two problematic points. The first is, why is talent emphasized to this extent? It is puzzling when you consider that the wage structure for animators is based on the number of frames they produce. In such a system, it is not clear that any talent other than speed will be reflected in an animator's paycheck. Why is such stock placed in talent, then? The second question is, how exactly do animators measure "talent"? When anime creators say that they prize things such as "knowing one's place in the process" and "not putting one's originality on display," it begs the question of what sort of empirical measure is being used to gauge the level of skill animators have. One hint can perhaps be found in the fact that the further down one goes in the hierarchy, the more likely it is that animators are working as freelancers. We go into more detail below, but suffice it to say here that an emphasis on raw talent serves as the wellspring that continually replenishes the flow of this freelance labor. This emphasis on artistic merit may seem strange from the perspective of people doing journeyman freelance labor, but we argue that it actually underpins a great deal of how the freelance system works.

With these issues in mind, we aim to investigate the following question in a historical context: In a system that prioritizes "talent" above all, what kind of "talent" was considered essential to the system? Here we are looking at the period of time during which the craftsperson model gained the upper hand and animators began to feel it was a good thing to be evaluated according to that model. In the next section we explore this shift, and place this change in the labor model in its historical moment.

A TRANSFORMATION IN THE WORKING MODEL FOR CREATORS

In this section, we look at three round-table discussions and one interview in light of the issues we have raised: (1) "Round-table: 70 Years of Animated Theatrical Releases: Looking Back at 'Our 'Dōga.'" Participants: Yabushita Taiji (1903–86), Daikuhara Akira (1917–2012), Mori Yasuji (1925–92) (*Animage*, December 1979, pp. 96–102); (2) "Characters Are Living Creatures," an interview with animation supervisor Ōtsuka Yasuo (1931–2021) (*Animage*, December 1979, pp. 37–38); (3) "Round-table: Komatsubara Kazuo." Participants: Rintarō (1941–), Katsumata Tomoharu (1938–), Komatsubara Kazuo (1943–2000) (*Animage*, March 1980, pp. 114–18); and (4) "Round-table: Sunrise." Participants (all job titles are from the time the article was published): Araki Yoshihisa (scriptwriter, 1939–), Iizuka Masao (planning, 1941–), Kanayama Akihiro (animator, 1939–), Tomino Yoshiyuki (unit director, 1941–), Hoshiyama Hiroyuki (scriptwriter, 1944–2007), Yamaura Eiji (board of directors, head of planning, 1935–2010), Sasaki Katsutoshi (unit director, 1943–2009) (*Animage*, January 1981, pp. 113–17).

The animators in (1) all started at Tōei Dōga before the war. In this panel, they looked back over their postwar careers and discussed the state of contemporary animation; (2) is an interview with Ōtsuka Yasuo, who was a mentor to Miyazaki Hayao from their time together at Tōei Dōga. The two had worked together on different animated versions of *Lupin III*, and the interview was promoted as "answering the question from a fan, 'If it's the same animation supervisor as it was in the old Lupin, why does the character look so different?'" The next roundtable (3) centers around Komatsubara Kazuo, famed as a craftsman-animator, discussing anime production in an age of commercialism, and (4) was a roundtable that took a retrospective look at the philosophy behind the production at Sunrise, a company that had been founded in the 1970s and quickly rose to become a fan favorite.

And so, (1) asked animators who had been active since before the war to comment on the changes of recent years; (2) was an interview with a veteran animator focusing on changes that were happening right then; and (3) and (4) were gatherings of a new generation of animators, centered around changing market forces.

EVOLUTION OF RESTRICTIONS ON ANIMATORS' INDIVIDUAL STYLES

One of the most important subjects in thinking about work models for animators has to do with their individual style. We can use item (1) to look at how animators who have been in the industry since before the era of television anime feel about individual agency.

As "looking back" and "our Dōga" indicate in the title of (1), this roundtable featured three animators thinking back to the prime of their careers and comparing life in the studio then to contemporary working conditions. Yabushita describes the differences between producing live-action films and animated features.[29] In a live-action film, Yabushita explains, it is fairly easy to do a retake when something goes wrong. Animation, however, is a different story:

Yabushita: In animation, that sort of thing simply isn't possible. You can't just go saying, "Yeah, I'm not crazy about this shot—let's go ahead and make another one," or, "Let's make this happen in two shots instead of one." If you do something like that, you're talking about days more work on the production schedule. So, no, you've got one chance to get it right. And meanwhile, live-action directors are looking at any number of takes and selecting the best one.

Daikuhara: I completely agree. That's why we're always thinking about animators' individual styles and personalities. If you don't know those things, you can't work with them. If you can't get through to the people you're working with—you know, this is the kind of work it is, and this is what we hope to achieve—you're simply not going to be able to get them to draw the kind of work you want to make.

Yabushita: It's similar to the way that live-action film directors need to really know the actors that they work with.

Daikuhara: The difference being, though, that even if they're a bunch of veteran animators, you can't just up and decide to make an anime with a group of people you don't know.

Yabushita: Yes, it would be unthinkable to gather a bunch of strangers together and try to make something. Film directors can put actors through their paces and make sure they have the chemistry needed for a particular work, but we don't have the luxury of testing people out in the anime world.

And so, Mori and Daiku here know each other really well, because they've been in the trenches together for a long, long time now, ever since they were together at Nichidō.[30]

This excerpt makes clear that the costs of redoing something in anime are far greater than in live-action film. It holds that there is a value placed on animators being able to explain what kind of work they are making and why, and for this reason they place a lot of value on getting a sense of the particular styles and personalities of the animators with whom they work.

From the perspective of being able to communicate intentions as efficiently as possible, having been "in the trenches together" is of far more importance than whether someone is a "veteran" or whether someone is a "good artist." This meant that they were frequently asking whether they could rely on their fellow animators as people and what kind of idiosyncrasies they had. The division of labor at the time was not very clear-cut, and individual animators had a great deal of latitude in managing things according to their own judgment.[31] This kind of organization, in which "individual styles and personalities" are the driving force, was very different from contemporary notions of organizing workers, in which they are brought into an organization and made to conform to its culture. Because everything was based on individual personalities, it was not a question of control so much as a question of trust. And the modern decline in this freedom is mourned, as we can see in the following exchange:

Daikuhara: Everything operates in such a rush these days. People staying up night after night to push things through. It's kind of amazing.

AM:[32] They can make an hour's worth of animation in only six months.

Daikuhara: We could never have done that. It's brutal.

Yabushita: Even the inbetweeners are more machine than artist. They are like automatons from the start.

AM: Has something been lost, do you think?

Yabushita: Yeah, something has been lost, for sure. These days, so many parts of animation don't require humans and can be done by machines. There's no longer anything you can point to as the sign of the artist.

AM: Is it possible for even inbetweeners to claim that they have had some influence on the work as a whole?

Yabushita: Probably not. The key animators are drawing their key frames with a certain concept in mind. They are explaining the vision to the people around them, and the people filling out the scenes have to stay faithful to what they have been told.[33]

We can see from this exchange that even if one wanted to maintain aspects of the old auteurism in the system of contemporary television production, the organization of labor makes it fundamentally difficult, if not impossible, to do so. It is simply considered to be something that has been "lost," and no one sees a realistic way to bring it back.

Ōtsuka Yasuo, a generation younger in animation terms, invokes this notion of individual style, with reference to Mori and Daikuhara. In the following excerpt, in response to the reader question, "Why is it that a character's design can change even over the course of a single work?" Ōtsuka draws a connection to "individual style." He explains:

In the old days, there was a lot more tolerance for variation within a single animated work than there is now. In the old Tōei works, such as *The White Snake Enchantress* (1958) and *Magic Boy* (1959), most of the drawings were done by two people, Mori Yasuji and Daikuhara Akira, but the design of the characters changes enough within a single work that it feels like a problem by today's standards.

This is something that only people on the production side really cared about; the general public didn't bat an eye at any of this. I think they were far more concerned about unnatural movements or problems with the way the story developed. But everything changed with the rise of television. Together with the rapid rise in requests came a dramatic rise in the need for key animators, and even if they didn't have a lot of experience they had to be thrown into projects. In order to protect the quality of the projects, someone needed to make up for this lack of experience. This, I think, explains the creation of the animation supervisor system.[34]

Here we have reference to how the system of production changed with television. In the theatrical releases produced by Tōei Dōga and mainly drawn by Mori and Daikuhara, movement and plot development were far more carefully scrutinized than any changes in style. It explains how, with the inevitable introduction of inexperienced key animators due to a rise in demand in the television era, the position of animation supervisor was created as a means of quality control. In other words, to animators, the rise of the process involving animation supervisors meant that character designs would be controlled over the course of a work.

CRAFTSMANLIKE EXPRESSIONS IN A SYSTEM OF CONTROL

Earlier, we saw how Komatsubara Kazuo and two other creators discuss what "craftsmanship" means in terms of the work performed by Komatsubara, considered by himself and those around him to be a "craftsman." In the course of their discussion, the following exchange occurred:

Komatsubara: To begin with the conclusion, I'd rather be a "craftsman" than an "artist."

Katsumata: Isn't he the epitome of a craftsman? . . . If I have to say it, it's because he's such a craftsman that he has no sense of creative ownership of his work. At this point, anyway. He doesn't have any one character that he can call his own. And he doesn't seem to have any desire to move in that direction.

Komatsubara: Not particularly.

Rin: What Katsumata is saying really gets at the heart of things. If I'm told, hey, we need you to work on *Tensai Bakabon*, I'm not just going to refuse straight out. Even if I can find only the most tenuous connection with the work, that's all I need. That's the essence of commercialism. If Komatsubara here came up with some original artwork, on the other hand, I'm not so sure I'd be interested in seeing it.

Komatsubara: And I wouldn't be interested in showing it to you. Now there's a terrifying thought. No, I want to work in a situation where things are laid out to a certain degree, and then I can show my genius within that framework.

AM: But you don't have any interest in drawing anything original? . . .

Komatsubara: At this point, if I were going to make anything original, it would have to be a private film that doesn't get out to the world. A real original means thinking up my own story, designing my own characters.[35]

Here, the keyword "commercialism" is strongly associated with restrictions on individual style that particularly limit original artwork. In connection to "commercialism," the "craftsman" and the "artist" are set up in opposition to each other. Komatsubara is positioned as a representative of the craftsman model of thinking, and the other two are discussing his stance toward his work. Although Komatsubara has a superior reputation as a craftsman, at the same time, he is considered to have "no sense of creative ownership of his work." This allows Rin to say that, in commercial animation, even if one feels that a particular job does not have much to do with one's previous work, if an offer comes in, it is quite easy to accept the work.

From this, Komatsubara suggests that a true craftsman takes the work as it comes to him, and that if he "were going to make anything original, it would have to be a private film that doesn't get out to the [commercial] world." But this should not be taken to mean that he does not feel any freedom. He speaks positively about his ability to carry out his work "in a situation where things are laid out to a certain degree," and no one seems to view this as a negative. What we need to explore is the context in which animators have these conflicted feelings about their own autonomy in the thick of this commercialism.

In the discussions we have looked at so far, the question of creative ownership has emerged, and "talent" as it has been traditionally defined has not mattered as much as a new conception of talent: the have-brush-will-travel craftman's notion of it. The discourses up to this section have explained that the development of a division of labor among processes has brought with it a new standard for measuring "talent." But it has not been sufficiently explained how talent-based hiring is achieved as a method superior to all others.

FREELANCE WORK ANCHORED IN A NETWORK OF PEERS

The final discussion is a conversation in which members of Sunrise, then a relatively new anime company garnering a lot of attention, discuss what makes it special vis-à-vis other animation companies. In this section of the conversation, Tomino, a key figure in the company, realizes that the other participants in the discussion, from the same company, do not know about the first projects he worked on with the company:

Tomino: That's because Dezaki (Osamu) was my unit director and he kept scrapping my work. I don't remember receiving any money back then! (laughs)

Iizuka: But, Tomino, you were doing work for various companies other than just Sunrise. Weren't you boasting that you would produce a thousand storyboards?

Yamaura: I've heard of the "thousand storyboards," too.

AM: And where was Yasuhiko at this point?

Yamaura: We were having him do various things for us starting with *Zero Tester*. As a unit director, scriptwriter, animation supervisor—he did it all.

Tomino: I have heard reports that at the time Yasuhiko didn't really understand everything that was involved in being a unit director, and that he really panicked a lot as a scene checker.

Iizuka: Sunrise was once a production site for Sōeisha.

Tomino: Yeah. The very best thing about getting involved in this company in the Sōeisha era is that it allowed me to meet everyone who is now part of Studio Nue.

AM: Why was that such a good thing for you?

Tomino: I'm talking about Takekawa and Matsuzaki—they were just a different species from everyone else who had ever worked in anime. They had this, I think it's fair to call it, obsession with getting the details right on things that the anime world really hadn't paid any attention to at that point— they made sci-fi feel accurate, they developed a whole visual language for mecha . . .

Yamaura: At the time, they were still college students. They were brought in by Numamoto (Kiyomi), who's now in the toy business at Takara . . .

Hoshiyama: From the old Mushi Pro way of looking at things, all of that new stuff was considered trashy.

Yamaura: Well, you can call it trashy or anything you like, but if we didn't take the work as it came to us, we didn't eat. We were all barely keeping our heads above water, myself included.[36]

From this excerpt, we can understand Sunrise's precarious situation from the way that if Tomino's storyboards were rejected, he did not get paid, a reality that forced animators working there to accept work from various other companies. And we can see that "doing work for various companies" and drafting "a thousand storyboards" are mentioned in quite positive terms. In other words, even essential staff at Sunrise, the studio that had the most attention from anime fans at the time, found themselves doing work that was very close to freelance. When they describe life as subcontractors for Sōeisha, they appear to agree that the very best thing they gleaned from the experience was the opportunity to meet the Studio Nue animators who "were still college students" at the time and shared their sensibility.

They have a sense of themselves as a generation of animators, and they insist that there is a disconnect between themselves and their predecessors; the Mushi Pro generation may well feel that their work is "trashy," but they have no compunction about working for a paycheck, and feel no need to see themselves as artists. They discuss how work was distributed, using as an example the way that celebrated Sunrise animator Yasuhiko Yoshikazu was made to fill positions even in which he had no experience. The way that various work is carried out with deference to the process of labor is spoken of approvingly as a standard working practice. Even when the creators do bring up the matter of restrictions on their various individual styles, the modes of expression that were possible within that system came to be understood as defining "talent." The rotation of work assignments, based on a new sense of what constituted "talent" completely at odds with the previous generation's understanding of it, played no small part in affirming that everyone who played a part in this system belonged to their own generation of animators. As the conditions of their labor changed, so, too, did their support for a system in which animators' individual ambitions were subsumed into the work process.

CONCLUSION

In this article, we have tried to show under what kinds of conditions a new model of labor able to support changes in the market that accompanied the anime boom came into being. In doing so, we have depicted a connection between Condry's two kinds of interactions, the first between the creators themselves, and the second between creators and consumers—here, the relationship between the rise of consumers in the 1970s and 1980s and the anime creators.

In other words, during the changing market conditions of the anime boom, various new avenues including direct-to-video anime opened up, and with them new forms of expression and greater labor needs. Talented animators were brought in through anime magazines, but what kind of skills did they need to carry out this work? A change in external factors— namely, the "anime boom"—brought about change in the workplace itself: a limitation on individual style for the sake of the commercial product. In the wake of this, animators appeared on the scene who were praised for demonstrating their abilities in terms of the way they managed to perform in a variety of positions within the system placing limitations on them. The freelancer's ethic that was based on this estimation of talent became the mainstream model. Thinking about this through the lens of labor-process theory, this shows that, although at first the limitations on individual style that were brought about by the commercialization of anime necessitated a move away from a model that privileged artistic agency, the model that prevailed over time was one in which producers of anime were able to fulfill various roles inside the system of limitations. In other words, the new labor model made changes in the industry possible to accommodate a rise in consumers, occurring as it did in a larger pattern of change in the commercialism of the anime business.

The situations that were discussed in these magazine articles showed changes in working conditions for animators that stemmed from changes in the market, but did so in a way that readers would find the work situation for animators after the great transformation appealing. In other words, the post-transformation work model is presented to readers of the magazine as a cultural shift. The working model that is praised in these pages is one in which, if there is a demonstration of authorial agency, it only occurs in a regime in which individual creativity is controlled, one which relies on labor which is very close to freelance work. In this model, what is valorized is the ability to perform various functions as each individual job requires, in a variety of workplaces and on a variety of projects. The workers are presented here as absolutely essential to the survival of the industry through the market changes involving the amount and quality of work owing to the introduction of direct-to-video anime and other innovations of the anime boom. We can surmise from these articles that changes in the market as a result of the anime boom brought about changes in the labor model, chief among which were the restrictions on individual style, and that through these articles this was conveyed to readers who might very well be joining the ranks of the animators in the near future.

We can imagine that those who joined the anime labor pool under these conditions would go on to play support roles in the creation of new anime and to influence the direction of new works. It is very possible that, since the new generation of workers would enter a system that was now largely freelance in nature, conditions were already ripe for a serious debate over working conditions. Any study of this would require researching those who entered the system during the anime boom, but an investigation of materials relating to what transpired after the readers of the above discussions entered the field themselves is beyond the scope of this article. We look forward to future research on this.

....

Kendall Heitzman is associate professor of Japanese literature and culture at the University of Iowa, where he teaches literature, film, theater, and the Japanese-to-English translation workshop. He is the author of *Enduring Postwar: Yasuoka Shōtarō and Literary Memory in Japan* (Vanderbilt University Press, 2019). His translation of Fujino Kaori's *Nails and Eyes* (Pushkin Press, 2023) received the Japan-US Friendship Commission Prize for the Translation of Japanese Literature.

....

Notes

1. Meaning, in focusing on labor, Lamarre neither treats Japanese anime as a particular film genre nor invokes theories of Japan's so-called uniqueness. See Thomas Lamarre, *The Anime Machine: A Media Theory of Animation* (Minneapolis: University of Minnesota Press, 2009).

2. Looking at the numbers of new anime programs produced for television: in 1970, there were 17; in 1977, the number reached 30; and in 1981, it peaked at 47. New productions dropped to 23 in 1985, but increased again to 60 in 1991. The market also rose dramatically, from 4.6 billion yen in 1975 to 106.9 billion yen in 1990. For more details, see Masuda Nozomi, Azuma Sonoko, Inomata Noriko, Tanimoto Naho, and Yamanaka Chie, "Nihon ni okeru terebi anime hōei dēta no bunseki: risuto no sakusei to sono gaiyō" (Analysis of Japanese television anime broadcast data: The creation of a list and its summary), *Kōnan joshi daigaku kenkyū kiyō: Bungaku, bunka-hen* 50 (2013): 33–40.

3. Many people point to *Space Battleship Yamato* as the symbol of the anime boom, and the attention anime magazines paid to its rebroadcast played a major part in starting the boom. The argument has been made that it was in fact the anime magazines that created the anime boom. See Nagata Daisuke, "'Anime otaku/otaku' no keisei ni okeru bideo to anime zasshi no 'kakawari': Anime zasshi Animage no bunseki kara" (Relations of video and animated cartoon magazine in animaniac: Otaku's formation from the analysis of the animated cartoon magazine Animage), Shakaigaku jaanaru (Tsukuba Daigaku Shakaigaku Kenkyūshitsu) 36 (2011): 59–79.

4. Masuda Hiromichi, *Anime bijinesu ga wakaru* (Understanding the anime business) (Tokyo: NTT Shuppan, 2007).

5. Nagata Daisuke, "Anime zasshi ni okeru 'daisan no media' to shite no OVA: 1980-nendai no anime sangyō no kōzō teki jōken ni chakumoku shite" (The "third media" OVA and anime magazines: Focusing on the structural conditions of the 1980s anime industry), *Soshioroji* (Kōrosha) 61, no. 2 (2017): 41–58.

6. Ian Condry, *The Soul of Anime: Collaborative Creativity and Japan's Media Success Story* (Durham: Duke University Press, 2013).

7. Kimura Tomoya, "Shōgyō animēshon seisaku ni okeru 'sōzō' to 'rōdō': Tōei Dōga Kabushiki Gaisha no rōshi funsō kara" ("Creation" and "labor" in commercial animation production: From the perspective of the Tōei Dōga Inc. labor disputes), *Shakai Bunka Kenkyū* (Kōyō Shobō) 18 (2016): 105–27.

8. Editor's note: While Pruvost-Delaspre's article on the invention of the *sakuga kantoku* or *sakkan* uses the translation of "animation director," this article translates *sakkan* as "animation supervisor." Instead of standardizing them, we have chosen to leave both translations as is. While this might invite confusion, the intent here is to distinguish between Mori's role as character designer and animation director for the Disney/Tōei model of theatrical full animation versus the role of quality control for the televisual model of limited animation. There is, of course, considerable overlap between the roles in both film and television production historically and today, though the preservation of two terms here allows us to continue the debate on the most accurate rendering of this complex job description into the English language.

9. Yamamoto Kenta, "Tokyo ni okeru animēshon sangyō no shūseki mekanizumu: Kigyōkan torihiki to rōdō shijō ni chakumoku shite" (An accumulation mechanism for the animation industry in Tokyo: Focusing on intercompany transactions and the labor market), *Chirigaku hyōron* (Kokusai Bunkensha) 80, no. 7 (2007): 442–58.

10. *Nihon animētaa enshutsu kyōkai* (Japan Animators Directors Association), "Animēshon seisakusha jittai chōsa hōkokusho 2015" [Animator labor white papers 2015], *Nihon animētaa, enshutsu kyōkai*, 2015.

11. Michael Burawoy, *Manufacturing Consent: Changes in the Labor Process under Monopoly Capitalism* (Chicago: University of Chicago Press, 1979).

12. P. K. Edwards, "Understanding Conflict in the Labour Process: The Logic and Autonomy of Struggle," in *Labour Process Theory*, ed. D. Knights and H. Willmott (London: Macmillan, 1990), 125–52.

13. Caroline Baker, "Ethnomethodological Analysis of Interviews," in *Handbook of Interview Research: Context & Methods*, ed. F. Gubrium and J. Holstein (Thousand Oaks, CA: Sage, 2002), 777–96.

14. Ōsawa Satoshi, *Hihyō media-ron: senzenki Nihon no rondan to bundan* (Critical media theory: The forum and literary world of prewar Japan) (Tokyo: Iwanami Shoten, 2014).

15. Of course, the creators who appear in anime magazines don't exactly represent the rank-and-file of the industry. But what is important here is that it is through these creators that the labor model is conveyed to others.

16. Ōtsuka Eiji, *Nikai no jūnin to sono jidai: Tenkeiki no sabukaruchaa shishi* (The second floor residents and their times: A personal history of a tumultuous subcultural period) (Tokyo: Seikaisha, 2016).
17. Nagata, "'Anime otaku/otaku' no keisei," 59–79.
18. Nagata, "Anime zasshi ni okeru 'daisan no media' to shite no OVA," 41–58.
19. Nagata, "Anime zasshi ni okeru 'daisan no media' to shite no OVA," 47–48.
20. Nagata, "Anime zasshi ni okeru 'daisan no media' to shite no OVA," 49–50.
21. Nagata, "Anime zasshi ni okeru 'daisan no media' to shite no OVA," 46.
22. Harry Braverman, *Labor and Monopoly Capital: The Degradation of Work in the Twentieth Century* (New York: Monthly Review Press, 1974).
23. Matsunaga Shintarō, *Animētaa no shakaigaku: Shokugyō kihan to rōdō mondai* (Sociology of animators: Models of commercialism and labor issues), (Mie: Mie Daigaku Shuppankai, 2017).
24. Matsunaga Shintarō, *Animētaa no shakaigaku*, 209.
25. The term "craftsperson" would ordinarily indicate a person who has gained skill through long experience, but Matsunaga is using the term as it was understood in the industry at the time.
26. Matsunaga Shintarō, *Animētaa no shakaigaku*, 111.
27. Matsunaga Shintarō, *Animētaa no shakaigaku*, 79.
28. Matsunaga Shintarō, *Animētaa no shakaigaku*, 127–29.
29. Yabushita uses the term "scripted film" (*gekieiga*), but it is clear that he is using it in the broader sense of "live-action film."
30. This refers to Tōei Dōga's predecessor Nichidō Eiga, and to its even earlier predecessor Nihon Dōga, *Animage*, December 1979, 99–100.
31. *Animage*, December 1979, 98–99.
32. The magazine's abbreviation for its own name, *Animage*.
33. *Animage*, December 1979, 101.
34. *Animage*, December 1979, 37.
35. *Animage*, March 1980, 117–18.
36. *Animage*, January 1981, 113–14.

Critical Production Platforms

Crafting Consensus in Anime's Writer's Room

Uchiawase *as Script Development*

BRYAN HIKARI HARTZHEIM

This article focuses on an aspect of a less-understood area of creative labor in commercial anime: script development. Through participant observation of two Tōei Animation Studio television series, I concentrate on the space where televisual screenplays are written by committee called *kyakuhon uchiawase*, or what can be thought of as anime's version of the "writer's room." Drawing inspiration from Eva Pjajcikova and Petr Szczepanik's study of committee-based writing for Czech television, this article sheds light on the "social logic" of script development by focusing on how the script mediates and is mediated by different "institutional frameworks, social relations, and aesthetic conditions."[1] To illustrate the social logic of this process, I adopt Clifford Geertz's culture as text model to "read over the shoulders" of three agents—sponsor, studio, and scriptwriter—and how they reflect distinct interests and subjectivities within the process of script development for serial television animation in Japan.[2]

Multiple studies on anime production have argued for the medium's exclusive emphasis on characters and worlds over narrative. While building compelling characters and worlds is certainly a strength of many anime productions, I argue that the most important aspect of script development in *uchiawase* committee-based TV productions is building stakeholder *consensus*. This consensus is often based as much on negotiated social values and relations as much as any particular creative choices. I use the script development of a single episode for a popular anime series as an example of how this consensus can be achieved in practice. In doing so, this article contributes to understandings of commercial anime production by showing how script development is an industrial *process* that is dependent on the real-time interaction of various cultural producers in the room.

Studying Writer's Rooms

Studies of screenwriting and script development have surged in the past decade, particularly within media industry studies. This article draws in particular on the small body of ethnographic literature that analyzes what in screenwriting circles is known as the "writer's room." In contrast to the solitary method of screenwriting often seen in novels or feature films, writer's rooms are a staple of Hollywood television production, where consistent weekly broadcasts necessitate a matching diet of scripts. The writer's room is industry shorthand for the collective workspace for the writers of a television series to brainstorm and facilitate the production of scripts for each episode of a television series. As Miranda Banks documents in her history of the Writer's Guild of America, "From the 1960s to the 1980s, a television writers' room generally included a hyphenate writer-producer, who was often also the creator of the series, a small team of two to four writers, and a story editor. In addition, freelancers might be hired piecemeal to write a couple of episodes."[3] The idea was that a team of writers would be necessary to create the required weekly output of content without having to rely on any single creative source. In the years since, "writing by committee" has become commonplace in various media productions where writers today are hired to "punch up" dialogue and scripts are created from a "menu" of narrative options.[4]

The writer's room is often viewed by professional screenwriters as a sacred space for idea generation, embodied by writer-producer Steven Bochco's exhortation that "what is said in the room, stays in the room." As such, the dynamics of these rooms have been sparsely chronicled due to difficulty of access, though productive academic works have emerged from Hollywood writer's room from insider perspectives. The limited number of studies of the television writer's room look at the negotiations that occur in the room, where ethnographic observation and interviews reveal how "occupational norms and learned expectations regulate relationships among writers."[5] Besides the ethnographic method, other studies mobilize the archive, digging out the beliefs and attitudes of writers and their employers through analyzing court cases or legal documents.[6] Such methods have been applied to documenting script development in Japanese cinema. Historical evaluation of script development departments (*kyakuhonbu*) and writer's "inns" (*joyado*) emerged in Japanese film studios in the 1920s where close-knit film crews engineered opportunities for collaboration.[7] Ethnographic analysis of television networks' production of "trendy" dramas in the 1990s meanwhile show how female scriptwriters butted heads with older male producers, with each side vilifying or complaining about the other as they work to reconcile differences in writing and composing plots.[8]

Using both historical and ethnographic methods, a growing body of academic work has emerged to examine the production cultures of anime. The most valuable of this work has focused on below the line workers instrumental to but often less publicly visible in the production process. Histories of finishing artists and colorists, for example, show the contributions of women creators.[9] Other sociological studies show animators as craft laborers, rather than auteur-like artists.[10] Comparatively less work has looked at labor processes "above the line," where script development falls under, though some scholars have examined producers and Cool Japan bureaucrats and their role in promoting and producing Japanese animation.[11] Ian Condry's ethnographic study of the "soul" of anime is one of the only works that looks at the process of script development, with extensive participant observation of script meetings of various children's television animation series. Condry's ethnography carefully acknowledges the levels of hierarchy in script development meetings, emphasizing a seemingly democratic process that is spurred by in-person interaction. In these meetings, the characters, premises, and worlds (as opposed to narrative) of anime productions harness an "energy" that "begins to give a sense of something larger than the media object itself, something emerging from a collective commitment among those who care."[12] These creative elements form a platform for social relations among staff—rather than any particular job duties or professional obligations—that create an intoxicating effect that makes the anime industry look and feel particularly attractive despite its tense labor conditions: "A certain social dynamic pulls you in, makes you feel the energy in the room, and—for some people at least—helps amplify a desire to be part of the action."[13]

What Condry describes as script meetings are examples of *uchiawase*, or consultations between different professional roles. *Uchiawase* are not exclusive to writers but are simply one leg of many between staff to build understanding among different creative roles. A productive *uchiawase* involves ironing out misunderstandings between parties that might have differing priorities, perspectives, and expectations regarding a particular transaction. *Kyakuhon uchiawase,* or script consultations, ostensibly function in similar ways to television writer's rooms in their focused discussion and revision of individual scripts, but they differ significantly in the occupants of the room, which is not limited to writers but includes any of the major stakeholders in an anime's production, including directors, producers, publishers, TV sponsors, ad reps, and other select personnel. Various professional personnel share the same physical space when dissecting scripts and the writer's perspective is not necessarily privileged over the roles of others. The function of collective writing in *kyakuhon uchiawase* are less to secure a sacred space for creativity than to build and shape consensus opinion among various professional roles, as the script comes to represent not just discrete characters or worlds, but also issues related to production financing, labor coordination, and franchise branding. In the following sections, I briefly describe how the interests of three such roles—producers, studio staff, and writers—are represented and negotiated in composite script development on two anime programs produced in 2012: *Smile Pretty Cure!* and *Saint Seiya Omega*.

The Script Development Process

Smile Pretty Cure! (henceforth *Smile*) draws from "magical girl" anime such as *Pretty Guardian Sailor Moon* and *Magical DoReMi*, revolving around schoolgirls who are granted magical powers to fight against evildoers. *Smile* was the ninth *Pretty Cure* (henceforth *PreCure*) series in the franchise, which still airs as of this writing, and followed a set formula for its construction. The first half of each episode in a series typically revolves around issues the girls face in their schools or communities. These conflicts are thematized by battles with villains in the second half of the episode, which are subsequently resolved by the girls transforming into superheroes and using fighting skills to overcome their enemies and/or self-doubts. As the show was also sponsored by toy manufacturer Bandai Namco, important narrative events in the show's composition revolved around the appearance of toy "items" in the broadcast and the simultaneous release of such toy merchandise in stores.

Saint Seiya Omega (henceforth *Omega*) is a spiritual successor to the television anime adaptation of *Saint Seiya* (1986–89), itself animated by Tōei Animation and based on Kurumada Masami's original *shōnen* manga (henceforth *Seiya*). The original story follows Seiya and his friends, a group of orphans called "Saints" who are able to harness their spiritual energy, or "cosmos," in battle. The Saints protect themselves with "cloth," a magic armor imbued with mystical powers derived from the constellations of Greek mythology such as Pegasus, Andromeda, or Cygnus. *Omega* begins several years after the conclusion of the original series and revolves around a new generation of Saints.

While *Omega* did not require the same close involvement of a toy sponsor and the necessary script integration of magical products, it also needed to stay faithful to the original world of Kurumada and get his approval for new concepts and characters, as well as how to handle the incorporation of existing characters and series' elements.

Script development for anime typically consists of three stages of development. The first, the "series composition" (*shiriizu kōsei*), acts as a narrative blueprint for the series by mapping story beats to a predetermined number of episodes. This is typically written and mapped by the production's lead writer. The next stage involves the creation of a "plot" (*purotto*), or a detailed outline of the episode's structure and action. For smaller productions, the lead writer might also write the plots and scripts, but for larger and longer-running series like the ones I observed, a team of writers split up the plot-writing duties. Once a plot is approved, the same writer creates a draft of the "script" (*shinario*) that is then distributed and collectively reviewed by the production staff. Depending on the quality of the script, which is determined by the criticisms or objections of the staff, the writer can create several more drafts. Strong scripts can be quickly approved, while scripts that need more polish can languish even while scripts further ahead in the narrative are being worked on. Multiple script revisions can create bottlenecks in production, as the animation staff must wait until the script is approved before even constructing storyboards and layouts.

While these are the basic building blocks of script construction, each studio or committee will have its own work pipeline and development method based on the nature of the production. Adaptations of manga or light novels will proceed very differently from original productions not based on any preexisting source. Even in cases of original productions, there are great differences in script development depending on the terms of the target audience, the source of funding, or the existence of a production committee that views the anime as but one part of an expansive transmedia entertainment. The two shows that I observed were both "original" productions in the sense that they were not based on any existing narratives, but both were extensions of established franchises that created limits and conventions that the writers and producers had to work from. Both also depended to a much larger degree on narrative continuity than the episodic series for children or families as outlined by Condry as they were broadcast for a year or more and required juggling multiple characters, storylines, and merchandise. Because of the scale and ongoing nature of production of Tōei's anime and other live-action television programs, the shows I observed might be viewed as atypical examples of tightly organized, well-managed script development within the anime industry. But neither should they be viewed as totally uncharacteristic of the industry as a whole, as many of Tōei's staff went on to found or work at anime studios of their own, and Tōei as an industry leader continues to exert an outsized influence on production practices, technologies, and networks.

The process of script development in *uchiawase* is conducted in real time, with the staff in the same physical or virtual office space. When I observed these meetings, they took place in Tōei's offices all over the city: in or across from the old studio in Oizumi Gakuen; in office buildings in Kagurazaka or Nakano; or in recording rooms in the now defunct Tabac recording studio in Okubo. Witnessing these meetings in person, one can see what different members of the production value and seek to emphasize based on their own professional obligations. Their comments, documented here via field notes and semi-formal interviews, can reveal the roles of each in the process of composite writing.

External Demands: Corporate Sponsors

Producers are often cast in a negative light in media portrayals of production work, injecting the creative process with corporate groupthink and risk-averse decision-making. While some of this kind of behavior certainly characterized some producers' actions during *uchiawase*, they were not at all uniform in how they approached script development. As salaried employees of companies, that is, *salarymen*, producers are gathered as representatives of their companies in the show's production committee. Production committees are formed to collectively finance and disperse risk among several complementary companies, and producers' roles in the room is to represent their corporate employer's interests and ensure any professional and contractual obligations are being kept. By working together on the same financing or production committee, the success of the series should ostensibly lead to collective financial success. However, as each producer represents a different corporate employer, these interests do not always align.

Of the shows I observed, producers represented three distinct interests: those of the advertising sponsor, television broadcaster, and the animation studio. The role of the advertising rep is to look at compositions and scripts to ensure that their client's product is being appropriately portrayed in the show. This meant that toy products needed to be persuasively woven into plots and dialogue; not simple product placement, but product *integration*, with entire plotlines revolving around the appearance of them. I have previously catalogued this process for *Smile*.[14] With the case of *Omega*, these products were essentially figurines, so simply portraying the characters attractively was the goal of the script. While the arrival of the toys in specific episodes followed a predetermined schedule, scripts could be altered to feature them more prominently if sales of specific products flagged. Scripts and scriptwriters needed to be ever attentive to the financials of merchandise sales in case they needed to make slight but significant alterations to developing scripts.

The television producers' supervisory role of the script is to ensure they meet several obligations to their corporate networks and the broadcast slot. As the majority of anime titles are broadcast late at night (*shinya*) for older, niche audiences, ratings are often an afterthought; such audiences often record or stream programs at their own leisure, so tactics like programming on a late-night broadcast slot or via regional broadcasters like Tokyo MX become ways to control cost and limit risk. But as TV Asahi was the network, and both programs aired during relatively more valuable Sunday morning broadcast slots, the ratings of the shows were important. Ratings not only mean increased advertising revenue, but a spectatorship that could translate into bolstered audiences for other related media (films, events, licensed goods).

With shows oriented toward children or families, the broadcast slot occupies a more prominent position in daily programming as the function of advertisements increases in importance. Analyzing the position of shows in the programming slot and the role of advertisements in such shows, what Nick Browne has called the program's "supertext," can reveal the relative importance and relationships of shows to studios, networks, and sponsors.[15] Both *Omega* and *Smile* were shows oriented toward children, and both shows occupied early morning slots on Sunday morning, but *Smile* occupied the much more desirable 8:30 a.m. slot versus *Omega's* 6:30 a.m. slot. *Smile's* prime viewing slot is understandable given its lengthy broadcast duration and lucrative partnership with Bandai Namco. *Omega's* less desirable slot can only be understood when looking at other shows that aired both immediately before and after *Smile*. The 7:30 a.m. and 8:00 a.m. slots on TV Asahi were occupied by the newest installments in the *tokusatsu* (live-action special effects) *Super Sentai* and *Kamen Rider* franchises, both produced by Tōei Animation's parent studio Tōei Company. The 9:00 a.m. and 9:30 a.m. slots, on the other hand, were occupied by two other Tōei-animated shows—*Toriko* and *One Piece*—which aired on the Fuji TV network. So, to avoid counter-programming against their own shows, the only remaining slots left were ones that were much earlier in the day. So why 6:30 a.m. and not 7:00 a.m.? Likely because the 7:00 a.m. slot was occupied by *Battle Spirits Heroes*, a show that was not produced by Tōei or Tōei Animation, but was financed by partner Bandai Namco, who had produced a lineup of toys that needed to be featured to an alert child audience. While *Omega* also was oriented toward children, its initial broadcast featured not toys, but high-priced collectable figurines. That is because its viewing audience consisted not only of preteen boys, but potential fans of the original 1980s series: their fathers, who have somewhat larger disposable income.

This secondary audience of "parents watching with their kids," what Matt Hills has called the process of "double coding," is in fact the audience that TV network producers are most aware of when overseeing script development.[16] Producers must imagine a broad, national domestic audience for the series, with the expectation that parents and children are viewing the broadcast together. This oversight does not necessarily extend to the broadcast's advertising to children. As Japan does not have the same legal restrictions to advertise to children as in the United States or parts of Europe, parents must act as a supplemental filter when watching programs like *PreCure* or *Anpanman* with their children. What TV network producers are instead attentive to are any potential scenes or situations that will invite parental "claims." This can often focus on dialogue or situations that might cause offense to specific viewing segments. In one meeting, the TV network producer objected to the inclusion of a game of *suikawari*, a pinata-like game played in the summer where blind-folded children try to bust open a watermelon, on the grounds that it might offend parents of visually impaired children. In another meeting, a scene of a flood had to be rewritten so as not to recall memories of the traumatic 2011 Tohoku earthquake and tsunami that was still fresh in the minds of the public at the time of production.

By this token, network producers carved out their own place in the room distinct from sponsor producers that also revealed their financing position within the *uchiawase*. By encouraging story themes that would avoid controversy and reduce claims, they helped to reinforce contemporary and conventional social attitudes. Moreover, while writers and directors initially objected to these "requests," they uniformly accepted them after several apologies and much pleading from the producers. Consensus here was achieved via an uneasy give and take where if producers pushed too much and too often, they risked offending the creative staff. Writers and directors, meanwhile, also needed to read and align script decisions to producer personalities in order to avoid unnecessary bottlenecks in development.

Internal Quality Control: Tōei's Producers and Series Directors

The second interest here is that of the studio itself, Tōei Animation. Tōei's producers must satisfy the demands of their clients while simultaneously producing a work that reflects the quality of the studio. A studio's brand is most often subjectively evaluated by viewers in aspects of production such as the animation or art design, but the script is also a significant element in projecting brand image. As stated previously, while both *Smile* and *Omega* were "original" productions, they were also extensions of existing franchises and needed to adhere to their established tropes and conventions.

Producers' involvement in the development of scripts can vary based on personality type and the nature of the production, but one consistency among both series I observed is how producers were expected to have a holistic knowledge of the franchise for which they were responsible. As Akahoshi Masanao has argued, this elongated supervisory role is somewhat unique to Tōei, which asks producers to supervise long-running franchises over lengthy periods.[17] The practice stems from the studio's history producing live-action television series like *Kamen Rider*, which are "rebooted" every year with new themes, cast, and crew, but which must reflect and build off of past series and conventions. The producer for *Omega*, Wakabayashi Goh, had formerly worked as a licensing manager in France and as an assistant producer for a previous installment of *PreCure*. These multiple perspectives allowed Wakabayashi to contribute significantly in *uchiawase*, drawing upon his understanding of the original work as a child manga reader and animation producer in Japan, but also as a young adult consumer in France where the original manga and anime were very popular. Wakabayashi was also responsible for establishing narrative and character continuity for the show after it was renewed for a second season and much of the writing and directorial staff was replaced. While not endowed with the total creative authority of a "showrunner," the term used in Hollywood for the writer-producer supervisory role of serial television productions, Tōei's studio producer can thus similarly establish and oversee the development of series and franchises across multiple media over time.

This often means that while the studio's producers were not responsible for any craft processes, their tastes, desires, and protracted understanding of Tōei's intellectual properties inflect narrative and character outlines in the planning stages. *Smile's* production came on the heels of the 2011 Tohoku earthquake and tsunami tragedy which claimed the lives of thousands and led to a long period of national mourning, so the story was designed as especially "forward-looking," with fairy-tale inspired villains and a more comical tone that broke from previous, darker installments. Conversely, the producers argued that a larger cast of heroes would allow for a greater range of character types and personalities, in the vein of large idol groups like AKB47 that were popular at the time. From a conceptual perspective, the producers' endeavored to create a series that would "pull everyone together to overcome" a national trauma through referencing contemporary music and fashion trends that targeted young and mainstream viewers.[18] In another example, once *Smile* producer Umezawa Atsutoshi took on the role of producer for multiple *PreCure* series, fans noted that characters felt more like junior high kids through their display of "clumsy" or "picky" tendencies. Umezawa, a former director of multiple Tōei Animation series himself, said he wanted to create "imperfect and vulnerable heroes" so that "kids could see themselves" in them.[19] These examples also show how certain emphases in series that are often attributed to directors or writers can be found in the tastes or inclinations of producers.

Studio producers and series directors are both employed by Tōei, though have very different jobs and job statuses. The former are responsible for franchise management and are salaried employees of the company; the latter are responsible for production management and are, in the case of Tōei, contracted employees. This creates different incentives for what directors look for in the script. While they work with producers and their corporate sponsors from the planning stages, they must also create scripts that translate to the production floor. This means that while also being aware of the sponsor's demands and history of the franchise, directors must think of their production staff and how they will read the scripts as animators and artists. Along with the lead writer, directors are one of the two people who are most closely involved with the construction of individual scripts and attentive to its details. Both directors I observed went through the script line by line to see if it aligned with the series composition, previous episodes in the series, and the franchise's history and conventions. They often asked for revisions, refinements, or clarifications if particular aspects of the exposition were confusing or if the dialogue was inconsistent. A description of an area or character might be clear for one writer but would often need further elaboration from the director who was thinking of translating the words into storyboards and layouts.

In both productions, directors frequently focused on character and setting continuity, as they could both pinpoint areas that needed additional input and then immediately follow up with concrete visual examples when required. In one *uchiawase* for *Omega*, a writer describes a character as "particularly cute," which prompts series director Hatano Morio to ask, "Aren't all of our characters cute?" When world details needed elaboration, Hatano's skill as a visual artist could bridge gaps in understanding; after reading one script that introduced a staging ground for a series of battles, Hatano whipped out a pencil and paper and scribbled a rough design for the entire room to see. The writer and Hatano tweaked this design in the room, but Hatano explained to me that because his production had fewer veteran staff on board than Tōei's marquee property, *PreCure*, there were often more instances where storyboard artists and episode directors needed further clarification. In these instances, Hatano would invite staff into the room to ask questions about visualized concepts. Series directors thus acted as bridges to production in multiple ways, both visualizing processes themselves and summoning production staff to *uchiawase* when scripts needed graphic clarification.

Both Hatano and *Smile's* series director Ōtsuka Takashi also argued that shows like *Pretty Cure* or *Saint Seiya* require a special attention to writing episodically, an effort described to me as trying to "consistently entertain" above all else. When asked if this means creating compelling characters or complex worlds, Ōtsuka answered, "Yes, but also stories that people want to watch every week. TV isn't like film; if our series has a poor beginning but a great ending, it won't matter if viewers have tuned out by episode four."[20] Ōtsuka here focuses on a key aspect of how anime is popularly consumed, at least among the family demographic that he is developing stories for: via weekly live broadcasts, one episode at a time. This calculus has changed somewhat with the popularization of on-demand streaming services, though the pressure to continually entertain audiences has magnified in the age of long-tail entertainment. Ōtsuka argues that the real value of anime lies as much in this broad appeal to the masses as the artistic aspirations of late-night fare; its ability to deliver consistently satisfying pleasures creates an everyday familiarity, like a snack. "I'm making Chocoballs," jokes Ōtsuka, referring to the cheap chocolate and peanut snack that children can buy with their pocket change (*okozukai*): "Godiva is a special treat you eat once a year, like Studio Ghibli."

But we spend more money on and time with Chocoballs. That's what anime amounts to. But I'll stake my life on making those Chocoballs."[21]

Beyond editing scripts for visual clarity and episodic entertainment value, directors must also manage the other demands in the room. I have previously written about how Ōtsuka carefully negotiates the opinions of sponsors and other stakeholders in the production of the show.[22] There is a stereotype that scripts created by consensus are bland, conservative, and formulaic, as a script that pleases everyone inevitably becomes diluted and predictable. But as Ōtsuka explains, this can be beneficial for series like *PreCure*, which are formulaic by nature and in constant need of fresh ideas: "It's not about taking everyone's ideas and incorporating them so that this pleases everyone, but hearing everyone's ideas and then going with the best one."[23] This approach takes some of the strengths of consensus-building—multiple voices, diverse perspectives, problem-solving—while also minimizing weaknesses like groupthink or conformity. This can lead to creative solutions to problems from unconventional sources, as I show later in the article.

But this involvement can also lead to creative frustration. *Smile's* rigid product release schedule and need for strong TV ratings meant that early scripts in the series frantically introduced a new character in each episode where the writers would have preferred an episode or two to flesh out the main character and her world. The need to appease all sources can also lead to creative impasses, particularly when producers water down scripts by anticipating potential objections as opposed to helping directors and writers resolve plots that bring out the themes of the show in consistently fresh or original ways. In summary, while studio producers and directors represent the studio, they do not necessarily look for the same things in *uchiawase*. Where producers are focused on the macro view of the franchise, directors must focus on how scripts work on the episode level. Negotiations between the two most often occurred when additional or unclear requests required significant visual redesigns or narrative rewrites.

The In-Between: Writing Teams

Writers are the only workers in the room who are not directly affiliated with a company. Where producers are salaried and directors are contracted, writers are paid per completed script, though like directors they receive royalties from broadcasts, DVD and Blu-ray sales, and streaming for completed scripts that are made into episodes. As such, writers are the most precarious participants in the room, occupying a range of positions on the labor spectrum; popular, experienced writers are constantly in demand, receive top billing, and receive significant secondary income from royalties; less popular writers juggle alternative writing assignments to keep busy until big jobs come in; and novice writers must claw for work, build up a reputation, and subsist on guarantees until royalties accumulate or a work becomes a hit.

There is a hierarchy among writers in the *uchiawase*. "Series composers" (*shiriizu kousei*), or lead writers, are at the top, responsible for managing all scripts of a series. For long-running productions like those at Tōei, which can run a year or more without a break, this involves managing the writing of multiple scripts at a time. Lead writers typically take the initial and narratively important episodes of a series, setting the tone for the series through establishing dialogue, tone, pace, and conflict. They then assign remaining episode scripts to writers based on their strengths and experience; more experienced writers will take other narratively important episodes, while novice writers might start out first observing and then be given "summary" episodes that are less creatively demanding and narratively important. The lead writer's role in script management depends on the type of production. On original series where there are only one or two writers, there is considerable leeway to write stories that they and the director find interesting and entertaining, though these types of productions are also riskier and less common. Most anime today are adaptations of existing works, which entails having a strong conception of the original title, understanding how many pages or lines of dialogue can fit into a specific episode, and the ability to restructure scenes into compelling individual episodes. *PreCure* and *Seiya* are creatively somewhere in-between original and adapted works, in that they do not have preexisting works that they must be faithful to but are still a new installment within an established franchise. Writers emphasized to me in discussion that while late-night anime could afford more creative freedom, the advantage of writing for established franchises was that the work was stable and for a much longer duration. While the opportunities for big windfalls from DVD or Blu-ray disc sales were smaller, the financials could be balanced by the opportunity to work on future long-running series from Tōei or other similar studios.

Like the series director, the lead writer went through each writer's script line by line asking questions or issuing corrections. In comparison to the series director, the lead writer's comments on these scripts focused on two aspects. The first revolved around the integrity of characters' dialogue,

actions, and relationships to one another. Similar to how an animation director might correct an animator's drawing of a character that was "off model,"
lead writers tended to ask for revisions in behaviors or phrases that were
out of character. Related to this, the second aspect concerned how scripts
bring out the themes not only of the particular series but of the franchise
as a whole. *PreCure*, for example, has a progressive image for a commercial
franchise, pairing its transformation products to future-oriented themes of
change. The series is known for promoting positive messages to young girls
and encouraging values such as friendship, independence, and hard work,
values that in Japan have traditionally been associated with action franchises
targeting young boys. As Akiko Sugawa-Shimada has argued, the series has
distinguished itself from previous magical girl series through deemphasiz-
ing romantic relationships and highlighting female autonomy and independence.[24] Magic devices then supplement these affirmative themes, becoming
tools for the schoolgirls to achieve their goals and commercial toys for school-
aged viewers to emotionally align with their idols. This future-oriented opti-
mism, however, is also balanced by a nostalgia that reaffirms the values of its
double-coded parental audience. Each season typically features nostalgic episodes that promote community, sacrifice, and empathy, values that seemingly
contrast with the franchise's focus on independence and consumption. These
values do not necessarily contradict one another, as the series "valorizes a
strong adherence to a sense of self tied always to the past, with any movement
forward based on looking backwards."[25] The franchise's larger themes thus
neatly pair aesthetics of transformation and change with stories that reaffirm
traditional community values.

In this way, parents tolerate the series' commercialism as long as it is
packaged with stories that encourage individual growth while embracing
traditional family values. In describing the writing process for *Smile*, lead
writer Yonemura Shoji said that the most challenging aspect of episode construction was, in fact, creating plots that reflect these twin social values: "If
we have a plot where the characters become invisible or there's a love story,
we also need a theme that we want the viewers to feel. We can't just end with
'that was fun but that's that.'"[26] In discussing an episode related to how one of
the characters, Yayoi, learns the origin of her name, Yonemura reveals how
a given episode reflects the franchise's penchant for pairing modern social
developments with traditional values. The character is both raised by a single
mother and loves making comics, two qualities that reflect changing demographics and career interests for young women in Japan. Yonemura's story,

however, emphasizes a theme of "deep familial love" through the character remembering her deceased father. The source of Yayoi's inner strength thus emanates from the love of her nuclear family, and her growth becomes tied to the protection of its memory. In such a way, *Smile's* writers connect broad changes in female identity and self-fulfillment with "unchanging" values such as protecting home and community.

Omega similarly kept to themes from the original manga and television series, which Tōei had produced in the 1980s, and from which the new series was based. These themes, like *PreCure*, revolved around friendship, determination, and the use of physical violence for resolution. Also similar to *PreCure* is a tension between seemingly disparate values; *Seiya* is known for the beauty and emotional intensity of its main characters, qualities more typically associated with manga and anime for girls. This emphasis on romantic undertones and attractiveness of the male characters has led to a strong popularity with female audiences since its serialization in the 1980s. Where *PreCure* promotes a wide range of alternative femininities, *Seiya* has been similarly recognized for its embrace of multiple alternative masculinities.[27] *Omega's* lead female writer, Yoshida Reiko, had developed a reputation for writing lively female character interactions in works such as *K-On!* and *Kaleido Star*, and she was hired specifically by series producer Wakabayashi to balance out *Omega's* action scenes with her ability to write "human relationships" and "portray human drama."[28] While Yoshida was brought in to give a more intimate touch, she also said she felt tremendous pressure in creating a pseudo-sequel to Kurumada's manga, likening the process to the trials and tribulations felt by Seiya and his friends as they are defeated and must get up again and again. Though the first season of the show introduced a new cast of characters, it was also heavily dependent on several characters and plotlines from Kurumada's manga, as if the writers were hesitant to deviate too far from the original formula. Thus, while *Omega* had fewer outside voices in the room, the writers still felt compelled to balance the series' themes as they related to the franchise's legacy audience and younger viewers.

This thematic pressure in both shows also extended to pressures from other creative forces in the *uchiawase*. Scriptwriters were responsible for flexibly balancing the corporate demands of producers and the craft needs of the director and production staff. From the sponsor side, this meant being sensitive not just to the removal of objectionable content, but to sudden requests to incorporate additional products, celebrity cameos from talent agencies, or promos for Edo-era theme parks from parent company Tōei. Scriptwriters would often need to think on the spot for alternatives to approved narratives due to producer proposals. In some cases, this could lead to a swift resolution. When the scriptwriter was asked to replace the flood in the script in the previous section, she quickly proposed a forest fire. This satisfied everyone in the room on the logic that such a natural disaster would not offend any viewers in Japan (international audiences were not considered). In other cases, both writer and director chafed when the requests or objections would lead to substantial changes in the entirety of the script. Upon being told by several producers that the idea of *suikawari* was a nonstarter, the writer (supported by the director) remained silent for several seconds before responding with a tone of exasperation: "We can't make anything if you think like that." This led to considerable haggling before alternatives were eventually proposed and accepted.

On the staff side, writers needed to consider plots that would translate smoothly to the screen. This meant not only writing clear descriptions and exposition, but also writing plots that would not command an excessive number of resources. Writing a complex action scene could be personally gratifying, but such scenes typically require specialized and talented animators, so their incorporation must be considerate of other staff. Asking for a character to be "extra cute" could seem like a simple request but would require a design order from the show's character designer instead of another animator, which could then create bottlenecks elsewhere as the character designer was already burdened by handling the show's animation direction. Monopolizing sizable chunks of the production staff for a single script could lead to friction from both the animation staff and other writers in the room, so writers needed to tacitly acknowledge the team and the entire production's resources when writing the script for even a single episode. In sum, the *uchiawase* for writers is incredibly pressure-laden and multilayered as they must balance the needs of external producers, production staff, the studio, and the larger franchise itself. More than any role, writers required the live format to immediately propose alternative ideas in order to proceed in their larger jobs as storytellers.

The Writer's Room in Practice

The interaction of these various professionals in the *uchiawase* is both controlled and dynamic; while each person in the room has a role and interest to represent, the interactions between them can create unexpected solutions to problems. In the following brief example of the script development of episode #36 of *Smile*, I show how this dynamism can disrupt these established roles and create solutions from unconventional sources.

The *uchiawase* is at a standstill; nearly an hour has passed, and no one can come up with an idea for the central conflict for the script. The premise for the episode in question is for a "summer romance" for Akané, the Osakan heroine, who must develop a crush on a boy at her school. Through her experience, she learns (and teaches young children) the lasting value of affection, as well as the pangs of separation. The staff, though, has considerable difficulty coming up with a love interest for Akané, as the character must be her age and a good match for her somewhat headstrong personality. Eventually, the director asks me for my opinion. Before I can express my thought, a producer for the show yells out, "A foreigner!" (*Gaijin da!*). The room erupts, realizing they have found a perfect solution to their dilemma: Akané will fall in love with a foreign exchange student.

The completed story is about the relationship that develops between Akané and Brian Taylor, a smiley foreign exchange student from England who is obsessed with Japanese culture. Brian visits the school of the *PreCure* students and Akané becomes responsible for showing him around the campus. She takes him to various campus clubs, and later, her family's restaurant, where she feeds him homemade *okonomiyaki*. She teaches him words in the Osakan dialect, and he also shares words with her in English. Brian and Akané become closer as they share more experiences, but she becomes dismayed when he says he will need to return to his country. Feeling betrayed, she avoids him until an evil henchman attacks her in an attempt to absorb the energy of lovestruck humans. She defeats the henchman and realizes that her time with Brian was memorable and valuable, even if their budding relationship ended prematurely. With the assistance of her friends, she rushes to the airport to see him off. The episode ends in the airport terminal, with Brian and Akané sharing a teary farewell. The narrative of the friendship of two "outsiders" is neat in its circular composition: it begins and ends with a meeting and departure, as well as the words "thank you" both in English and in the Osakan dialect (*ōkini*).

On one level, the assembled construction of Brian shows the dynamism behind script development in anime, where a story about a student love-interest can double as a lesson in international relations. The "social energy" that Condry describes in his observations of script meetings is on display here in the collaborative effort of the room to solve a particular problem

Figure 1. Brian Taylor from Episode #36 of *Smile PreCure!*

in the script. This problem is solved not by the designated creative roles of director or lead writer, but by the TV network producer and, by extension, the presence of the foreign participant observer. The collective enthusiasm behind the idea is anything but stale and conservative; indeed, as the approach is unconventional for the series, it is immediately greeted with approval from the staff. I even get roped into the script development and its implementation: I proofread and change some of the English phrases in the script, help Brian's voice actor—the German transplant Kakihara Tetsuya—with his English delivery in voice recording sessions, and even pose for character designs, though only my thick glasses are adopted in the end. Such an example shows that anything and anyone in the room can provide creative juice given the right circumstances. It also shows how consensus in script development is generated through the introduction of a fresh idea, not from a list of options.

On another level, however, a closer read of the room reveals subtle social dynamics that enabled the "solution" to materialize. While Yonemura was the lead writer for the series, the writer for this particular episode was Narita Yoshimi, a seasoned writer for *PreCure* having served on every writing team of the series since its inception and as a lead writer on three of those seasons. She thus commanded respect with regards to the types of themes and values the series' propagated since she had been responsible for helping to establish them. The episode also dealt with an experience—a heroine's first love—that lent her gravitas in decision-making. While the male writers proposed ideas for love interests for Akané, many of these were shot down by Narita as unconvincing or out of character. Thus, Narita's presence in the room steered the ideation of the "correct" love interest in a particular direction that drew on her experience as both a woman and a *PreCure* vet, helping to create a more convincing, logical, and interesting character that aligned with the show's themes of progression and tradition. Her commandeering of the script also facilitated a smooth process in its development, as the final draft was approved with only a single revision. In this instance, the room's hierarchies were reversed: a freelance writer stood at the top, while salaried producers deferred. While collective in the sense that the room approved of Narita's elevated status, it nonetheless required the tacit acceptance of others in more senior positions to relinquish their authority for the sake of the script.

Consensus: Negotiating Work and Values

As the above example illustrates, while the collective members of the *uchiawase* might desire an entertaining script, how that end result is shaped depends on the interactions and relations of the individuals in the room. Of course, scriptwriting's contingency on larger social relations is not unique to anime or to *uchiawase*. In studies of Hollywood writer's rooms, for example, collective writing becomes a microcosm of American dysfunction, where rooms are described as stressful workplaces, where staff engage in competitive "one-upmanship," where artistic freedom butts heads with commercial studio demands, and where writers are othered based on their gender, race, and class identities.[29] Such tense production relations can be observed in chronicles of writing and editing in Japan's creative industries as well. Gabriela Lukacs and Sharon Kinsella argue creativity is a contentious process in television and manga production, where authors feud with producers or editors over how to shape cultural meaning and representation.[30] In these script meetings, Lukacs argues that patriarchal values and "notions of identity and womanhood" are negotiated, with the results inflecting the material that appears on the page and screen.[31]

Like the spaces described by Condry, the *uchiawase* I observed were typically convivial and collegial, if mostly sedate and methodical. Observing these meetings and having discussions with its participants over several months, however, I argue that their productive working environments stem from two complementary factors constantly being negotiated by its participants. The first is the need to maintain productive working relationships. Eva Novrup Redvall's ethnographic study of writer's rooms for Danish television has mapped less combative environments, whose harmony depends on "casting" established writers or showrunners who can preserve the "chemistry" or spirit of "family collaboration" in the room.[32] While no staff I observed ever referred to the production as a "family," there was a tacit understanding that the industry is relatively small and *ningen kankei,* or the "human relationships," of creative industries are as important as any prodigious writing ability.[33] As invitations to future projects can come from any positive relationships developed in *uchiawase,* writers and directors worked to find ways to incorporate requests from sponsors, viewing them as necessary compromises that could lead to being viewed as good "team players" who would be invited to work on other productions. Producers, to their credit, were judicious with their interventions and worked with writers and directors to find solutions to sudden changes in scripts.

Much of this desire to accommodate the other side depends on the liveness of *uchiawase,* which was always conducted in real time in offices all over the city. Even during the COVID pandemic, such meetings were conducted live via Zoom meetings. This forced interaction between different hierarchies of production staff is less common in the "sacred space" of the Hollywood writer's room but can reduce opposition between management and creative staff. Producers rarely deliver revisions to scripts via notes, a system common in writer's rooms that create resentment from writers toward "distant" producers. Such an appearance of harmony in *uchiawase,* moreover, reveals the different purposes of script meetings, which is to create broad agreement on the direction of the script itself. While disruptive or patronizing outbursts directed at staff can occur in *uchiawase,* more direct communication would more often spill into *nomikai* drinking parties after the *uchiawase* that go late into the night. It was here where producers could grumble about dull plots or directors chafe at producer demands. Writers could also negotiate issues among themselves, depending on their career position, with young writers aiming to make a good impression and experienced writers regaling the crew with war stories, career advice, or pointed rebukes. For consensus, what is important is that everyone *feels* that their voice has been heard and respected, and that a solution to their criticism has been proposed and accepted within the limited time constraints set by the meeting, rather than if the accepted solution is actually the best or more appropriate one for the script and series. It is understood, moreover, that the script is a blueprint that will be adjusted according to the interpretations of the episode director, storyboard artist, layout and key animators, and so on down the line. If a problem is not completely resolved within the script, it has multiple areas where it can continue to undergo revision and refinement in what Stevie Suan has termed the "distributed agency" of anime's production pipeline where "all parties involved have different degrees of power in this hierarchical structure."[34]

Secondly, and connected to working relationships, is how a sense of respect for the experiences and knowledge of others pervaded script discussions. As the case study demonstrated, the crafting of each episode reveals such processes of negotiation in the staff hierarchy, where individuals can rise or fall within the room based on their backgrounds and experiences. In the production of *Smile*, the opinions of series director Ōtsuka and the voice actor for Akané often took precedence when conceiving plots and dialogue for the character as they were both Osaka natives and were able to convince the staff that their readings and interpretations were sound. Osakan characters are often stereotyped in Japanese media, and while *PreCure* also engages in stereotypes of Kansai culture—Akané's parents operate a restaurant that specializes in *okonomiyaki*, a Japanese pancake that is ubiquitous in Osaka—such character portrayals tended to focus on humanizing Akané's family and their working lives. Unlike the contentious battlegrounds of one-upmanship over race and gender seen in Hollywood writer's rooms, the shifting power relations in these instances of script development were handled with professionalism, and consensus was achieved via trust and reputation. Akané, like Brian Taylor, is initially Othered, but also incorporated into the franchise's legacy of heroines with sensitivity due to the experience and relative diversity of its staff. Values in the program that ostensibly connect contemporary audiences are thus a reflection of disparate cultural and regional interests prioritized within script development.

These working dynamics, of course, apply to committee-based televisual script development of various kinds in Japan. Still, it is worth considering how script development for anime franchises like *PreCure* or *Seiya* can reflect the diverse values of its stakeholders. Despite the idea that anime production might foster more caring or committed staff than other media industries, script development of the shows I observed reflected the same territorial anxieties over returns on investment, production budgets and schedules, and future opportunities for precarious work that characterize many global creative industries today. In recent years, moreover, management at various studios have been condemned for creating varying degrees of poor working conditions. Tōei Animation, for example, pays above industry average rates and gives directors and animators significant latitude in developing their careers; but the studio also has a checkered history with regards to worker rights, from its opposition to labor unions in the 1960s to present day allegations of animator overwork, power harassment, and LGBT discrimination.[35]

In spite of this stress, its staff continue to reinvent past works in thoughtful and considerate ways, particularly via the *PreCure* series which in recent years has been praised for its progressive gender representation and plots critical of contemporary corporate work culture. While *uchiawase* are not "sacred spaces" sequestered from financial concerns, their broad and professionally diverse participation means they can address parent company management practices within the structures of the franchise. Corporate producers have a stake in the scripts, but so too do the voices of directors, writers, and other personnel who can provide perspective and criticality beyond the board room. While these voices, too, can conform to established and conventional social beliefs and practices, their presence and agency allow for potential to branch off into unexpected directions. It is true that this is somewhat inherent to all kinds of genre or franchise production, as repetition must allow for stylistic or thematic variation and deviation for continued relevance. But even if the franchise reverts to a more conventional form following a more experimental or progressive iteration, the longer it goes on, the more playful, ironically, it can become. Thus, rather than portraying writer's rooms of anime production as utopic or toxic, it is more instructive to see what creators do in such generative workspaces and how these actions translate to allegorical reflections or responses to their sources of capital and control.

....

Bryan Hikari Hartzheim is Associate Professor of New Media at Waseda University's School of International Liberal Studies and Graduate School of International Culture and Communication Studies. His research specializes in the style, histories, and industries of video games and animation in and around Japan. He is the author of *Hideo Kojima: Progressive Game Design from Metal Gear to Death Stranding* (2023) and the coeditor of *The Franchise Era: Managing Media in the Digital Economy* (2019).

....

Notes

1. Eva Pjajcikova and Petr Szczepanik, "Group Writing for Post-Socialist Television," in *Production Studies, The Sequel!: Cultural Studies of Global Media Industries*, ed. Miranda Banks, Bridget Conor, and Vicki Mayer (New York: Routledge, 2016), 106.

2. Clifford Geertz, "Deep Play: Notes on the Balinese Cockfight," in *The Interpretation of Cultures* (New York: Basic Books, 1973), 452.

3. Miranda Banks, *The Writers: A History of American Screenwriters and Their Guild* (New Brunswick: Rutgers University Press, 2015), 166.

4. John Thornton Caldwell, *Production Culture: Industrial Reflexivity and Critical Practice in Film and Television* (Durham: Duke University Press, 2008), 213.

5. Patricia Phalen and Julia Osellame, "Writing Hollywood: Rooms with a Point of View," *Journal of Broadcasting* 56, no. 1 (2012): 11.

6. Josh Heuman, "What Happens in the Writers' Room Stays in the Writers' Room? Professional Authority in *Lyle v. Warner Bros.*," *Television & New Media* 17, no. 3 (2016): 195–211.

7. Lauri Kitsnik, "Scenario Writers and Scenario Readers in the Golden Age of Japanese Cinema," *Journal of Screenwriting* 7, no. 3 (2016): 289–91. Directors Kurosawa Akira and Ozu Yasujiro were two of the more well-known directing luminaries to employ the method.

8. Gabriela Lukacs, *Scripted Affects, Branded Selves: Television, Subjectivity, and Capitalism in 1990s Japan* (Durham: Duke University Press, 2010), 104.

9. Diane Wei Lewis, "*Shiage* and Women's Flexible Labor in the Japanese Animation Industry," *Feminist Media Histories* 4, no. 1 (2018): 115–41; Rayna Denison, *Studio Ghibli: An Industrial History* (London: Palgrave Macmillan, 2023).

10. Matsunaga Shintaro, *Animeetaa no shakaigaku: Shokugyō kihan to rōdō mondai* (Sociology of animators: Occupational norms and labor issues) (Tsu: Mie University Press, 2017).

11. Ryotaro Mihara, "Involution: a perspective for understanding Japanese animation's domestic business in a global context," *Japan Forum* 32, no. 1 (2020): 102–5; Kukhee Choo, "Nationalizing 'Cool:' Japan's Global Government Policy Towards the Content Industry," in *Popular Culture and the State in East and Southeast Asia*, ed. Nissim Ozmatgin and Eyal Ben-Ari (London: Routledge, 2012), 85–105.

12. Ian Condry, *The Soul of Anime: Collaborative Creativity and Japan's Media Success Story* (Durham: Duke University Press, 2013), 12.

13. Condry, *The Soul of Anime*, 144.

14. Bryan Hikari Hartzheim, "*Pretty Cure* and the Magical Girl Media Mix," *The Journal of Popular Culture* 49, no. 5 (2016): 1059–85.

15. Nick Browne, "The Political Economy of the (Super) Text," in *Television: The Critical View*, 4th ed., ed. Horace Newcomb (New York: Oxford University Press, 1987), 585–99.

16. Matt Hills, *Triumph of a Time Lord: Regenerating Doctor Who in the 21st Century* (London: IB Tauris & Co., 2010), 119–39.

17. Akahoshi Masanao, "Tōei Dōga no kenkyu" (Tōei Animation Research), in *Zusetsu Terebi Anime Zenshō* (Complete book of TV animation: Illustrated), ed. Misono Makoto (Tokyo: Hara Shobō, 1999), 215–19.

18. Hasegawa Masaya, interview by the author, June 2012.

19. Yoshioka Yuu, ed., *Smile PreCure! Complete Booklet* (Tokyo: Gakken Publishing, 2013), 94.

20. Ōtsuka Takashi, interview by the author, March 2014.

21. Ōtsuka Takashi, interview by the author, March 2014.

22. Bryan Hikari Hartzheim, "*Pretty Cure* and the Magical Girl Media Mix," 1067–73.

23. Ōtsuka Takashi, interview by the author, March 2014.

24. Akiko Sugawa Shimada, *Girls and Magic: Representations of Magical Girls and Japanese Female Viewership* (Tokyo: NTT Shuppan, 2013).

25. Anya Benson, "Loss in the Land of Toys: *Purikyua* and the Marketing of Childhood Nostalgia," *Japanese Journal of Policy and Culture* no. 26 (2018): 40.

26. Yoshioka Yuu, ed., *Smile PreCure! Complete Booklet* (Tokyo: Gakken Publishing, 2013), 89.

27. Lorna Piatti-Fornell, "Blood, Biceps, and Beautiful Eyes: Cultural Representations of Masculinity in Kurumada Masami's *Saint Seiya*," *The Journal of Popular Culture* 46, no. 6 (2021): 1133–55.

28. Wakabayashi Goh, interview by the author, July 2012.

29. Caldwell, *Production Culture,* 211–16; Felicia Henderson, "The Culture Behind Closed Doors: Issues of Gender and Race in the Writers' Room," *Cinema Journal* 50, no. 2 (2011): 145–52.

30. Sharon Kinsella, *Adult Manga: Culture and Power in Contemporary Japanese Society* (Honolulu: University of Hawaii Press, 2000).

31. Lukacs, *Scripted Affects, Branded Selves,* 94.

32. Eva Novrup Redvall, *Writing and Producing Television Drama in Denmark* (London: Palgrave Macmillan, 2013), 154–56.

33. Jennifer Prough, *Straight from the Heart: Gender, Intimacy, and the Cultural Production of Shojo Manga* (Honolulu: University of Hawaii Press, 2011).

34. Stevie Suan, "Consuming Production: Anime's Layers of Transnationality and Dispersal of Agency as Seen in *Shirobako* and *Sakuga*-Fan Practices," *Arts* 7, no. 3 (2018): 78.

35. Kim Morrissy, "Toei Animation Refuses Labor Negotiation With LGBT Union Member," *Anime News Network,* January 27, 2021, https://www.animenews network.com/interest/2021-01-27/toei-animation-refuses-labor-negotiations -with-lgbt-union-member/.168819.

Platforming the Studio

Kaname Production, Original Video Animation, and the Politics of the Amateur

BRIAN MILTHORPE

Founded in 1982, the animation studio Kaname Production released seven Original Video Animations (OVAs) during its short lifespan of six years. The fluctuating standards of this rapid video output and its consistent courtship of the bishōjo and sci-fi genres bound the studio as a symbol to the early energy and eventual fizzle of the 1980s OVA boom. While Kaname Pro contributed production assistance to many notable titles across television and film, including *Transformers* (1984) and *The Wings of Honnēamise* (1987), the studio garners attention today mainly for the celebrity names checkering its OVA credit rolls. Besides playing temporary host to esteemed subcultural creators, including Sorayama Hajime and Nagai Gō, the studio's posthumous identity largely resides in Kanada Yoshinori's auteur animation of *Birth* (1984) or the gamine appeal of Inomata Mutsumi's character designs in *Leda: The Fantastic Adventure of Yohko* (1985). To an extent, this checkering is natural. Staff circulated between projects to keep the fledgling studio afloat, investing labor and talent where needed but ultimately dwindling until the studio dissolved in 1988 from financial loss.

However, this argument begins from the conviction that Kaname Pro deserves an introduction in scholarship as a distinct entity on par with more prominent studios particularly for the *stability of its unstable symbiosis* with the OVA format. While Studio Ghibli or Kyoto Animation can sustain the attribution of consistent aesthetic, thematic, and directorial programs or signatures across film and television, the formalization of similar transtextual symmetries is absent in treatments of less popular, stable, or prosperous studios. Indeed, this evaluative bias appears hardwired into the OVA format itself. For decades, fans in and outside Japan have noted how the format tended to anchor limited technical éclat, shallow scenarios, inhospitable runtimes, or titillating eroticism to the detriment of the kind of narrative complexity, character development, or world-building found in longer format or bigger budget affairs.[1] The "O" in OVA even hides a biting irony: a significant portion of these titles were hardly "original," instead compiling conceptual tropes from Hollywood films or extending extant TV and manga series.

This asymmetry can be attributed in part to the unique correspondence between product-technology platforms like the VHS and Beta videotapes or LD and VHD videodiscs on which OVAs were distributed and the platform-like structure of the studios in which they were created. The product-technology platform of video is a "fundamentally open and hence transformable . . . device whose end result is not determined from the outset."[2] It exists on a continuum with the range of startup animation studios like AIC and Gainax appearing in the early 1980s alongside Kaname Pro as "contained and bounded space[s] shaped by, and shaping, distributed creation processes."[3] In each studio, technical constraints nonetheless engender indeterminate content potential when compared to the tendencies of preexisting media pathways. In his recent discussion of transmedia genre, Thomas Lamarre gestures toward this homology between studio and video in the early 1980s in his focus on how the OVA "created expectations for discontinuity or divergence" in departure from film and television, licensing programs of expression unsubordinated to the linear economic rationality of clean serialization or consistent aesthetics.[4] As stable yet fragile sites of diverse production, small studios like Kaname Pro meld into the video format, transforming into transmedial entities that, like the technology platform, become capable of placing forms of expression "into relation (imperceptibly) and ensuring that they remain distinct (perceptibly)."[5]

At the same time, however, the comparative freedom granted by direct-to-video production counterintuitively depended on closely tailoring this latitude to niche consumer tastes. As Nagata Daisuke has shown in analysis of contemporary anime periodicals, the close relations enabled by the OVA contributed to the discursive construction of the otaku, a hyperconsumer whose repetitive tape viewing built a repertoire of sociotechnical knowledge about anime and its industry.[6] While Nagata's study of the discourse networks circling the early OVA depends on the platforms nested in the concurrent expansion of the consumer electronics economy, it neglects a vital dimension of this nesting in accepting Hiroki Azuma's database model as its formal conclusion.[7] Following Azuma to frame subcultural invention in the last decades of the twentieth century as preparation for a self-referential digital repository in which the otaku "database animal" combines, recombines, and organizes informatic tidbits, Nagata leaves unexamined the psychopolitical dynamics of the very sociological knowledge he discovers.

Recontextualizing the OVA as a studio-platform through analysis of the platform-studio Kaname Pro leverages Nagata's findings away from Azuma's asocial postmodernism. Such theories about the novel subjectivity of the "dissociated human" at the end of history obscure the debilitating consequences of psychotechnical dissociation, what Bernard Stiegler has called "the destruction of associational media through development of psychotechnologies eradicating psychic and social faculties."[8] Refusing to confront media's mesmeric ability to shape the sociality of knowledge and imagination, leaves it to degrade attention, social agency, and historical consciousness. At best, the result is generalized addiction.[9] Azuma diagnoses this disease but refuses treatment. For him, the otaku is forever an uncritical addict craving doses of stereotyped affect. Closer consideration of the studio-platform and the platform-studio reveals in opposition how creators through studios and fans through platforms resisted dissociation by investing in the OVA as a discontinuously associated medium that doubles as a social platform supportive of the formation of technical and historical knowledge.

To explore how the studio-platform of the OVA departs from the database model, the first section of this article outlines the early history of Kaname Pro, concentrating on the productive sphere to highlight how the studio invested in a platform for user-creator relations. The following section shifts its focus to consumers to assert that the replay of OVAs enabled by fan-creator platforms gestures toward an alternative to the hyperconsumption of the otaku by sublimating acquisitive impulses into knowledge formation proper to the "amateur," a loving practitioner of technical media. Hinging together these two sections, I plot a trio of images showcasing a selection of Kaname Pro's OVA works. These synoptic vignettes inspired by Walter Benjamin's writings on spectacular commodities in the *Arcades Project* attempt to evoke the historical topical breadth introduced within the self-contained asymmetrical content of the studio-platform. My design suggests that a relay among narratives, media forms, and histories emerges from these images "in a flash" through the discontinuity of video media to cast illuminating sparks of a past analogue struggle for associated communities of amateurs. In doing so, I propose a way of reading anime that can counter the dissociative tendencies posed by our digitally networked and socially mediated present in allowing tropes and technologies to produce novel connections across time.[10]

The Birth of the Distributed Studio

Kaname Production was founded in January 1982, by a small group of former Ashi Production staff members from diverse roles who left to create their own studio. Each of these initial members was under thirty years old, unmarried, and enthusiastic about the undertaking. First setting up shop in a two-bedroom apartment (moving to a more manageable office building in the Suginami Ward of Tokyo the following year), early members included manager Nagao Akihiro, director Yuyama Kunihiko, scriptwriter Takegami Junki, mechanical designers Kohara Shōhei and Toyomasu Takahiro, and animators Kageyama Shigenori, Inomata Mutsumi, Ochi Kazuhiro, and Watanabe Mayumi.[11] Despite their métier in animation, an amateurish cinephilia pervaded the core staff. Kageyama shot Super 8 footage in high school, Nagao previously worked in the film industry, and discussions at the studio ran the gamut from Hollywood blockbusters to B movies.[12] There were even expectations that Kaname Pro would balance animation and live-action recording as a hybrid studio; but a dearth of live-action opportunities quickly forced their concentration on animation.[13]

This pressure led to the studio first contributing keyframes to Tomino Yoshiyuki's *Combat Mecha Xabungle* (1982), a mecha TV series like those on which members honed skills while at Ashi, such as *Space Warrior Baldios* (1980) and *GoShogun* (1981). Kaname Pro stayed close to this genre in producing their first in-house title with Toho, a manga-based TV series called *Plawres Sanshiro* airing on TBS beginning in June 1983. The show chronicled the trials of a boy who enters his miniature fighting robot into wrestling matches and benefitted during its run from a strong merchandising campaign that materialized its competitive vigor into a variety of plastic model kits and soft vinyl toys marketed by Bandai. A significant following bubbled around this first TV voyage, owing to Inomata's attractive models and stylized animation from Kanada Yoshinori, Itano Ichirō, and Ochi, remediating wrestling's delicate anatomic choreography into expressive robotic form.

Around the airdate of the final episode of *Plawres Sanshiro* in February 1984, the Kaname Pro Fan Club (FC) was established to keep fervor around the studio alive. The club operated out of Kaname Pro's headquarters, published a bimonthly serial that announced new projects and sweepstakes for studio merchandise (including pencil boards and calendars), and released a bound-volume series titled *Viva! Kaname,* which contained production sketches, conversations, comics, original illustrations, and studio updates.

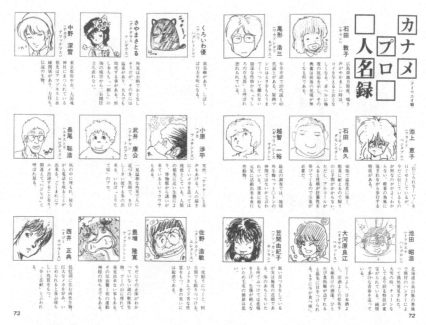

Figure 1. The "Kaname Pro Directory" featured in *Viva! Kaname,* Vol. A (Tokyo: Kaname Pro, c. 1983), 72–73, introducing Kaname Pro staff alongside self-portraits and short biographies.

These periodicals opened a studio structure often invisible or undervalued by presenting a relaxed profile of self-driven and personal creativity (Figure 1). On April 3, 1984, Kaname Pro FC opened this structure further by holding the first major event of the club, Excite Kaname. A flier advertising the gathering features diagonal lineation, fluorescent color, and a sketch by Inomata, delivering a rhetoric of inclusion, familiarity, and, of course, excitement (Figure 2). The program included *Plawres* viewings, boxed lunches, musical performances, and staff and cast Q&A. In exchange for membership dues, which supplied another revenue source to pay wages and fund side projects, like a manga by Ochi, members received the ability to share a space with creators whose presence would have otherwise been entirely mediated by broadcast signals. Early in its course, publications, and events of this type distinguished Kaname Pro by offering a multimedia infrastructure that tended to "customers, advertisers, service providers, producers, suppliers, even physical objects," that is, a transmedial platform that embedded animation, studio, and fandom.[14]

Figure 2. "Kaname Production Event: EXCITE Kaname!" leaflet (Tokyo: Kaname Pro, c. 1984).

This intimate model of fan-creator relations combined with Kaname Pro's thwarted desire to enter the film industry fostered their next production, *Birth* (1984), a SF action OVA based on a 1982 manga written by Takegami, illustrated by Kanada, and planned for television by the studio in the year of its founding. After Studio Pierrot gained widespread notice from the successful direct-to-video release of Oshii Mamoru's *Dallos* in 1983 (like *Birth*, a scuttled TV project), production companies began testing projects in the video market, selling OVAs either directly to consumers via mail order or in batches to the hundreds of video rental shops then around Tokyo. An industrial narrative began to take hold that video-production sanctioned a field for creators to shape works with "individual character" unconformable to the mass appeal of standard anime. Banking on the enthusiasm proven by the activity of Kaname FC, the decision to follow *Plawres* with *Birth* in the OVA market presented a method for not only recouping costs but capitalizing on tape technology's precision of distribution and physical intimacy to reinforce relationships between studio and fans.

Jonathan Clements's recognition of the fact that many early OVAs also received theater screenings simultaneously elucidates and sidelines a more complex media profile.[15] The OVA acted as a means of developing small-scale studio production that bore a closer resemblance to film than TV, but independent from theatrical circuits. Neither spruced-up TV episodes nor undercooked blockbusters, the format engendered the generics of a focalized cinematic production-content matrix akin to the B movie or exploitation film on video. *Birth* can be framed as both a testing ground for Kaname Pro's turn away from a strict TV market and toward a video production model based on the studio as "a multilinear machine articulated at once across media" that could assimilate diverse tones and subjects.[16] Complementing the platform capacity of Kaname FC, the OVA was capable of "binding open exchanges between self-directed users," and proscribing a medial space of niche interaction.[17]

Small studio projects, while still relying on divisions of labor and merchandising contracts, also condoned more lateral movement in terms of collaboration, ideation, and execution. Speaking as a representative of Kaname Pro in 1985, Kageyama articulated this ethos: "In our studio, every member aims to be a creator; we see everything as 'footage' . . . and work together to come up with ideas."[18] Reacting to an industry in which "it feels like everyone is isolated within their own category," the young animator elsewhere expressed the virtue of the transdisciplinary experimentation possible in small studios: "Rather than only working within your own section, it's good to meddle in others. Like animators writing screenplays and vice versa. You find all kinds of unexpected connections and stimuli with this."[19] For Kageyama, an animator interested in traditional ink painting, such versatility encouraged more refined animation capable of "sharpening viewer's eyes," training their awareness of animation as a self-conscious medium with its own language and practice emulating raw video footage.[20]

Kageyama's comments also elucidate a contrast to traditional studio production, which originated in the hyperspecialized labor segmentation required for massive animation projects at Disney in the 1930s and was replicated by Tōei Dōga in the following decades.[21] The studio form often exhibited static section scaffolds focused on "broader systems of production, not necessarily on individual career paths."[22] Less restricted coordination combined with fewer personnel endowed low-level Kaname staff with more influence in, for instance, the opportunity to reinterpret key frame lines to express personal invention.[23] While corrections sometimes preserved hierarchies, as Inomata notes, an atmosphere of experimentation pervaded production, owing partly to competitive comradery: "Everyone had an excessive desire to improve, and wanted to flaunt how well they could draw."[24] With this cross-sectional collaboration, Kaname Pro solicited the potential for its staff to advance "individual career paths" from *within* the studio system, combining a valuation of member's art with the OVA's direct pathway to fans looking for unique touches and tropes, such as dynamically animated hovercraft chase scenes carried across multiple projects. The decision to premiere a preview of *Birth* at a FC meeting formalized this pattern: the studio outfitted its productions with a community-oriented service environment joining staff, fandom, and media.

Birth, however, left many fans unsatisfied; complaints about the incoherent plot and shoddy photography prevailed. The OVA's authorization of content unsuited for film or TV proved in this case both blessing and curse. Inomata's crystalline designs and Yuyama's directorial whimsy picked up the slack with a subsequent project that formalized the beautiful fighting girl trope popularized in magazines like *Fanroad* and the 1984 independent animation short *Bakusō Flash Gal*. The production was the fantasy epic *Leda: The Fantastic Adventure of Yohko* (1985) and boasted a hundred-million-yen budget funding five thousand key frames on 35 mm film stock (Figure 3). Second in sales only to the OVA megahit *Megazone 23*, the success of *Leda* ignited Kaname Pro's production schedule with simultaneous serial OVA projects harboring pastiche thematics and the spectacular thrills of Hollywood cinema: the aura of B-movies enveloped *Dream Hunter Fandora* (1985–86); elements of *Taxi Driver* (1976) and *The Terminator* (1984) entered *Bavi Stock* (1985); and the decade's cyborg obsession infected *The Humanoid* (1986) (Figure 4).[25]

Each of these multi-installment video series emerged in partnership with Shibasaki Hiromasa's production company Hiro Media in a project focused on distributing OVAs in the North American market. Advertised alongside other OVAs in Shibasaki's magazine *Globian*, these co-productions embodied a precocious ancestor to the simulcast dynamic of modern anime distribution not only in their transpacific mindset but also in recognition of the distinct transmissibility inherent in the format. Indeed, the Kaname-Hiro international OVA partnership employed the medial logic of video cassettes to thread the gap between feature standards and overseas broadcast contracting. Yet the full scope of these plans never came to fruition. One explanation for this failure is the fact that Kaname and Hiro bypassed the expanding US rental industry in favor of direct mail-order sales to individual consumers reluctant to spend nearly a hundred dollars on a single cassette.[26] Sole attention to economic factors, however, downplays the importance of the platform capacity Kaname Pro exercised through periodicals and events. Voided in the Kaname-Hiro international strategy was the concern for viewers that Kageyama expressed from within the studio through the OVA as a platform. Hiro Media neglected to consider they were selling more than animation on video; they were selling a new social media platform that hosted the profile of newly formed amateur studios within a specific sociotechnical discourse intervening in Japan's media ecology.

Extension into unfamiliar markets and demanding production schedules for several post-*Leda* releases led the studio into difficult straits. Profits during this middle period, as Inomata recalls, barely warded off a dip into the red.[27] Balancing work on *Windaria* (1986), a major feature headlined by Inomata and Yuyama, together with sequels to Hiro Media video projects and a stalled *Leda* follow-up subtitled "Taste of Honey" created conditions in which labor stretched and debt accumulated.[28] Hyperextended and disheveled, members of Kaname Pro regrouped before the release of their final OVA in partnership with Konami, *The Story of Watt Poe* (1988), only to buckle around the time of its release (Figure 5).[29] During the production of *Windaria*, Nagao recognized both the precarity of the studio and the bond between their fortunes and video: "If we dabble in [TV series] incorrectly, it'll be a death blow. Based on this situation, we'll likely be concentrating on video anime for now. As far as the direction of our anime, we'd like to consider doing SF anime with our own touch."[30]

Yet if it is true that the viability of anime studios depended on maneuvering between "adopt[ing] a recognizable style . . . relying on the help of a well-known director" and "pleas[ing] the general public by adapting a popular manga . . . with media-mix projects," Kaname Pro's commitment to the OVA market to enable the production of original projects "with our own touch" exposes the inherent risk of the video platform.[31] It also raises questions around the consequences of a lateral studio structure. If directors, writers, and animators are all "creators," and if these creators work across sections while conversing, collaborating, and editing others' work, how does the studio emerge from the list of individual names? Who exactly is the "our" in Nagao's statement?

Recent work in the field of studio studies answers these questions in attending to the peculiarities of the studio as a distinct yet complicated form. Conceptualizing art studios as experimental laboratories, Ignacio Farías and Alex Wilkie propose the concept of "distributed creation" as a notional tool to identify "creativity as a sociomaterial and collective process, in which no single actor holds all the cards."[32] Such an approach moderates the tendency to see the studio as the playground for the sovereign skill of a solitary genius or as fodder for social processes hovering above these sites of cultural production. The ultimate benefit of this distributive studio model is that by "paying attention to the variegated events in which the potentialities of materials, artefacts, bodies, images, and concepts unfold empirically," the studio becomes stable yet flexible, concatenating persons, objects, and actions without erasing the specificity of its organizational or material inputs.[33] The distributed studio thus resembles Benjamin's Bratton's definition of the platform as a paradoxical structure, "a strict and invariable mechanism . . . providing for an emergent heterogeneity of self-directed uses."[34] Relying on standardized technologies, common materials, and engrained techniques, the studio-platform nonetheless mediates functionality to achieve undetermined output.

In such a view, the surplus of variables combining to *make* a given production depend on diverse times, media modes, and events which may not enter into relation with the studio in an apparent way. If "an emphasis on the creation of cultural artefacts cannot be separated from the settings in which such entities are brought into existence," this opens a vast parametric field.[35] These settings may be semiotic, historical, or mnemonic, existing as possible nodes of connection beyond individual consciousness to be established elsewhere, in historical hindsight or political foresight. Like Walter Benjamin's dialectical practice of reading multiple temporalities into the simultaneity of the commodity as an historical image, the studio "involves taking the risk of assembling alternative relationships between objects, people, and spaces, introducing alternative propositions, imagining a different world."[36] If the "touch" of Kaname Pro, along with other small studios, becomes tangible through this model, the most pressing questions to entertain after its dissolution must be: what relationships and propositions did they assemble in their video productions? What times and memories did they bring with them? What worlds did they make and what worlds made them?

Figure 3. Still frame from *Leda: The Fantastic Adventure of Yohko* (Kaname Production and Toho Co. Ltd., 1985).

Leda: A Transmedial Love Letter

- Leda was violated by Zeus after he took the form of a swan, unleashing the lust intensified by admiring her from afar in a sexual violence immortalized across ages in diverse media forms from vases to tapestries and prints. She gave birth to Helen of Troy, who, in Homer's telling, exhibits strange powers of imitation and, in a fragment from Sappho, epitomizes singular desire.
- On a scintillating boulevard, a young girl loses herself in a cassette player, sinking into the depths of a piano composition recorded for her unrequited lover. Fate places its beneficiary on the same boulevard, but her courage to confess her love flags. Suddenly, she is transported into an alternate world threatened by a maleficent sorcerer. Learning that she is an ancient warrior named Leda and that her cassette holds a strange power to open worlds and subdue this evil, she gathers her lost bravery and endeavors to do the impossible.
- In 1979, Sony released the TPL-S2 Walkman, the first portable cassette player, commodifying auditory memory, emotion, and culture in a private, controllable, and exchangeable form.

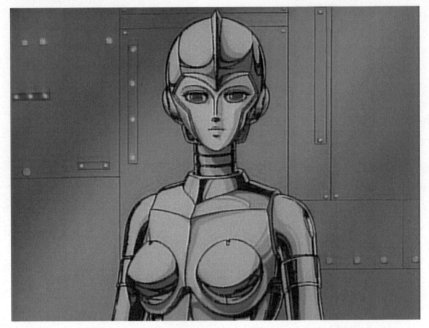

Figure 4. Still frame from *The Humanoid* (Kaname Production, Hiro Media Co. Ltd., and Toshiba EMI, 1986).

The Humanoid: Ghosts in Marie's Shell

- In 1772, two decades before her guillotining, Marie Antoinette commissioned Pierre Kintzing and David Roentgen to build a miniature tympanum-playing automaton in her likeness, reputedly using her own clothes and hair.
- A supply ship crewed by workers whose only respite in the senseless depths of space is the scent of coffee delivers commodities to the planet Lazeria, sanctuary to an alien emperor escaping war. There they meet a woman with a machinic body and biological mind named Antoinette whose Geppetto believes she will harmonize nature and technology. As Antoinette falls in love a crew member, a dissenting imperial faction plots to use ancient technology to return to their home and destroy Lazeria in the process.
- The artisanal cafe experienced a boom in 1980s Japan. Decadent gold leaf coffee accompanied exploitative novelty cafes where waitresses in revealing office attire acted as erotic props for lecherous businessmen constrained at work by new sexual harassment laws.

Figure 5. Still frame from The Story of Watt Poe (*Watt Poe to Bokura no Ohanashi*) (Pony Canyon, and Konami, 1988).

Watt Poe: Eco-apocalyptic Memorandums

- In 1977 Paul Watson founded The Sea Shepherd Conservation Society, considered an ecoterrorist organization by the Japanese government for their disruption of Japan's whaling program. In 1982, *Asahi Newspaper* christened Watson "the messenger of the dolphins."
- A boy named Jam lives in an impoverished fishing village whose tutelary deity, a horned whale name Watt Poe, was abducted by flying monsters. Orphan notes of a mysterious flute one day beckon the boy to the forest where he discovers Selene, a girl whose instrument comforts Watt Poe, living sequestered in a caldera. Jam learns the whale's captors are technologically advanced humans, survivors of a nuclear apocalypse who, having lost the ability to reproduce, sought Watt Poe's intercession.
- In 2010, census data on the Japanese population registered a statistically significant decline for the first time. Fertility fell to almost half the replacement rate. Economic inequality and social alienation accelerated by neoliberal deregulation number among the causes.

Amateur Desires and Periodical Platforms

Approaching such questions around Kaname Pro requires recalling that the OVA boom occurred within the larger context of an economic expansion owing to a steady increase in manufacturing exports in the automobile, semiconductor, and consumer electronics industries in the first half of the 1980s. In this regard, the studio-platform comports with a wider post-recessionary market strategy to "test innovations" with "small firms exploit[ing] new products, processes, [and] technologies" in concordance with reinvestments in domestic consumer desire.[37] Located within this thrust toward innovation and application of new technologies, the OVA was not simply a conduit for creative expression. The medium itself arose within a sphere framing it as an exemplum of "restoring prosperity largely through the exploitation of consumer power."[38] Indeed, video production models only became feasible after sharp declines in electronics manufacturing costs multiplied VCR ownership among Japanese households from 2 percent in 1980 to approximately 65 percent in 1989.[39]

Rising purchasing power among the middle classes quickly befriended private video media, a technology harboring an inherent decentralization of media control formerly reserved in broadcast corporations' manipulation of information entertainment streams.[40] In the nascent anime periodical industry, this medial dehierarchization found an intellectual counterpart in a series of critical misprisions equally set on usurping control in favor of mass politics. After a failed vanguardism in the late 1960s, leftist student groups in Japan abandoned material for semiotic revolution, clinging to children's entertainment as a reversal of cultural hierarchies and hawking the theories of Foucault and Derrida in magazines like *Animage* to lend their *ressentiment* a sheen of intellectualism.[41] Inventing the notion of otaku subjectivity in this way, as Ōtsuka Eiji admits, the editorial work of this New Left intelligentsia amounted to little more than "marketing theory," acting as if consumers watching anime could become radical or transgressive through consumption.[42]

Flickering in the hope born by a boom economy glowed hints of the social isolation and hyperconsumption that would come to characterize the post-bubble otaku in the following decade. The OVA studio-platform thus registers a distinct contradiction: the consumer culture accelerating in the 1980s engendered a collective and collaborative structure of economically privileged fan support that exposed yet intensified the atomized labor of the anime industry. Ōtsuka, however, fails to appreciate how the ironic misapplication of French philosophy in elevating Japanese subcultural practice to "high theory" proceeds from and perpetuates this same contradiction, a consequence of the phenomenon Derrida himself theorized under the term *mondialization*, a globalized regime of cultural commodification illuminating and flattening idiomatic differences. The guilty pleasure of distorting low and high culture began as a "joke," but globalization enjoyed the first and last laugh. Ōtsuka's previous and Azuma's recent postmodern rhapsodizing only signal the psychopolitical deprivations clearing the way for the addictive hyperconsumption of contemporary global otakuism initiated in the voracious commodity consumption and alienation of the 1980s anime industry.

The OVA studio-platform, however, also potentiated resistance to social fragmentation through methods of social and technical engagement not reducible to consumption. This tense logic shapes the video format into what Bernard Stiegler calls a *technology of transindividuation*, one of many "relational technologies, of which 'social networks' are the latest avatar."[43] Relying on symbols as tools of massification segmenting individual desires into consumer profiles like "the otaku" or "fan," these technologies are fundamentally agonistic. On one hand, they dampen the singularity required for maintaining desire, reducing *unique* attachments to whatever drives *mass* consumption. Yet, on the other, as social networks routed through technical objects, they provide open space for methods of invention and communication that "struggle against becoming audience of the public."[44] Only care and knowledge prevent the opposition between unthinking consumption and devoted association from leading to toxic individual and collective disorders.

Stiegler deploys the term "amateur" in its etymological sense of "lover" to shape a figure of this care, which formulates a language capable of understanding how technologies work, creating media spaces from within where judgment, appraisal, and knowledge unfold. Studious in distance yet amorous in proximity, the amateur "who loves because, in his own way and by his own practices . . . his senses are wide open to sense" learns to differentiate, individuate, and analyze through practices depending on the communication between biological and technical organs.[45] Azuma's repetitive database consumption haunting the otaku exist for Stiegler in audiovisual media technologies as "repetitive machines" turning thinkers into consumers through "loss of participation [and] living knowledge."[46] And yet these same devices can resist this tendency in configuring "a new epoch of repetition which is productive of difference," itself forming new interpersonal and intellectual associations. Through participative aesthetic experience, the amateur finds that life in a hyperconsumerist society is, despite its own degrading pathos, still worth living.[47]

A willingness to confront otaku subjectivity as a global media phenomenon in which all of us participate sits at the center of Stiegler's thought. As Claire Colebrook explains, for Stiegler "the individual becomes complex and capable of care for the world through images that are archived, repeated, and constitutive of long circuits of memory."[48] Yet these same images are also subject to deadening "stereotypes and the waning of the power to establish individuating circuits," that is, the ability to produce interpretive communities of care routed through longer trains of historical thought.[49] The stakes of the otaku's interest in trope-dense images palpable here expose the inflexibility of both Azuma and Ōtsuka's analyses. A "desire for identity and place" evinced in the otaku subculture emerging in the 1980s fascinated with animation and animators does not inherently indicate a desperation for conservative "grand narratives."[50] Rather these evince a struggle for knowledge-making practices within an economic industrial machine programmed to turn consumers into automated data banks, victims of a kind of alienation still active today on digital platforms whose use requires no particular knowledge of their underlying technology or operation.

A prominent example of this knowledge practice exists within specialty magazines treating the OVA as a distinct format, most notably *AnimeV*, an *Animage* supplement turned independent publication in 1985. Skimming any issue of *AnimeV* delivers a universe of expertise, cultural reproduction, and technical knowledge driven by insiders and outsiders alike. Besides collocating interviews with creators alongside reader contributions, including character sketches, fan mail, and passionate letters airing judgments and praise, *AnimeV* individuated itself through directly addressing the OVA's platform capacity to organize and influence amateur desires. Spotlighting new releases and upcoming projects with colorful glossy images, each issue also devoted consistent attention to the technical specifications, management, and functionality of VHS, Beta, and LD formats hosting this content while auguring the affordances, limitations, and futures of each. Users guided users into a knowledge practice of indexing, comprehension, and preservation opposed to disposability and unthinking consumption (Figure 6). In this, *AnimeV* foregrounded a practice of technical-aesthetic participation, a form of intervention through patterns of reinterpretation, evaluation, and differentiation, that constituted sensible engagement with technical media.[51]

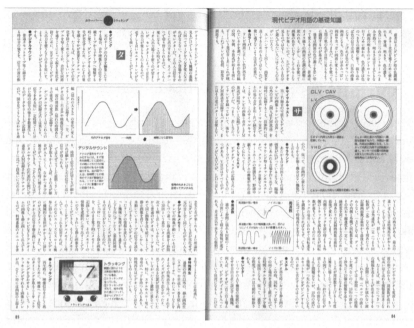

Figure 6. A video glossary article from *AnimeV* (1986) detailing video waveform frequencies, simulcast recording, constant linear/angular velocity, tracking, and trick play functionality.

Essential to focalizing practices of care subtended by the product-platform of the OVA were intentional statements submitted by OVA fans to contribution columns. Perused by industry insiders gauging the desires of consumers and fellow fans eager for serialized debate or comradery aware of the limited number of industry personnel, as Nagata asserts, column activity discursively positioned the OVA as a self-conscious "third medium" intervening between TV anime and theatrical anime film.[52] Reviewing *AnimeV* fan submissions, Nagata shows how readers conceptualized the OVA as presenting a kind of animation impossible in these other mediums, inaugurating distinctions between generalist and otaku "literacy."[53] In tandem with the development of such literacies, *AnimeV* exemplified how platforms "set the terms of participation according to fixed protocols . . . [gaining] strength by mediating unplanned and perhaps unplannable interactions."[54] Playback abetted amateurism through explicit mechanisms taking the form of special columns like "Ah! Scenes," a section of the magazine dedicated to indexing moments whose repetitive viewing shed light on animation techniques or trans-textual allusions, such as the discovery of a copy of Dazai Osamu's novel *No Longer Human* (1948) in Studio Gainax's *Gunbuster* (1989).[55]

The Studio's Aesthetics-in-Action

By the end of the 1980s, OVAs proliferated, multiplying more than tenfold since 1983.[56] A concurrent increase in the quantity of video rental shops siphoned sales from a relatively stable and growingly selective pool of purchasers. Taketomi Yukako suggests that during this period the OVA market began to steer away from niche otaku content and catered instead to general interest traffic attracted to video rental stores associated with corporations like Japan Home Video. Newly produced titles "differed completely from the type of work fans demanded. Creator mentality [began] to shift away from creating a single volume worth 10,000 yen and toward something enjoyable at a 500-yen rental fee" with an emphasis on "quality entertainment, enjoyable by wide ranging demographics, from kids to adults."[57] Such a stance chaffed against specialty discourses and amateur eccentricities circulating around the OVA, cultivating a sense that the singularity of the medium had begun to wane.[58] Buttressing this trend was a stronger embrace of adapting pre-existing properties: in 1988, 67 percent of OVAs produced were derivations of manga or TV series.[59]

Gluts of mediocre OVAs, new satellite and rental services, and the introduction of the production committee system together fail to sufficiently explain the decline of the OVA boom. As the discussion above indicates, a complex imbrication of factors led to a situation wherein the demands of a profit-driven model of consumer massification superseded the local desires and discursive networks of a relatively stable number of fans and creators who invested in the OVA as a social media platform. Like the digital platforms succeeding it, capital incentives drove the OVA to "strike a different balance between safe and controversial, between socially and financially valuable."[60] This revised conception of OVA production late in the decade suggests that the profit-motive undergirding platform architecture outstripped the activity of "self-directed" amateurs whose aesthetic proclivities and undynamic purchasing were perceived as capriciously unprofitable. Taketomi's supposition that "if we only target maniacs, we can't expect any further development for the OVA" poignantly summarizes the change.[61] A generalized industrial output capable of hosting more bodies exceeded the bounds of a platform model organizing a specialized knowledge discourse focused on thinking the intricacies of the novel "third medium."

None of this is to endorse a nostalgic resuscitation of the OVA or romanticize studio labor. Rather it is to notice how the "selfish" interests of Kaname Pro's original productions glimpse an alternative production-consumption model based not on the generalized database consumerism of *homo informaticus*, but on an open platform animating the discovery of unexpected configurations across discontinuous media emerging with and organized by studio profiles. In this, Kaname Pro instantiates the notion of the studio proper in that it "involves a form of aesthetics-in-action, of assembling, improvising and manipulating cultural artefacts in view of producing affective attachments to future users, audiences, spectators and publics."[62] Hyperfixation on certain expressive forms designed to "sharpen" viewers' eyes between and within works lends itself to a "rewind" opportunity for the cultivation of an amateurism based on holding desire and know-how. Instead of a novel database subjectivity, the methods of analysis, knowledge production, and practices of care exemplified in periodicals like *AnimeV* constitute limited tactics in a battle against the massifying tendencies of global technoeconomic capital on its own terrain, an antagonism still visible where online discourse networks influence media mix strategies or animation studios outsource creative labor to overseas fans.

Organizing fan desires and creating networks of exchange in the medial form of a cassette tape to be viewed, reviewed, and preserved elicited the potential for a process of individuation, critique, and longer circuits of attention. As a platform rooted in analogue media technologies, the OVA offers an example of how "a work of art is at once free of any attachment to its own time . . . and at the same time formed uniquely in, by, and out of its age."[63] This distributed temporality outside of linear time defines both Kaname Pro as a distributed platform-studio and the OVA as an open studio-platform. The superficiality and standardization of content elevate an awareness of form and technicity as pivots into a more expansive awareness. In this sense, the studio-platform condenses and makes available an undertheorized aspect of all social media platforms. The paradox of open spaces abbreviated by restrictive standards or massifying stereotypes insistently asks users to become not one of a mass, but, like the youthful staff of Kaname Pro and early OVA fans, disciplined amateurs experimenting with open senses, discovering reasons to live, think, and care through relational technologies.

Brian Milthorpe is a postdoctoral fellow at the University of Wisconsin-Madison. His research concentrates on eighteenth-century working-class poetry, romanticism, and media technologies of the eighteenth and nineteenth centuries. He is particularly interested in reevaluating from a media studies perspective the tradition of romantic natural genius within the context of emerging divisions between mechanism and organicism, logics of prosthesis and supplementarity, and the invention and diffusion of visual technologies related to film and animation incorporated into visual modernity. He is currently developing a book project based on these topics that investigates points of convergence between romantic poetic theory and the aesthetic practices and media technologies of animation.

Notes

1. Fred Patten, *Watching Anime, Reading Manga* (Berkley: Stone Bridge Press, 2004), 277; Gilles Poitras, "Contemporary Anime in Japanese Pop Culture," in *Japanese Visual Culture: Explorations in the World of Anime and Manga,* ed. Mark MacWilliams (Milton Park: Taylor and Francis, 2014), 54.
2. Mark Steinberg, *The Platform Economy* (Minneapolis: University of Minnesota Press, 2019), 78.
3. Ignacio Farias and Alex Wilkie, *Studio Studies: Operations, Topologies, and Displacements* (New York: Routledge, 2016), 7.
4. Thomas Lamarre, "Transmedia-genre: Non-continuity, Discontinuity, and Continuity in the Global 80s," *New Review of Film and Television Studies,* 20, no. 1 (2022): 129.
5. Lamarre, "Transmedia-genre," 124.
6. Nagata Daisuke, "OVA as 'The Third Media' in Anime Magazines: Focusing on the Structural Conditions of the Animation Industry in the 1980s," *Soshioroji,* 16, no. 3 (2017): 41–58.
7. Hiroki Azuma, *Otaku: Japan's Database Animals* (Minneapolis: University of Minnesota Press, 2001).
8. Bernard Stiegler, *Taking Care of the Youth and the Generations* (Stanford: Stanford University Press, 2010), 134.
9. Maxime Derian, *Cognitive Prosthetics* (London: ITSE, 2018), 140–42.
10. Walter Benjamin, *The Arcades Project,* trans. Howard Eiland and Kevin McLaughlin (Cambridge, MA: Harvard University Press, 1999), 462.
11. Nagao Akihiro, "Kaname Pro Special," *Ji Anime,* September 1985, 24.
12. Kageyama Shigenori, "Anime Ningen Intabyū" (Humans of Anime Interview), *Ji Anime,* October 1985, 120.
13. Nagao, "Kaname Pro Special," 24.

14. Nick Srnicek, *Platform Capitalism* (Cambridge: Polity Press, 2017), 43.
15. Jonathan Clements, *Anime: A History* (New York: BFI, 2017), 167.
16. Lamarre, "Transmedia-genre," 128.
17. Benjamin Bratton, *The Stack: On Software and Sovereignty* (Cambridge, MA: MIT Press, 2016), 42.
18. Kageyama, "Kaname Pro Special," 24.
19. Kageyama, "Anime Ningen Intabyū," 121.
20. Kageyama, "Anime Ningen Intabyū," 122.
21. Tze-Yue Hu, *Frames of Anime* (Hong Kong: Hong Kong University Press, 2010), 83.
22. Susan Ohmer, "Classical Hollywood" in *Animation* (New Brunswick: Rutgers University Press, 2019), 62.
23. Inomata Mutsumi, *Ima dakara katareru 80 nendai anime no hiwa: Bishōjo anime no hōga* (Secrets of 80s anime finally revealed: The budding of bishōjo anime) (Tokyo: Yosensha, 2012), 137–64.
24. Inomata, *Ima dakara katareru 80 nendai anime no hiwa*.
25. Kageyama, "Kaname Pro Special," 14–16.
26. Fred Patten, "My Time with Hiro Media Associates," *Cartoon Research* (2015), https://cartoonresearch.com/index.php/my-time-with-hiro-media-associates. Accessed 15 January 2023.
27. Inomata Mutsumi, *Inomata Mutsumi shiryōshū* (Collected works of Inomata Mutsumi), ed. Tamura Hideki, (Tokyo: Horoyoi zadankai, 2013).
28. Mobsproof, *Orijinaru bideo anime 80's* (Original video anime 80s) (Kobe: Shuppanworks, 2018), 21.
29. *Anime V*, July 1989, 37.
30. Nagao Akihiro, "The 21 Prophets of Anime," *Newtype*, January 1986, 49.
31. Giannalberto Bendazzi, *Animation: A World History* (New York: Routledge, 2016), 222.
32. Farias and Wilkie, *Studio Studies*, 5.
33. Farias and Wilkie, *Studio Studies*, 7.
34. Bratton, *The Stack*, 47.
35. Farias and Wilkie, *Studio Studies*, 8.
36. Farias and Wilkie, *Studio Studies*, 12.
37. James Matray, *Japan's Emergence as a Global Power* (Westport, CT: Greenwood, 2001), 41.
38. Matray, *Japan's Emergence as a Global Power*, 43.
39. Toru Higuchi and Marvin Troutt, *Life Cycle Management in Supply Chains: Identifying Innovations Through the Case of the VCR* (Hershey: IGI, 2008), 323–24.
40. Andrew McKevitt, *Consuming Japan: Popular Culture and the Globalizing of 1980s America* (Chapel Hill: North Carolina University Press, 2017), 148–53.
41. Eiji Ōtsuka, "Otaku Culture as 'Conversion Literature,'" in *Debating Otaku in Contemporary Japan*, ed. Patrick Galbraith, Thiam Huat Kam, and Björn-Ole Kamm (New York: Bloomsbury, 2015), xxi.
42. Ōtsuka, "Otaku Culture as 'Conversion Literature,'" xix.

43. Bernard Stiegler, "The Quarrel of the Amateurs," *Boundary 2* 44, no. 1 (2017): 49.

44. Stiegler, "The Quarrel of the Amateurs," 50.

45. Bernard Stiegler, *Symbolic Misery*, vol. 2 (Cambridge: Polity Press, 2015), 13.

46. Stiegler, *Symbolic Misery*, 108.

47. Stiegler, *Symbolic Misery*, 48.

48. Claire Colebrook, "Impossible, Unprincipled, and Contingent: Bernard Stiegler's Project of Revolution and Redemption," *Boundary 2* 44, no. 1 (2017): 223.

49. Colebrook, "Impossible, Unprincipled, and Contingent," 223.

50. Ōtsuka, "Otaku Culture as 'Conversion Literature,'" xxvi.

51. Stiegler, *Symbolic Misery*, 31.

52. Nagata, "OVA as 'The Third Media' in Anime Magazines," 49.

53. Nagata, "OVA as 'The Third Media' in Anime Magazines," 53.

54. Bratton, *The Stack*, 44.

55. "'A' no shiin," *Anime V*, July 1989, 82.

56. "AnimeV hakusho" (AnimeV white paper), *AnimeV*, February 1989, 110.

57. Taketomi Yukako, "OVA reki 005 nen ha senryaku no jidai" (The fifth year of OVA history is the age of strategy), *Animage*, November 1988, 13–14.

58. Daisuke Nagata, "OVA to iu hyoumei" in *Sociology of Anime*, ed. Daisuke Nagata and Shintaro Matsunaga (Kyoto: Nakanishiya, 2020), 171–73.

59. "AnimeV hakusho," 110.

60. Tarleton Gillepsie, "The Politics of Platforms," *New Media & Society* 12, no. 3 (2010): 359.

61. Taketomi, "OVA reki 005 nen ha senryaku no jidai," 19.

62. Farias and Wilkie, *Studio Studies*, 12.

63. Stiegler, "The Quarrel of the Amateurs," 19.

Animation Platforms

Yoshiyama Yū, Tropical Rouge! Pretty Cure, and Sakuga *as New Media*

ALEX TAI

Some animation yells, "Look at me!" Ambitious sequences showcase appealing motion: unique, recognizable, original. Recently, animator Yoshiyama Yū has garnered much attention from fans of anime's animation (known as *sakuga fans*) for her outstanding sequences on the magical girl series *Tropical Rouge! Pretty Cure* (2021). This article examines how sakuga fans see animation and how Yoshiyama responds to their viewing practices. I explore the critical potential of nontraditional viewing modes by engaging with Yoshiyama's work through the websites sakugabooru and Twitter. On these platforms, we encounter small parts of anime—clips and screenshots rather than full episodes—allowing us to more clearly understand that individual sequences and frames are created by animation workers. Considering fragments of animation both in isolation and in relation to the overall work, I show that new meaning can be generated by the fan practices of *framestepping* and sharing screenshots. I argue that sakuga fandom establishes an epistemology of anime production, constructs an evaluative critical framework, and drives a labor movement. Although this study examines sakuga fandom by way of its favored gathering spots, it is important to recognize that digital platforms must be understood as open systems, that websites are not perfectly representative of users' values, and that fan communities are not monolithic.

Tropical-Rouge! Pretty Cure (2021) is a recent installment of the long-running *Pretty Cure* magical girl franchise produced by Tōei Animation. The series follows five middle school girls banding together to fight against the Witch of Delays and her servants Chongire, Nemuri, Elda, and Butler, who sap motivation from civilians for nefarious purposes and create monsters called *Yarane-da* out of miscellaneous items. Of particular importance for this article is the oldest member of the team, a third-year student named Takizawa Asuka. Asuka's cool demeanor, stylish design, and independent streak conceal a traumatic past involving her exit from the tennis team and estrangement from her doubles partner, the strong-willed Shiratori Yuriko (who also happens to be the student council president). After meeting the other Pretty Cures, Asuka learns how to work with other people again and joins the team as Cure Flamingo. Asuka's most important scenes—her transformation sequence, her finisher attack sequence, and the climax of a tennis match with Yuriko that resolves her arc—are all animated by Yoshiyama.

Sakuga, which in Japanese simply refers to drawn animation, has been appropriated in Western fan discourse to refer specifically to "particularly good animation."[1] As the popularity of sakuga spread to the West, the website sakugabooru was built from the template provided by the *moebooru* anime image board system.[2] On sakugabooru, users upload clips of standout pieces of animation and tag them with information to make the database searchable. The video player built into the site features five speed settings (from 0.2x up to normal speed) and a framestepping function. There are social features as well, a comments section on every post and a forum. Posts on sakugabooru are often downloaded and reshared on Twitter (and other social media sites) to a broader audience. The sakugabooru uploads for Yoshiyama's work on the series can be found by a search for her name with the series title.[3] I examine Yoshiyama's animation by engaging in sakuga viewing practices, with attention to what the affordances of certain platforms do and do not reveal about the way sakuga fans build knowledge of anime production, make value judgments, and act as labor agitators.

Ways of Seeing

Wandering the Modern Wing of the Art Institute of Chicago, we may come across a Rothko. Aside from the painting itself, we might consider the way it is framed (or not), the way it is lit, or its position with respect to other works in the gallery. Recalling the artist's famous statement that his work should be viewed from a distance of only eighteen inches, we might try to step closer to the canvas so that we may feel the effect of its size.[4] But get too close and we may draw a warning from museum staff. In short, the experience of spectatorship is always intertwined with physical and social contexts of exhibition. Personal context is also important—for instance, a security guard's experience may be impacted by their being "on the job." John Berger, Walter Benjamin, and others have explored how the contexts of exhibition can change our experience of a work of art.[5] Today, the consumption of animated media is not limited to the cinema or the television; the media experience of animation is increasingly digital. What bearing do new modes of spectator-ship have on our understanding of animation? Can platforms of distribution also be considered media with forms worth exploring?

Sakugabooru and Twitter are both examples of what Marc Steinberg calls "contents platforms," hosting user-generated content and facilitating social interactions, though the former is noncommercial and obviously has a much smaller userbase.[6] Neither has a secure future; sakugabooru is in a state of precarity due to its reliance on user donations and vulnerability to copyright claims while Twitter is subject to the whims of its impetuous leadership. Since these developments are ongoing, I do not attempt to predict the fate of either platform. Instead, I examine how they have already functioned: as sites of (knowledge) production, distribution, and consumption, but also as "new media" experiences that enable alternative modes of perception. Here I understand "new media" as "computer based artistic activities" that "[privilege] the existence of potentially numerous copies, infinitely large number of different states of the same work, author-user symbiosis (the user can change the work through interactivity), the collective, collaborative authorship, and network distribution (which bypasses the art system distribution channels).'"[7]

Of course, as Thomas Lamarre shows in his genealogical account of tele-vision animation, what is called new media is usually nothing new.[8] This is also the case with what I have been calling "sakuga." While the rise of sakuga fandom outside Japan is a relatively recent phenomenon, a similar move-ment had already developed in Japan in the 1980s.[9] The advent of the VCR allowed fans to see their favorite works of animation over and over and to slow them down significantly or pause them on single frames. This allowed for the intense study of the formal elements of anime on the level of drawings and motion. The study of the animation revealed the unique characteristics of individual animators, giving rise to the "charisma animator" movement, which celebrated the uniqueness and artistry of a handful of top animators, especially Kanada Yoshinori. Many of these early sakuga fans would go on to make their marks on the world of Japanese animation, where they continued the tradition of enabling and celebrating the individuality of the animator. Today, the practices of repeated viewings, slower viewings, and framestep-ping remain significant aspects of sakuga spectatorship, as does the practice of identifying animators by their individual quirks. This celebration of stylis-tic particularity dovetails nicely with the *Pretty Cure* franchise's portrayal of diverse kinds of femininity and *Tropical-Rouge! Pretty Cure*'s message of being true to yourself.

Yoshiyama's animation is particularly suited for the viewing practices of sakuga fans. One of her most distinctive traits is her placement of "Easter eggs" in her effects and impact frames. These drawings, shown only for a split second, contain sly nods to other anime she has worked on (Figure 1), shapes that pertain to the traits of specific characters, and so on. In an interview with the sakuga fan website artist_unknown, she revealed her motivation for practicing such a high-effort technique: "I'm aiming for you all to look at my parts over and over, it's essentially bait for you to do so. To me an impact frame is the Jack-in-the-box of animation techniques (Yoshiyama laughs). I just hope people who spot them will find them funny to look at."[10] Special effects and impacts are flashy in the sense that they are explosions of color and movement that demand your attention, but also in the sense that they "flash" by quickly, such that it is only possible to get a real good look at them by breaking the animation down frame by frame. Yoshiyama leaves messages hidden in plain sight for those who are willing to see in a different way. Admittedly, such a practice is not new to animation or to television anime—in one corner of the twenty-sixth frame of a cut from episode 19 of the anime *His and Her Circumstances* (1998, *Kareshi Kanojo no Jijō*) uploaded to sakugabooru, we find that Ogura Nobutoshi has drawn the character Rasa from *Birth* (1984), an OVA with animation direction and character designs by Kanada.[11] What sets Yoshiyama apart is the sheer number and density of secret delights she leaves for the discerning viewer, such that they are not just quick jokes, but a core element of her aesthetic identity.

It is also notable that Yoshiyama frequently takes to Twitter to invite fans to search for her Easter egg frames, even leaving extra clues and confirming correct identifications for fans who post screenshots of her cuts. Keenly aware of the platforms through which her work will be experienced, she knows that sakuga fans will use their video players (on sakugabooru or elsewhere) to pore over every frame of her work and that they will then rush to Twitter to post their findings in groups of four pictures. Given Yoshiyama's acknowledgement and encouragement of sakuga fans, we might ask: are framestepping her cuts on sakugabooru and viewing her frames in isolated Twitter posts not also intended (albeit optional) viewing experiences? What critical frameworks and discourses might we build around this new type of animation appreciation and distribution? To fully explore these questions, we need to take a closer look not just at Yoshiyama's animation, but also at the platforms on which sakuga fans experience them.

Figure 1. An impact frame in episode 40 of *Digimon Adventure* (2020) depicting Cure Flamingo. Notably, this episode aired before Asuka made her first appearance. *Digimon Adventure* episode 40; animator: Yoshiyama Yū (2020); available on Crunchyroll.

Here Comes Senpai! Burn, Cure Flamingo!

Characters in the *Pretty Cure* franchise change from civilians to "legendary warriors" in lavishly animated transformation sequences. Magical girl series ride on these scenes, which repeat in every episode; they are important moments of characterization that are also crucial for selling toys and filling up runtime. In the following section, I examine the sakugabooru upload for Cure Flamingo's transformation sequence to explore new possibilities for viewing animation on digital platforms.[12] I also hope to demonstrate the critical potential in thinking about transmedia flow beyond the production committee and its approved commodities, which have been the primary focuses of scholarship on anime's transmediality since Steinberg's pioneering study on media mix.[13]

Of course, official products and modes of distribution remain important. As a starting point, let us consider the platform on which anime are first seen: live broadcast television. Obviously, there are aspects of the television experience that are not reproduced on sakugabooru. Viewers who do not watch the Japanese broadcast will not see the commercials for toys and other items that are vital to *Pretty Cure*'s media mix strategy.[14] There is also the digital clock in the corner of the screen, always reminding us that television is on a schedule.

Pretty Cure gets its half-hour; then it makes way for something else. The temporal flow of the moving image is completely out of viewers' hands.

Streaming offers more control. The video can be paused, specific passages can be replayed, opening themes can be skipped, and sometimes the viewer can even change the playback rate. Still, for the most part the viewer on a streaming platform will be watching the animation uninterrupted and at normal speed. Of course, this viewing mode is possible on sakugabooru as well. For fans simply looking to find a specific sequence they enjoyed, "the *booru*" (as it is referred to by users) is often the most convenient place to look, and they need not do anything more than press play to see (but not hear) the scene again. I will now view and analyze the Cure Flamingo transformation sequence in this way. I encourage the reader to do the same.

On a first viewing, the most striking feature of the animation is the snappiness of the movement. This stands in sharp contrast to the magical girl convention of using fluidity of motion as a showcase of beauty and grace.[15] Because the spatial distance between consecutive poses is large while the number of drawings is kept high, it feels like Asuka is three times faster than her peers. Other distinct visual elements include dynamic poses and colorful effects. Because these elements are common to the animation style pioneered by Kanada Yoshinori, many sakuga fans have labeled Yoshiyama part of the "Kanada school." Yoshiyama herself identifies most closely with Ōbari Masami, considered by some anime historians to be "the most famous representative of . . . 'the second-generation Kanada school.'"[16] The flamboyant and unconventional approach to movement championed by animators in the Kanada lineage is a significant element of the characterization of Asuka and Cure Flamingo. Like the animation itself, the character is charismatic, spontaneous, and stylish. Like her animator, Flamingo has an individualistic streak, but nonetheless must embrace working as part of a team to realize her goals. Yoshiyama's special attachment to the character, then, comes as no surprise; Asuka/Cure Flamingo embodies her animation philosophy, and, in the sense that animators "act" by putting the body of a character in motion, Yoshiyama is Cure Flamingo.

One controversial characteristic of sakugabooru is that it forbids the inclusion of sound in uploads. This stems from a desire to focus on animation: sound effects might change our impression of a heavy impact, voice acting may or may not match the character animation, or music might heighten the emotion of a scene. In short, sakuga fans want to view animation on its own terms. If we watch the transformation sequence on sakugabooru, we will miss Cure Flamingo's catchphrase ("Fluttering wings! Cure Flamingo!"), delivered with gusto by voice actress Seto Asami. We will also not hear the sound effects accompanying each step in her makeup routine (perhaps some of the same sound effects generated by the toys). We will not be swayed by the eager and upbeat music, and if we *only* watch transformation sequences on sakugabooru we might overlook how this music, serving as the background for every character's transformation, emphasizes the sense of teamwork so vital to the *Pretty Cure* franchise and especially to Asuka's character arc. Indeed, when individual transformation sequences are combined into a group transformation in later episodes, the collation works in part because all sequences already use the same background music.

It cannot be denied that sakugabooru's no-audio policy prevents, at least temporarily, a holistic reading of *Tropical Rouge! Pretty Cure*, as it eliminates the sound-image relationship, the sound-narrative relationship, and the role of sound in *Pretty Cure*'s media mix. To address this, we could leave sakugabooru and watch the Cure Flamingo transformation on CrunchyRoll's YouTube channel.[17] But is it possible to gain something by ignoring sound? Let us consider the conditions of anime production. Specialization and dispersion of labor means that the animator may only have a vague sense of sound effects and music. They must imagine these elements on their own and hope that their animation mixes well with everything else. Viewing animation on sakugabooru, we might share in this act of imagination, or even imitate the sound design of *The Wind Rises* (2013) and *Keep Your Hands Off Eizouken!* (2020) by making the sounds with our own mouths. We might fill in the snapping of Flamingo's costume implied by the sharpness of her motion; the twinkles and jingles suggested by crosses and circles flashing across the screen; the ruffle demanded by the toss of her voluminous red hair (Figure 2). By removing the sound of *anime*, *sakugabooru* reveals the "sound" of *animation* in our mind's ear. We find that the sound-image relationship does not have to originate entirely from an external cinematic object because moving images *seem* like they should make certain noises.

In losing the whole we gain a new part, a different mode of perception. It is not the view from the living room couch or the director's chair, but from the animator's desk. It turns out that what we might typically think of as the "whole" work—the final product, the TV anime—is itself only a part of the larger experience of *Tropical-Rouge! Pretty Cure*. Of course, it must be acknowledged that we are not actually looking over Yoshiyama's shoulder, much less seeing into her head. But however far we may remain from the real act of animation, the sakugabooru viewing position brings us closer than any other, and

Figure 2. Asuka tosses her hair. *Tropical Rouge! Pretty Cure*, animator: Yoshiyama Yū (2021); available on Crunchyroll.

we can ultimately combine our experience of sakugabooru with other ones to paint a more interesting critical picture of anime and its animation.

Let us move to other features. Sakugabooru is not just a repository for clips but also a site of critical evaluation. While posts are visible as soon as they are uploaded, they are subject to a moderation process to determine whether they are notable enough to be on the site and may be removed for lacking in quality or originality, not fitting the site's focus on the drawn portions of animation, or simply for handling video improperly (changing the frame rate, for instance). Moderation prevents the site from being overrun with excessive clips of the most popular superpower fighting shows, but tensions can arise around uploads for older anime and Western animation, which moderators have less experience viewing and evaluating. Articulation of a critical framework for evaluation also happens in the comments of uploads. For Cure Flamingo's transformation, reactions range from mild disappointment to effusive praise (Figure 3). One user finds it jarring that the sequence cuts frequently between Yoshiyama's animation and 3DCG shots of the compact, an accessory that allows the Pretty Cures to transform. Of course, the series must include shots of the compacts if it is to sell plastic toys, and, as Bryan Hartzheim has noted, 3DCG offers a way to "render the contours and movement of the Pact as close to the real toy Pact as possible."[18] These comments point to the uneasy relationship between the series' expressive ambitions and its commercial obligations in the form of a gap between 2D and 3D. But if the tension between art and

Figure 3. Screenshot of the sakugabooru upload for Cure Flamingo's transformation sequence. *Tropical Rouge! Pretty Cure,* key animator: Yoshiyama Yū (2021); available on Crunchyroll.

commercialism exists within the animation itself, it does not seem to be a problem for Yoshiyama, who frequently posts her *Pretty Cure* merchandise on her Twitter account. Like most of anime's animators, Yoshiyama is an anime fan engaged simultaneously in production and consumption, often playfully combining Pretty Cures with Gundam figures, model insects, and other paraphernalia in a sort of unscripted play with toys.

Perhaps the most important of sakugabooru's features are the tags, listed in a column on the left-hand side of the page for each upload. They function to provide basic production information and describe uploaded sequences in technical language, but they can also be used to search for other uploads; each tag can be clicked to bring up search results for other posts labeled with the tag. It is tempting to say, then, that sakugabooru users engage in literal database consumption, responding to specific repeated aesthetic features (here, *yutapon_cubes, smears, running* instead of cat ears, blue hair, glasses) existing outside of narrative.[19] We see later that the situation is more complicated, but let us first take a closer look at the tags for the Cure Flamingo transformation sequence (Figure 3).

The first tag on each post is the name of the animator. Sometimes, cuts are identified by reading through interviews, artbooks, and so on. Otherwise, fans piece together their knowledge of the traits of individual animators with the names written in the credits to guess the animators responsible (when this happens, they add the presumed tag). Because Yoshiyama announces what she did on Twitter whenever she has worked on an episode, guessing is not necessary. Still, authorship in anime is never as simple as assigning a sequence to a key animator. Like the Pretty Cures, animators work as part of a team, with each member contributing specialized skills. However, unlike the Pretty Cures, the teams that make anime are hierarchical in structure and geographically (and usually transnationally) dispersed. And sometimes, to the disappointment of sakuga fans and animators alike, the final product does not fully reflect the key animator's intent—the chief animation director changes how something is drawn, compositing obscures the details of a smoke effect, and so on. Yoshiyama, as an animator pursuing bold expressions, is no exception to anime's system of supervision.[20] Animation style in an industrial environment is thus always negotiated (though not on equal terms) between many agents in a way that the tagging system obscures.

Of course, sakuga fans are quite sensitive to the importance of people like animation directors and layout artists in determining the visual qualities of a scene. There have been discussions around including labels for animation directors and layout artists within the tagging system.[21] This is nontrivial from a technical standpoint, but the situation would remain complicated even if these changes were implemented; conversations on Twitter and the sakugabooru forums reveal that tagging practices vary by uploader and are sensitive to the highly specific conditions of anime productions. For example, sometimes an animation director is tagged when the uploader strongly feels their "hand," sometimes as an actual tag and sometimes in the "source" field of the upload.[22] Uploaders work within a conception of creativity as individual expression. Thus, sakugabooru tags are not simply committed to recognizing just any kind of labor, but specifically to the production of distinctively drawn movement.

This becomes clearer when we look down the list of tags for the Cure Flamingo transformation sequence and come across another complication: the *cgi* tag. Although many uploads have this tag, CGI as such is not the focus of sakugabooru. For instance, *Beastars* (2019), despite its popularity in general anime fandom, has only four uploads on the site, only one of which involves CGI. But the situation gets more complicated still: *Sakuga Blog*, which is directly affiliated with sakugabooru, published an article in 2019 celebrating the animation of *Beastars* specifically for its creative use of CGI.[23] Again we find that the sakuga community is not a monolith but rather a complex network of people, platforms, and publications.

The incongruity between the values suggested by the affordances of sakugabooru and the actual attitudes and practices of sakuga fans can be further illustrated by considering more information that is not tagged: roles that are visual but not strictly animation (art direction, compositing, storyboards), below-the-line "noncreative" roles (cel painters, in-between animators, camera operators), information pertaining to anime-as-business (studio, production staff, production year, release year, format). Again, sakugabooru, as a platform, seems to support a miniature auteurism that values key animation at the exclusion of all else. But the platform is not a closed system. Among the list of items running between the header and the video player is a link to *Sakuga Blog*. Examining the publications of this and other sakuga fan sites like artist_unknown and Full Frontal reveals much more complexity. To varying degrees, they are interested in animation specifically, but they are *also* interested in visuals in general, committed to the labor rights of below-the-line staff, and bitterly familiar with the economic aspects of anime production.[24] As they have published articles discussing these issues on sakuga-oriented sites, it seems fair to label these concerns as sakuga-related, even if sakugabooru's design pushes them to the periphery. Limitations in the site architecture of sakugabooru (sometimes the result of technical challenges, but sometimes intentional) belie sakuga fans' underlying understanding of the complex problems of authorship and labor in anime production.

Asuka Strikes!

In his study of transnational sakuga fandom, Stevie Suan makes the interesting claim that sakuga fan viewing practices are "estranged from narrative."[25] For Suan, sakuga's non-narrativity deemphasizes the "Japaneseness" of anime and dovetails into greater awareness of the transnational nature of anime production. The supposed non-narrativity of sakuga is a powerful and provocative concept. It does seem fair to regard sakugabooru as a platform for non-narrative media. After all, it collects decontextualized excerpts of animation sorted by default in reverse-upload order for viewing by animation enthusiasts who have not necessarily seen the source works. Still, awareness of animation aesthetics should not imply ignorance of narrative. In the rest of this article, I explore how Yoshiyama's animation challenges the separation of sakuga from narrative and resists the subsumption of the part under the whole.

The *Pretty Cure* franchise makes heavy use of *bank cuts* (animation sequences meant for reuse in multiple episodes) in transformations and in special "finisher" attack sequences. Like the transformation sequence, the finisher carries a high level of prestige and presents an opportunity to flex production muscle while also selling toys (in the case of *Tropical-Rouge! Pretty Cure*, lipstick). Cure Flamingo's finisher, in which Asuka uses a tennis racket to smash a flaming red comet that chars the monster of the week, has two uploads on sakugabooru as a result of a modification to the sequence.[26] In episode 38 of the series, Yoshiyama added a new effect layer and an impact frame to the attack, which was enough to justify an additional upload of a clip long enough to cover the changes, listed as a "child" post to the "parent" upload of the original attack as seen in episode 5. Building on Ida Kirkegaard's examination of how the usage of bank cuts can operate not simply as a cost-saving measure, but also as an artful way to generate meaning, I examine the difference between these two uploaded sequences.[27] The reader is encouraged to use sakugabooru to framestep these posts and try to spot the new frames on their own before continuing.

The two added frames are shown in Figure 4. The first one is very abstract: eight jagged red lines on a black background, paired and angled to direct our line of sight towards a small V-shape in red and a small upside-down V in white. Based on this frame alone, it is difficult to determine what additional meaning is generated by the insertion of the impact frame, even for those who have seen the show. In the next frame, however, the abstract and distant V-shapes burst into the foreground as a flamingo and a swan. A yellow tennis ball also comes into view. If we were "watching" *Tropical Rouge! Pretty Cure* exclusively on sakugabooru, this image would hardly have any more meaning than the last one. It would "only" be a very nice drawing of two birds. But if we were following the television series, we would know what occurred in the narrative to induce this change in the animation. In an emotional tennis match between Asuka and Yuriko, Yuriko reveals that she has always longed to play with Asuka again. Years of estrangement and resentment dissolve with the swing of a racket and the two resolve to aim for the top of the world of high school girls' tennis together at Phoenix Academy. With this context, the meaning of the added frames becomes obvious—the flamingo and the swan (a reference to Yuriko's family name, Shiratori) attack together once more. Revealed only through sakuga viewing practices, the added frames are a visual representation of both characters' development.

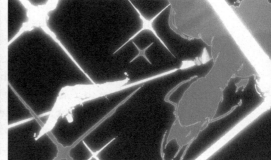

Figure 4. Frames added to the finisher bank sequence in episode 38. *Tropical Rouge! Pretty Cure* episode 38, animator: Yoshiyama Yū (2021); available on Crunchyroll.

In retrospect, we can read the repeated use of the unmodified finisher sequence in earlier episodes of the show as a representation of Asuka's stagnation. Indeed, much to the disappointment of her fans, the plot of the series gave Asuka very little attention for most of its run, focusing instead on the charismatic mermaid Laura and the sunny protagonist Manatsu. As early as episode 5, Asuka had embraced working as part of the Pretty Cure team, but from then until episode 38 she was still missing her partner, as she had not truly moved on from her past trauma. Although the character takes a backseat from a plot perspective, Asuka's story is represented throughout the show in the form of the bank cut and the impact frame. This is sakuga-as-narrative. What we have here is not the choice between the whole (the television anime *Tropical-Rouge! Pretty Cure*) and the part (Yoshiyama Yū's sequence on sakugabooru), but the nonhierarchical presentation of the whole *and* the part as mutually reinforcing but freestanding media forms. If we do not watch the show, we will still have a nice drawing of a bird; if we do not framestep, we will still feel the overall impact of the scene on the level of movement and character writing. But experiencing whole and part *together* gives us even more. In this way, Yoshiyama challenges both conventional and sakuga modes of consumption by asking fans to engage in both. Indeed, just as conventional viewing can lead to sakuga viewing when fans review their favorite cuts at slower speeds, sakuga viewing can lead to conventional viewing when fans see sakugabooru posts that introduce them to new anime.

PARS CON TOTO

As we have seen several times, sakugabooru is not a closed system. Sakuga fans use the site to find good animation, but there is also a strong culture of sharing this experience with other fans, especially on Twitter. There are several Twitter accounts dedicated to (re)posting clips downloaded from sakugabooru, but I want to focus here on another common form of sharing in sakuga fandom: posting screenshots, usually in groups of four, of particularly amusing or interesting frames, often without commentary. When this is done with Yoshiyama's animation, the results are particularly striking. In this section, I return to a non-narrative framework, turning to the form of individual screenshots. After all, is there any real harm in enjoying an image just because the shapes are sharp, and the colors are bright? No—a case could be made for an alternative animation viewing practice: treating screenshots of Yoshiyama's work as whole pieces of art, taking up the study of the single frame inaugurated by Hannah Frank.[28]

To framestep on sakugabooru is to consider the single frame, but never in isolation. Although we control the speed, we still follow the sequential logic of animation: each image responds to its predecessor and anticipates its successor. Mash the forward button quickly enough—clickclickclickclick—and the illusion returns: still drawings come back to "life." Thus, there is always the potential for (re)animation in the video player. Impact frames and camera cuts can be considered disruptions to the flow of the motion, but such an understanding still grounds them in the context of the broader movement. Is it even possible, then, to view distinctive frames like impact frames in truly standalone fashion? Frank presents some of them this way in *Frame by Frame*, but as the curator of these frames she would have already seen them in context.[29] While her descriptions of the pure forms of single frames are brilliant, she could not have completely forgotten what they were really depicting. But what if Frank had a few thousand friends, equally as enamored of the art of the single frame and eager to spread the word about their favorite artists? In sakuga Twitter, there is potential for a new media experience that Frank did not get: single frames, fully removed from the perceptual gestalt of animated movement. This is an even smaller part of an anime than we find on sakugabooru, which removes the sequence from the episode and cleaves sound from image while still preserving the movement and the order of frames. The Twitter screenshot abandons movement altogether, and for any given post we have no way of knowing the relation of any image to any other: what order they appear in, how close in time, etc. Individual frames are so small that they do not "threaten" conventional viewing in the way that sakugabooru uploads are perceived to. That is, it seems silly to say that we look at a screenshot *instead* of watching the whole work. It is easier, then, to entertain a consideration of single frames on their own terms, outside of their function in the larger work.

This is the opportunity that sakuga fan Kevin Cirugeda offers us in a Twitter thread, retweeted by Yoshiyama, highlighting the climactic battle of the series.[30] Noting the increased intensity of Yoshiyama's effects and impact frames, he states that "at some points the scene becomes a jaw-dropping expressionistic spectacle," posting eight exemplary frames in two Tweets (Figures 5 and 6). Chaotic bursts of colorful shapes, the frames have little to no relation to any real-world referent. Impact frames *could* refer to the moment when one object collides with another and effects *could* refer to physical phenomena (fire, light beams, etc.), but these relations are considerably weakened when the frames are decontextualized. Therefore, we can consider them not as parts of a TV show, but as standalone works of abstract art. Confrontation with abstraction is the experience of pure form: shapes and colors that will, per Kandinsky, carry certain affective associations.[31] Impact frames become striking frames; they grab our attention on a Twitter feed instead of representing a collision. Effects become affects; they make us feel the sublime in abstraction instead of representing natural elements. It's not anime! It's a curious feeling.

Figure 5. The first set of screenshots posted by kViN: *Tropical Rouge! Pretty Cure,* episode 45, animator: Yoshiyama Yū (2021); available on Crunchyroll and Kevin Cirugeda. Twitter, 22 January 2022. https://twitter.com/Yuyucow/status/1485098722199486468.

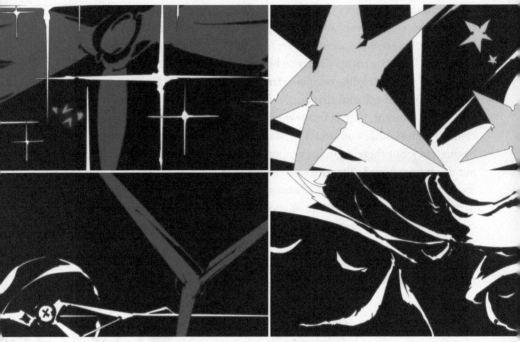

Figure 6. The second set of screenshots posted by kViN: *Tropical Rouge! Pretty Cure*, episode 45, animator: Yoshiyama Yū (2021); available on Crunchyroll and Kevin Cirugeda. Twitter, 22 January 2022. https://twitter.com/Yuyucow/status/1485098847005290497.

At this point, we are engaged so much with animation "as such" that it is worth asking whether sakuga forms of spectatorship are merely *l'animation pour l'animation*. It is clear to me that they are not. As Suan has shown, there is a strong commitment to labor advocacy engendered by sakuga as a viewing practice, wherein fans "become somewhat critically engaged, mainly in concern to the terrible work conditions of the animators themselves."[32] In a *Sakuga Blog* article titled "Anime's Present And Future At Stake: The In-Betweener Problem," Cirugeda describes the conditions faced by in-between staff as "hellish" and decries "how the delegitimization of an essential job is ruining lives and putting anime's present and future at risk."[33] Similar articles outline "anime's collapsing mentorship," the "layout crisis," and "the unrewarding nightmare to assemble a high-profile team."[34] On Full Frontal, Matteo Watzky has launched a series of articles titled "Anime Numbers," which attempts to understand the industry's labor problems from a quantitative and historical perspective.[35] And when productions begin to visibly collapse partway through a show's run (a frequent occurrence), sakuga fans are quick to point out the problems in Twitter threads. It is important to note that several of them are engaged in sakuga-like activity—that is, they post clips of impressive sequences and often name the animator(s) responsible—who do not identify as "sakuga fans" because they do not agree with the established culture of maintaining a critical position toward the industry's labor practices. For these fans, the experience of consumption takes priority over concerns about working conditions, such that sakuga fans' tendency to complain about production problems is simply elitist nitpicking. There is a distinction, then, between the enjoyment of animation as a "purely" aesthetic endeavor and the more labor-oriented position of established sakuga fandom.

When sakuga fans see animation, they do not just consider form as an end-in-itself; they always know they are looking at labor. Consider the Rothko again. His name is nowhere to be found on the painting. And yet, the instant we see it, we know who made it, which changes how we feel about it. Indeed, I spoke not of a specific work but of a "Rothko" in the abstract, and even his name instantly calls up a mental image of large painted rectangles with soft edges. The same is true of Pollock, Mondrian, and so on. Our aesthetic experience of a work by a well-known figure, from the moment it catches our eye to the moment we leave it, and even our recollection of our encounter with it, is shaped by art historical knowledge, which is not just a history of works (*No. 5*, 1948), but also a history of work (for instance, art historical accounts tend to stress the physical intensity of Pollock's painting process). Similarly, when we see a Yoshiyama cut or frame we recognize her style, which becomes synonymous with her name. We might pick out her energetic hand shapes, jagged effects, intense shading that recalls the shell of an insect, erratic timing, dynamic poses, or of course her Jack-in-the-Box frames. When we see that she has hidden Cure Flamingo in a *Digimon Adventure* episode that aired *before* Cure Flamingo's first appearance in *Tropical Rouge! Pretty Cure*, we are reminded that animators work on multiple shows at the same time. Keeping the name of the artist in mind, we are always reminded that artwork is work. We are always looking at labor.

In chapter 3 of *Frame by Frame*, Frank poses a question about animation's potential for revealing the labor involved in its production by invoking a construction metaphor: "What if every brick, every tile, bore the traces of the hands that touched it?"[36] Frank speaks here not just of the hand of the key animator, but of anonymous animation workers: the colorist, the in-betweener, the camera operator, and so on. It must be acknowledged that sakuga fans do not dive below-the-line in quite the same way that Frank does; they do not share the radical aesthetic interest in "noncreative" labor that caused her to painstakingly search every frame for specks of dust and misarranged cels, because their notion of creativity is based on the artistic *choices* of individuals.[37] Still, sakuga fans do have an intimate knowledge of the conditions of dispersed and transnational anime production. Given that the world of industrial animation is highly unlikely to ever produce a film or series in which in-between animators and colorists enjoy total creative freedom, sakuga fandom's view of anime— that is, anime as a collection of sequences drawn by stylistically differentiable animators and other animation artists with varying levels of creative agency— may be the closest existing approximate answer to Frank's question.

Coda

Sakugabooru's exclusive focus on animation, especially its hardline policy against the inclusion of audio, has been controversial in popular discourse because it seems to foreclose on the holistic experience of a work. But if sakugabooru's exclusive focus on animation is a problem, it is only because there are not equivalent sites for other aspects of anime production (except for music). Difficulties of site maintenance notwithstanding, there would be much to gain from a *backgroundbooru*, a *soundeffectsbooru*, and so on. The momentary fragmentation of our sense of perception allows us to focus specifically on individual elements. A different mode of perception is made possible. I have experienced *Tropical-Rouge! Pretty Cure* in whole and in part: the standard way (as television), the sakugabooru way (as clips), and the Twitter way (as screenshots), and each time I have only gained for it. Of course, this could be attributed to Yoshiyama's consciousness of sakuga viewing practices. A similar approach may not work as well for other anime or animators. Still, Yoshiyama proves that the potential is there. Just as the invention of the camera did not render our eyes obsolete, the existence of sakuga fan viewing practices does not preclude other ways of seeing. Each way of seeing has something unique to contribute to the experience of animation media. The intentional partiality of sakuga challenges the dominant paradigm wherein animation is framed exclusively in terms of its function in the overall work, showing that we can engage in viewing practices on sakuga platforms *in conjunction* with conventional spectatorship to discover new critical potentials. The whole may be greater than the sum of its parts, but the sum of the whole *with* the parts is greater still.

Alex Tai is an independent animation theorist. By day, he is a PhD student studying computational materials science at the Massachusetts Institute of Technology, though this article was written when he was an undergraduate at Northwestern University.

Notes

1. *Sakuga Blog,* "Sakuga," https://blog.sakugabooru.com/glossary/sakuga/, accessed 19 April 2023.
2. *danbooru,* "Danbooru," https://github.com/danbooru/danbooru, accessed 19 April 2023.
3. https://www.sakugabooru.com/post?tags=yuu_yoshiyama+tropical_rouge_precure, accessed 19 April 2023.
4. Jeffrey S. Weiss, John Gage, and Mark Rothko, *Mark Rothko* (New Haven: Yale University Press, 1998).
5. *Ways of Seeing,* Season 1, Episode 1, "Camera and Painting," dir. John Berger and Michael Dibb, aired January 8, 1972, on BBC 2; Walter Benjamin, "The Work of Art in the Age of Mechanical Reproduction," in *Aesthetics: A Reader in Philosophy of the Arts,* ed. David Goldblatt, Lee B. Brown, Stephanie Partridge (New York: Routledge, 2017), 66–69.
6. Marc Steinberg, *The Platform Economy: How Japan Transformed the Consumer Internet* (Minneapolis: University of Minnesota Press, 2019), 72.
7. Lev Manovich, "New Media from Borges to HTML," *The New Media Reader* 1, no. 2 (2003): 13–25.
8. Thomas Lamarre, *The Anime Ecology: A Genealogy of Television, Animation, and Game Media* (Minneapolis: University of Minnesota Press, 2018).
9. Thomas Lamarre, *The Anime Machine: A Media Theory of Animation* (Minneapolis: University of Minnesota Press, 2009), 144–54; Matteo Watzky, "Exploring Sakuga—Part 1: Birth of Otaku, Birth of Sakuga," https://animetudes.com/2020/08/22/exploring-sakuga-part-1-birth-of-otaku-birth-of-sakuga/, accessed 19 April 2023.
10. Federico Antonio, "Exclusive Interview with Yuu Yoshiyama: Impact Frames as Surprise Boxes?!" https://artistunknown.info/2020/09/21/exclusive-interview-with-yuu-yoshiyama-impact-frames-as-surprise-boxes/, accessed 12 July 2022.
11. https://www.sakugabooru.com/post/show/37224, accessed 19 April 2023.
12. https://www.sakugabooru.com/post/show/149738, accessed 19 April 2023.
13. Marc Steinberg, *Anime's Media Mix: Franchising Toys and Characters in Japan* (Minneapolis: University of Minnesota Press, 2012).
14. Bryan Hikari Hartzheim, "*Pretty Cure* and the Magical Girl Media Mix," *Journal of Popular Culture* 49, no. 5 (2016): 1059–85.

15. Kevin Cirugeda, https://twitter.com/Yuyucow/status/1376272606542884873, accessed 28 March 2021.

16. Antonio, "Exclusive Interview"; Matteo Watzky, "Artist Spotlight: Masami Obari," https://animetudes.com/2021/05/02/artist-spotlight-masami-obari/, accessed 2 May 2021.

17. *Crunchyroll* Collection, *Flamingo Cure Transformation / Tropical-Rouge! Precure*, https://www.youtube.com/watch?v=xiD8l2L_RlA, accessed 15 July 2022.

18. Hartzheim, *"Pretty Cure."*

19. Hiroki Azuma, *Otaku: Japan's Database Animals* (Minneapolis: University of Minnesota Press, 2009).

20. Kevin Cirugeda, https://twitter.com/Yuyucow/status/1305205977969561603, accessed 13 September 2020.

21. Kraker [@kraker2k], https://twitter.com/kraker2k/status/14229414208397 51682, accessed 4 August 2021.

22. Ukrainian Z'gok [@BlackSeaAMS], https://twitter.com/BlackSeaAMS/status /1422938718256631808, accessed 4 August 2021; Matteo Watzky, https:// twitter.com/anime_gaku/status/1422940203170373635, accessed 4 August 2021; "Crediting the *Sakkan / Sakugabooru*," https://www.sakugabooru.com/forum /show/1225, accessed 19 April 2023.

23. Kevin Cirugeda, "BEASTARS: Traditionally Excellent Modernity," https://blog .sakugabooru.com/2019/12/04/beastars-traditionally-excellent-modernity/, accessed 4 December 2019.

24. Dimitri Seraki, "Sakuga Espresso—*Heike Monogatari*," https://fullfrontal.moe /sakuga-espresso-heike-monogatari/, accessed 13 December 2021; Jamal, "Scale, Space & Ranking of Kings' Visual Worldbuilding," https://fullfrontal.moe/scale -space-ranking-of-kings-visual-worldbuilding/, accessed 21 January 2021; PurpleGeth, "*Neon Genesis Evangelion* 3.0 + 1.0: Deho Gallery and Tatsuya Kushida's *Post-Apocalyptic Eden*," https://artistunknown.info/2021/08/27 /neon-genesis-evangelion-3-0-1-0-deho-gallery-and-tatsuya-kushidas-post -apocalyptic-eden/, accessed 27 August 2021; Kevin Cirugeda, "Anime's Present And Future At Stake: The In-Betweener Problem," https://blog.sakugabooru .com/2020/06/24/animes-present-and-future-at-stake-the-in-betweener -problem/, accessed 24 June 2020; Kevin Cirugeda, "What Is An Anime's Pro- duction Committee?" https://blog.sakugabooru.com/2017/05/02/what-is an -animes-production-committee/, accessed 2 May 2017; Kevin Cirugeda, "What Actually Is Anime Outsourcing?—The Historical Context And Current Reality Of Anime's Life Support," https://blog.sakugabooru.com/2021/06/09/what -actually-is-anime-outsourcing-the-historical-context-and-current-reality-of -animes-life-support/, accessed 9 June 2021; Kevin Cirugeda, "*Hoshiai No Sora / Stars Align*: A Story About Corporate Betrayal, But Also A Lot More," https:// blog.sakugabooru.com/2020/01/12/hoshiai-no-sora-stars-align-a-story-about -corporate-betrayal-but-also-a-lot-more/, accessed 12 January 2020.

25. Stevie Suan, "Consuming Production: Anime's Layers of Transnationality and Dispersal of Agency as Seen in Shirobako and Sakuga-Fan Practices," *Arts* 7, no. 3 (September 2018): 27, https://doi.org/10.3390/arts7030027.

26. https://www.sakugabooru.com/post/show/149739, accessed 19 April 2023; https://www.sakugabooru.com/post/show/172472, accessed 19 April 2023.

27. Ida Kirkegaard, "Play It Again, Hideaki: Using the Cel Bank in *Neon Genesis Evangelion,*" in *Anime Studies: Media-Specific Approaches to Neon Genesis Evangelion,* ed. José Andrés Santiago Iglesias and Ana Soler-Baena (Stockholm: Stockholm University Press, 2021), 49–83.

28. Hannah Frank, *Frame by Frame: A Materialist Aesthetics of Animated Cartoons* (Berkeley: University of California Press, 2019).

29. Frank, *Frame by Frame,* 91.

30. Kevin Cirugeda, https://twitter.com/Yuyucow/status/1485098120744783884, accessed 23 January 2022.

31. Wassily Kandinsky, *Concerning the Spiritual in Art* (New York: Dover Publications, 1977).

32. Suan, "Consuming Production," 14.

33. Cirugeda, "Anime's Present and Future At Stake."

34. Kevin Cirugeda, "The Long Quest To Fix Anime's Collapsing Mentorship: The Young Animator Training Project, And Its Legacy 10 Years After LWA & Death Billiards," https://blog.sakugabooru.com/2023/03/31/the-long-quest-to-fix -animes-collapsing-mentorship-the-young-animator-training-project-and-its -legacy-10-years-after-lwa-death-billiards/, accessed 19 June 2023; Kevin Cirugeda, "The Layout Crisis: The Collapse Of Anime's Traditional Immersion, And The Attemps To Build It Anew," https://blog.sakugabooru.com/2022/08/05 /the-layout-crisis-the-collapse-of-animes-traditional-immersion-and-the -attemps-to-build-it-anew/, accessed 19 June 2023; Kevin Cirugeda, "The Anime Industry Bottleneck: The Unrewarding Nightmare To Assemble A High-Profile Team," https://blog.sakugabooru.com/2022/02/22/the-anime-industry -bottleneck-the-unrewarding-nightmare-to-assemble-a-high-profile-team/, accessed 19 June 2023.

35. Matteo Watzky, "Anime Numbers—1: How Many Anime Are There?," https:// fullfrontal.moe/anime-numbers-1/, Accessed 19 June 2023; Matteo Watzky, "Anime Numbers—2—The Situation of Anime Studios," https://fullfrontal.moe /anime-numbers-2/, accessed 19 June 2023; Matteo Watzky, "Anime Numbers— 3—Working Conditions through Time," https://fullfrontal.moe/anime -numbers-3/, accessed 19 June 2023.

36. Frank, *Frame by Frame,* 98.

37. Frank, *Frame by Frame,* 80.

Transnational Frictions

Media Mix and Taiwan Bar

Taiwan for Sale to Selling Taiwan

AI-TING CHUNG

The animated short from Taiwan Bar Studio starts with a seven-minute anima-tion about "selling (out) Taiwan." Titled "Episode 0: Taiwan for Sale?" (2014),[1] the short film features cute IP (Intellectual Property) characters discussing the position of Taiwan in the colonial period (1895-1945). For the Imperial Japanese government, Taiwan was a dead-end product that they wanted to sell to France. Introducing colonial Taiwan from the standpoint of the Japanese colonizer, the animated short approaches colonial history from a different perspective than the school curriculum in Taiwan, which adopts a China-centered narrative of Taiwan as a cession of territory of Qing China (Qing Ruling of Taiwan, 1683-1895). With the rising demand for citizen media and the strained China-Taiwan relationship in the 2010s, "Taiwan for Sale" earned over two hundred thousand views in forty-eight hours and 1.8 million views in four years.[2] Encouraged by the viewership, the studio produced an English remake of this episode in 2018, as well as a video of English speakers in Taiwan watching the English remake.

Founded in 2014, the same year when the student-led, sociopolitical Sunflower Movement took place, Taiwan Bar premiered as a studio devoted to providing e-learning animated videos on YouTube, earning profit via crowd-funding, merchandising its animated character designs, cooperating with other enterprises, and promoting animated advertisements for companies in Taiwan. The founder of Taiwan Bar, DJ Hauer (Hsieh), claims that they are a new media company able to translate complicated concepts into fun messages for the e-generation to discuss.[3] Graduating from National Taiwan University, the top university in Taiwan, Hauer regards his mission as edu-cating the people in Taiwan to "think critically." In the pilot episode, Hauer and three other founders—Buchi, Jiajiach, and Thomas Xiao—encourage the local e-generation to be more engaged in foreign affairs by examining world history outside of the Qing China-centered narrative of the colonial history in Taiwan. The "critical thinking" Hauer pursues is an alternative narrative to history textbooks and a counter discourse to the politicians who exploit TV broadcasting for leadership and power.

The studio has profited from social media platforms such as YouTube, Facebook, and Instagram, which have plugged into the daily lives of the populace. As of 2022, Taiwan Bar has over one million YouTube followers, 400,000 Facebook followers, and 35,000 Instagram followers. The YouTube channel regularly updates new series discussing different issues, from local history to Bitcoin, from Hakka migration to philosophy. Currently, the studio is updating the history of pornography, sex, and gender education in Taiwan on the YouTube channel with animated shorts. They also have a project of filming children interviewing Muslims and migrant workers from Southeast Asia in Taiwan on Facebook. Instagram provides a space for followers who want to chat with the creators of Taiwan Bar. The official website of Taiwan Bar also updates its blog regularly for its audience. Taiwan Bar aims at educating Taiwanese by inserting the discourses it encourages into the daily life of its audience. Targeting the younger generation, it has started to publish audio books and board games. I reveal the meaning of Taiwan Bar Studio in the context of both the contemporary media mix and Taiwanese-ness, especially the role of Taiwan's colonial identity plays in the formation of its nation-state discourse.

Different from traditional media consumption logic, the media-mix world leads its consumers to a new participatory cultural logic, where seeking out new information and making connections between dispersed media content is encouraged. When the expansion of the media environment penetrates the life-worlds of human subjects, the consumption of media can become a force to shape the people and reinforce a form of national and cultural identity, or vice versa. The local consumption of the animated shorts guarantees the discourse of the national identity discussed in the video. Let me contextualize the relationality of "selling Taiwan" and "Taiwan for sale." The former refers to the animation media mix practice of the studio, namely the marketing of the nation as a consumer product, while the latter points to two layers of meaning: the colonial identity the studio discusses in its pilot episode; and a term that Taiwanese nowadays use to describe the betrayal of politicians who are submissive to powerful regimes. To further contextualize the animated short "Taiwan for Sale," I (1) analyze the design of the IP characters in relation to the influence of Japanese popular culture in Taiwan and the formation of Taiwanese identity; (2) grapple with how the pilot episode's counter-narrative of colonial history compares to history textbooks in Taiwan; and (3) examine the multilingual aspect and (un-)translatability of the pilot by analyzing its subtitling and dubbing in Chinese, Japanese, and English alongside video of the watching experience of English speakers in Taiwan.

Via its broad merchandising of images and franchising across media and commodities, Taiwan Bar not only successfully developed a brand with cute IP characters but converged this capitalist model of media mix with social media and civic discourses in Taiwan. The episode "Taiwan for Sale" is selling Taiwan to the domestic and international audience, seeking the chance to gain visibility via social media to earn international support for Taiwan's sovereignty under political pressure from China. Examining Taiwan Bar in its earlier stage in 2014, I untangle the complexity between the capitalist media-mix business model and a national discourse in pursuit of Taiwanese-ness by rearticulating its coloniality. In this context, media mix is an excess of a business model that sells a kind of national discourse, which Taiwan Bar indulges in and encourages. Taiwan Bar is a media-mix case study of a convergence of business, entertainment, education, and political advocacy.

To delineate the influence of Japan on Taiwan culturally, economically, and politically, I illustrate how the Japanese media-mix model led to the success of Taiwan Bar's IP characters, and how Murakami Haruki's *shōkakkō* was interpreted as a motif for the sociopolitical movement that addresses democracy with nationalism against the rise of China. To problematize the national discourse of coloniality in Taiwan, I investigate the sociopolitical environment, animation industry, and history textbooks in Taiwan as a backdrop for the studio to publish "Taiwan for Sale" on YouTube as an alternative venue of local identity. To understand the implications of the establishment and swift success of the launch of Taiwan Bar in 2014 and its relationship with the young adult generation in Taiwan, it is necessary to look at the political tendencies of the past decade. In the next section, I contextualize the political environment in Taiwan and the IP characters of Taiwan Bar.

Why 2014? From a Sliver of Happiness (*Xiao que xing*) to the Birth of *Hei Pi* (Beer)

Along with the development of high-velocity capitalism, the Taiwanese younger generation confronts an imbalance between the abundant material lifestyle they grew up with and the current increasing living expenses, poor working conditions, deficit of social welfare systems, and growing economic influence of Mainland China. Given the weariness of unsolvable social problems and loss of faith in both political parties in Taiwan—DPP (Democratic Progressive Party) and KMT (Koumintang)—the younger generation was indifferent to politics and instead indulged in the pursuit of what is known as *xiao que xing*, a translation of the Japanese term *shōkakkō*, or "a sliver of happiness." The existence of the term could be traced back to the turn of the twenty-first century, when the translation of the novelist Murakami Haruki and illustrator Anzai Mitsumaru's illustrated prose collections *The Afternoon of Islet of Langerhans* (*Rangeruhansu tō no gogo*, 1986, translated into Chinese in Taiwan in 2002) and *Finding the Whirlpooling Cat* (*Uzumaki neko no mitsuketaka*, 1996, translated into Chinese in Taiwan in 2007) were introduced to Taiwan. In Taiwan, the term "a sliver of happiness" came to refer to a state of the tiny but guaranteed satisfaction that replaced the no longer possible life dreams of working hard for the future. The trend of people indulging in "a sliver of happiness" could be associated with the popularity of Japanese *iyashi* (literally meaning "soothing or healing mentally or physically") designs, which encourage satisfaction with both the cuteness of commodities and the status quo. The phrase of *xiao que xing* started to pop up in newspapers and transformed into a sociopolitical implication that reflected the anxiety and melancholy of young people around the 2010s.

The year that Taiwan Bar was founded signals a critical moment in Taiwan: sharing similar anxieties of the PRC depriving the political autonomy of local governments in Taiwan and Hong Kong in the 2010s, both the Sunflower Movement in Taiwan and the Umbrella Movement in Hong Kong were student-led movements against their local governments' cooperation with the PRC government in 2014. In March, the Taiwanese young generation took to the streets in protest, despite their characterization as a group of people indulging in "a sliver of happiness" and *iyashi* designs, who do not need to work hard for their future since they, although not rich and luxurious, are living well enough to enjoy a convenient lifestyle in Taiwan. The protest, known as the Sunflower Movement, was driven by a coalition of students and civic groups and opposed the KMT's "selling (out) Taiwan" to Mainland China. The KMT declared the CSSTA (Cross-Strait Service Trade Agreement) as a treaty favorable to the economy of Taiwan. Unwilling to damage the international credibility of Taiwan by withdrawing from the trade pact, the party forced the treaty's passage without a clause-by-clause review. Upon hearing this, the protesters accused the KMT of letting the PRC government hurt the already vulnerable economy in Taiwan and demanded that the CSSTA be reviewed "transparently." On March 18, the Taiwanese legislature was, for the first time in its history, occupied by citizens, mostly students. The movement reveals the weariness and lack of trust in the KMT as well as the DPP, tension between generations, and young adults' anxiety for a future of Taiwan that was threatened by the power of the PRC.

While it is no longer a Japanese colony, Taiwan is still immersed in Japanese culture. The influence is evident in both the transformation of the Japanese translation term "a sliver of happiness" into a Taiwanese sociopolitical context, as well as the existence of the Japanese media mix practice that has made it possible for Taiwan Bar to create its "ideal commodity" of animated IP characters. As Marc Steinberg beautifully illustrates the relationality that character consumption generates via media mixes in *Anime's Media Mix* (2012), the character is not just a consumed material but is an entity in-between production and consumption.[4] To maintain the construction of a capitalist society of mass consumption, the equilibrium of production and consumption is the key to success. Namely, to work around the contradiction between economic, political, social, and cultural arrangements in order to maintain this delicate equilibrium, anime characters as "ideal commodity" act as not simply a media-commodity but also a convergence of promotion, production, and consumption.

The concept of "ideal commodity" was introduced by the French Regulation School (FRS), which illustrates the models of development in reaction to the contemporary societies in nation-state, international, and global levels. Dominated by new media, the ideal commodity in the twenty-first century is redefined by Steinberg as "the character" in the Japanese media-mix model, ensuring consumers not only consume the character but produce the narratives of the character in multimedia forms.[5] Among FRS scholars, Robert Boyer believes that the current era is a diversity of national capitalism. In 2000, Boyer edited *Japanese Capitalism in Crisis* with Toshio Yamada, looking into the trajectory of Japanese society in the 1990s and its systemic capitalist crisis. Boyer argues that rather than a convergence into a global market, each nation-state has a model of development suitable for the local industrial structure, political system, and financial markets.[6] Using the case study of Taiwan Bar Studio to respond to Steinberg and Boyer, I argue that the multimedia commodity of the IP character creates a civic space for consumers to develop their imagined community.

In the case of the IP characters Taiwan Bar creates, they are both products and advertisements, as well as a connecting point of transmedial relations. Through the eye of the characters Taiwan Bar creates, audiences are encouraged to think about the meaning of Taiwan. The characters create relationality between media, consumption, and civic discourse. Taiwan Bar's production of animated episodes facilitate consumption of the IP characters who encourage a debate on Taiwan's national identity. Built upon the popularity of Japanese cultural practices such as local mascots (e.g., local mascot *Kumamon*) and anime (e.g., the character Kudō Shin'ichi from TV anime *Case Closed*), Taiwan Bar successfully engages in the cultural and national discourse among younger generations in Taiwan. The local consumption of this "ideal commodity" (the seemingly apolitical animated IP characters) involves a political awareness that makes Taiwan visible in the international arena with its colonial identity.

The term "IP (Model)" has been commonly used in Mandarin as a part of daily vocabulary since the 2010s, generally referring to merchandising character-related commodities (e.g., LINE stickers). Partially supported by the government, IP character merchandising has become a part of the local economy in Taiwan. Taiwan Bar's IP characters are modeled on rare species in Taiwan, including the Formosan black bear ("Beer"), the Formosan rockmonkey ("Mijo"), the Mikado pheasant ("Brandy"), the Formosan landlocked salmon ("Rosé"), and the leopard cat ("Shaoxing"), all of which are named after different kinds of alcohol standing for Taiwanese culture. Mijo and Shaoxing, for example, are two kinds of alcohol that Taiwanese love to use when cooking. The studio took their naming quite literally. In fact, there was a real bar in the studio.

There is no direct reference why Taiwan Bar decided to introduce drinking culture with the naming of the characters, especially when it promotes itself as an educational studio oriented to children and teenagers who are not legally allowed to drink. My (over-)interpretation of this choice is associated with Paul Barclay's analysis of indigenes being portrayed as alcoholic due to the history of "wet diplomacy": the diplomatic drinking banquets of Taiwanese indigenous tribes and earlier imperial Japan. The narrator of this animated series, Buchi, happens to be an Amis (one of the indigenous tribes). As Barclay argues in his book, *Outcasts of Empire,* it is possible that the studio tried to incorporate local identity by promoting indigenous identity.[7] Sharing this marginality, the rare species connotes an endangered Taiwanese national identity. The characters are designed in an *iyashi* style, which corresponds to the tastes of the current Taiwanese younger generation who relate to "a sliver of happiness," a concept that assures people the right to feel and catch every tiny bit of happiness in daily life without worrying about an unattainable or unstable future. The Chinese name of Beer, *hei pi,* sounds like the English word "happy," which coincidentally corresponds to the "sliver of happiness" atmosphere.

Figure 1. The IP characters Taiwan Bar creates. Courtesy of Taiwan Bar Studio.

The nuance of the term *iyashi* in Taiwan is also worth mentioning. In Taiwan, *iyashi* has little to do with the Japanese *iyashi-kei*, which tends to describe certain types of people, especially women, who can warm one's heart or calm one's mind in times of sadness, or certain types of literature, such as the novels of Yoshimoto Banana. The usage of *iyashi* in Taiwan is not limited to describe people and is often related to the cuteness that the character arouses. Derived from the *iyashi* boom around 1990s in Japan, *iyashi* in Taiwan ties to "sliver of happiness" consumerism via spiritual trips and cute goods. Hsin-I Sydney Yueh, the author of *Identity Politics and Popular Culture in Taiwan: A Sajiao Generation,* has conducted a micro-analysis of "cute" language in the Taiwanese media to examine layers of discourse about marginal, national, and local identity.[8] Similar to Yueh's observation, I suggest the cute and *iyashi* culture in Taiwan is a key to understanding how Taiwan struggles to gain its visibility with coloniality in the shadow of hegemonic China. The *iyashi* characters of Taiwan Bar, especially Beer (*hei pi*), delineate how coloniality is exploited in national discourses via mass media and consumerism.

The business model of using cute animated and mascot characters to represent government agencies, brands, and localities can be traced to the media-mix practice in Japan. The 2010 Kumamon, a character developed in Kumamoto prefecture in western Kyushu, became an internationally known ambassador of Japanese tourism. Considering the prosperous tourism developed between Japan and Taiwan, Kumamon was influential in Taiwan as well.

While I have no intention to prove the influence of Kumamon in Taiwan, it is not coincidental that the Formosan black bear had been chosen to be the central IP character in Taiwan Bar series. In fact, in 2013, a year before "Beer" was born in Taiwan Bar, the Tourism Bureau of the Ministry of Transportation and Communications in Taiwan also created the character "Oh! Bear" as the ambassador of Taiwanese tourism.[9] The name is a pun that mixes Taiwanese and Mandarin, which means black bear. What I want to emphasize here is that the media-mix world is transnational. The power of capitalism harnesses national and cultural identity to intra- and interstate business models. The business models based on existing animation consumption culture and high-velocity tourism help to form national and local identity both in Japan and Taiwan.

Discourses of Civic Media and Textbooks

Opening with an appeal for crowdfunding, Taiwan Bar studio stated clearly that it depends not on the support of government but on digital consumers who are potentially representing "mainstream public opinions" that the civic groups of the Sunflower Movement also appeal to. As an alternative venue for Taiwanese history, the episode of "Taiwan for Sale" is arguably from the perspective of the Japanese colonial government, rather than the standard textbook focusing on how the colonized Taiwanese adjust to the new regime. Due to economic and political suppression from the PRC government, Taiwanese tend to experience a nostalgia toward Japan and colonial Taiwan (1895-1945). The narrator states at the beginning of the short film, "Gotō Shinpei thought the Taiwanese nationality was money grubbing, death fearing, and face saving. As Taiwanese, we find such characterization a bit awkward yet spot on" (0:10), portraying a colonizer looking down on the colonized.[10] The short does not explain who Gotō Shinpei is, assuming students in Taiwan are familiar with him in a very different context. According to Taiwanese history textbooks, Gotō was the Japanese colonizer who respected Taiwanese customs and successfully pushed the modernization of Taiwan. Gotō Shinpei's name is mentioned in the second of the six volumes in the current high school textbook. The first two volumes of the textbook are on Taiwan's history. Instead of putting this narrative into the fifth or six volume, which covers world history, Gotō Shinpei is a part of Taiwan history for his contribution to modernizing Taiwan.

The textbook I refer to was created after the education reform led by Yuan-Tseh Lee, the former president of the Academia Sinica in Taiwan. The high school history textbooks are divided into three parts: Taiwan, China, and the rest of the world, each with two volumes. There is a repetition (or gap) for the first- and second-year history textbook: one stresses colonial history, while the other covers premodern ruling systems and the "enemies" each Chinese dynasty faced. The description of historical events in the fourth volume about Qing (and Taiwan) is often China-centered. Interestingly, in the first two volumes, the image of Taiwan is shaped as an immigrant society, with many colonizers, including Qing and Japan; however, there is no mentioning of "colonialism" (*zhimin*) for those periods. The absence of *zhimin* discourse in the textbook illustrates the controversy of the debate on defining colonialism among Taiwanese scholars.

Introducing Gotō Shinpei in the context of Taiwanese history in the textbooks, the government focuses more on how the Taiwanese resist the foreign regime and shifts quickly toward the modernization of Taiwan, giving credit to people who contribute to Taiwanese progress. For example, Zheng Chenggong, or Koxinga, the pirate leader of the Ming forces against the Manchu conquerors of China, is characterized as a "national hero" for modernizing and establishing Taiwan, whereas his "national hero" identity for the communists of Mainland China stems from his victory over Dutch specifically and Western imperialism generally. The two volumes of Taiwan history introduce different regimes and people who were dedicated to advancing Taiwan, while Taiwan Bar reveals the sentiment of these different powers and tries to provide more historical information behind those rulers' decisions. For instance, Taiwan Bar successfully tells history from a different angle and recharacterizes the historical figures in its first seven-and-half-minute animation to build up the logic and sentiment of "selling Taiwan." Framed from Japan's perspective, ruling Taiwan was considered to be worthless. The narrator points out the hygiene problem on the island by comparing Japanese deaths in the southern expansion of 1895 and to Japanese plague deaths in Taiwan. The narrator also shows the historical data of the unbalanced income and expenditure of the Japanese government at the time. The animation displays the reluctance of Japanese people to be sent to Taiwan, as if such an assignment was a form of exile. On the other hand, the narrator illustrates shirtless and shoeless Japanese rulers and points out the terrible situation of corruption, robbery, and undisciplined police to explain the anti-occupation sentiment the Taiwanese shared. Rather than giving credits to the colonizers for the modernization of Taiwan as the history textbook does, Taiwan Bar seems to open a debate on how to rearticulate the colonial history of Taiwan.[11]

The Taiwanese historian Huai-Chen Kan suggests that history textbooks are where nationality is constructed and represented. Kan argues that Taiwanese history textbooks are written in the context of preserving the greatness of traditional Chinese culture against the PRC government.[12] This context of reinforcing the superiority of Chinese history and culture in order to "save the nation" in the postwar period has been changed with the devastation of KMT being the sole party in Taiwan.[13] In the 1990s, Taiwan underwent a series of education reforms which ended the policy of the government as the monopoly publisher for school textbooks, known as "one-guide one-textbook." Instead, "one-guide multi-textbook" started to flourish, which opened the right for private companies to publish textbooks. According to Gan's observation, the history textbooks after 1990 put more emphasis on de-systemization and depoliticization, which reflected the uncertainty of Taiwan's international position and its struggling relationship with the PRC regime.[14] The biggest change in these new history textbooks was the high ratio of Taiwan's history, which, Gan argues, is a political issue for legitimizing the authority of the current regime.[15]

What Taiwan Bar tries to do in this series of animation is not in complete opposition to the grand narrative that the history textbooks construct. Rather, it provides an alternative narrative that promotes an understanding of the nuances of historical incidents to lead the discussion of how to define Taiwan in world history. It declares that the "Japanese government apparently ran a rational analysis as a colonizing nation but also wanted to show guts to western powers, . . . We [Taiwanese?] should avoid emotional judgments in order to get closer to the truth."[16] Who the "we" in this statement refers to is unclear, as it targets both domestic and international audiences.

The narrator's line, "Speaking of selling out Taiwan, it seems to be current events,"[17] resonates with the 2014 "current" issue of the KMT compromise with the PRC. Released soon after the Sunflower Movement, the episode encouraged a dialogue relating current political issues with historical incidents. The studio consciously "sells" Taiwan history in animation to the domestic audience to make visible the political situation of KMT "selling out Taiwan" to the PRC. By annotating the colonial history of Taiwan in animation, the episode tones down tensions between Taiwan and China to form a space discussing the power dynamics in East Asia with *iyashi* IP characters.

Animation and Global(?) Taiwan

Animation in Taiwan, once a media industry that made Taiwan famous in the international market in the 1980s, has no longer been competitive in the past few decades even though there are many experienced animators in Taiwan. In fact, the Taiwanese animation industry—led by Chinese Cartoon Production in the 1950s to '60s and Wang Film Productions (also known as Hong Guang Animation/Cuckoo's Nest Studio) in the 1980s—has earned international fame for cooperating with studios such as Tōei, Hanna-Barbera, Warner Bros., Disney TV, and DiC Entertainment in the US, Europe, and Asia. However, the industry declined rapidly in the 1990s. While there are several reasons, the main one, as pointed out by Taiwanese animator and former Cuckoo's Nest employee Shyh-Chang Chen, is that even though Taiwan does have some of the best animators in the world, it does not have its own brand since it never moved beyond its role as an OEM (Original Equipment Manufacturer), or a site of outsourced labor.[18] This environment limited Taiwanese animators to low-budget outsourced uncredited work.

Most of the people, even Taiwanese themselves, do not know that Taiwan was exporting animation. In choosing animation as *the* medium to "sell Taiwan," Taiwan Bar Studio rebuilds the image and association of Taiwan as both consumer *and* producer in the global animation market through recognition of its animation made in and about Taiwan on YouTube. Targeting both domestic and international audiences, the studio made Chinese, English, and Japanese subtitles for the series and published an English remake of the pilot episode. Sadly, as James Hevia suggests in *English Lessons,* to be taught, persuaded, and coerced by "guns and pens," the colonized peoples as agents are as active as the colonizers in the colonial processes.[19] The colonial process continues even after the end of colonialization. It is a hegemonic project that brings the conquered populations into relation with the colonizers and the coloniality changes their relationship terminally.

The choice for Taiwan Bar to make English and Japanese subtitles for its pilot episode suggests that there is an acquiescence of the power dynamics between the West and the East, as well as Japan and the rest of East Asia. Responding to the YouTube comments, Taiwan Bar even published a video of English speakers in Taiwan watching the English remake.[20] The video demonstrates the Taiwanese desire to be seen in the Euro-American world to earn respect and support from the West for their national sovereignty as a bulwark against political pressure from China.

The challenges of a media-mix environment are not only industrial, political, and social but also cultural and linguistic. In their book *(Multi)Media Translation: Concepts, practices, and research,* Yves Gambier and Henrik Gottlieb proposed to study translation and convergence between media by redefining the "text" as not only a string of sentences but an integration of images, sounds, and graphics.[21] Following this concept of "text," I turn to the analysis of the episode "Taiwan for Sale" through a close reading of the Mandarin version with subtitles, the English remake, and the video of the English speakers. Before going into subtitling and dubbing analysis, I want to make clear that, unlike English and Japanese speaking cultures, subtitling in Taiwan is not meant for translation. Rather, it is a routine practice. Almost everything is subtitled, even news reports. Besides Mandarin, the languages that do not have a writing system, such as Taiwanese and aboriginal languages, are also subtitled in Chinese characters. Rather than translation, the multilingual environment adds nuance to the subtitling; as a common practice, subtitling can be a paratext enriching the watching experience without destroying the visuals, akin to Markus Nornes's concept of "abusive subtitling."

Nornes points out in the Japanese cinema context that subtitling is an intrusion interrupting the viewer's eye flow and corrupting the aesthetics of the mise-en-scène. However, he defines "abusive subtitling" as a change in how the audience receives the mise-en-scène and perceives the process of filmmaking: with an experimental way of subtitling, "the 'unlucky' translator [and/or subtitler] who is absent from both popular and scholarly discourses" is able to be seen.[22] According to Nornes' observation, animation is suitable for abusive subtitling since the medium itself is transgressive and innovative.[23] Following Nornes' observation, I found several examples of abusive subtitling in the production of "Taiwan for Sale."

The episode "Taiwan for Sale" exemplifies abusive subtitling as paratext. Rather than corrupting the aesthetics of the mise-en-scène, Taiwan Bar adds affect to the written words through the insertion of ellipsis, swung dash, and other features common to texting. The Chinese subtitle perfectly matches with the voiceover, sound effect, and animation:

goto shinpei thought/the taiwanese nationality was (0:07–0:08)
後藤新平認為／台灣人的民族性就是
money grubbing, death fearing, and face saving/as taiwanese (0:10–0:13)
愛錢 怕死 愛面子[sound effect + graphics]／這句話此時此刻／身為台灣人
的我們聽起來 . . .

we find such characterization a bit awkward yet spot on (0:14–0:15)[24]
似乎有點害羞又還算中肯~

Unfortunately, the English subtitle is visually too long and fails to catch up with the speed of the voiceover. As Nornes suggests, "the film's utterances are segmented by time; natural breaks in speech are marked for the temporal borders of the subtitle."[25] He further introduces the technique of "spotting," which requires the translator to determine the length of each unit of translation down to the frame. The following example demonstrates another failed spotting in English subtitling, yet a successful abusive subtitling in Chinese. In Mandarin, the sentence is chopped into three segments with several characters in larger font size (as the boldface below) while the English subtitle was left fixed on the screen:

> nearly we would greet each other with bonjour bonjour like frenchman
> (0:23–0:25)[26]
> 只差那麼一點點／我們見面就要像**法果**／**扔**一樣**碰啾碰啾**地喊了

The word-for-word translation preserves the sentence structure by starting with "nearly," creating a grammatically weird but understandable sentence; however, the humor is lost in English subtitles. In Chinese, the last two characters of the second segment, *fà guǒ*, and the first character of the third segment, *rēng*, is translated into "Frenchman." The meaning is translated, but the play of the tone is lost: the narrator intentionally mimics a foreigner's tone of speaking *fà guó rén* (Frenchman) as a funny tone of *fà guó rēng*, creating the imagination of being colonized by the French. The untranslatability results from the flow of time, the determined linguistic difference, and the cultural imagination.

Supposing Taiwan could have been colonized by either France or Japan in the late nineteenth century, Taiwan Bar puts little effort into criticizing imperialism. Instead, it considers the colonial relationship as an opportunity for cultural exchange that shapes a multilingual environment. The studio imagines its domestic audience, regularly immersed in Japanese cultural input, as therefore able to understand some phrases in Japanese:

> seriously? (0:30)[27]
> 紅豆?! [with azuki-bean graphic]
> 紅~豆~~~?

The pronunciation of red bean in Chinese *"hóng dòu"* sounds like Japanese *hontō* (seriously?). The Japanese subtitle is surprisingly captioned with the "wrong" kanji: neither using the kanji of hontō nor *azuki* (where the first character is different), it copies the Chinese characters. Rather than adopting the YouTube machine-generated subtitle, the Japanese subtitle Taiwan Bar creates projects an imagined Japanese audience having a "mutual" understanding of Taiwanese culture and language. In the English remake, the play of the languages between Japanese and Chinese is erased. Instead, the narrator mocks himself by saying "spill the bean." Both English subtitling and dubbing are disappointing because they erase the dynamics between Japan and Taiwan. Ironically, the subtitling and dubbing parallels the cultural distance between the East Asian area and the Euro-American world.

The cultural distance reflected in the subtitling and dubbing echoes the studio's emphasis on the colonial identity of Taiwan. Though the syntax of Japanese is different from those of Mandarin and English, the Japanese subtitle keeps most expressions with similar word order as the Chinese; yet the English subtitle omits some expressions:

> japan could prove to all the mighty western powers/that they can run a
>   colony just fine (3:24–3:29)[28]
> 日本就可以向船堅炮利的／歐美列強證明 自己也擁有／治理殖民地的能力／
>   並以此拿到 脫亞入歐的門票
> 日本は欧米の列強達に自分たちも植民地経営ができるのだと証明し／脱亜入
>   欧のチケットを 手にすることが出来るだろう

In the remake, the dubbing narrator is given two more seconds to interpret the animation that the subtitling fails to capture:

> Japan could prove to the Western world that/it also has what it takes to
> colonize countries/and get the golden ticket to be one of the/cool kids
> (3:41–3:48)[29]

Different from the East Asian context, in which the concept of *"Datsu-A Ron"* (leaving Asia) is clearly transmitted, neither the English subtitling nor the dubbing translates the term *Datsu-A* literally. Rephrasing the term, the subtitle describes the West as "mighty powers" that Imperial Japan desires to join, while the dub "domesticates" Imperial Japan by comparing Japanese to the "cool kid who gets the golden ticket" to join the West.

Nornes argues that dubbing adaptation is "an extreme form of domestication."[30] But in the case of the remake, it is Taiwan Bar itself that made the episode into English. How "domestic" could it be for the non-English speaking Taiwan Bar to domesticate the English translation? We may see the English remake of Taiwan Bar in 2018 as a paratext or an abusive translation of the 2014 pilot episode "Taiwan for Sale." In the remake, there are some creative adaptations: the Japanese general Nogi Maresuke, who committed suicide on the day of the emperor's funeral, has a famous quote of how to rule Taiwan that was translated into an English proverb in the 2018 remake with the sound play of "death/*desu*."[31] The remake tries to preserve the multilingual pun with exoticization. However, whether viewers are convinced remains an open question (Figure 2). While the studio made efforts to conquer untranslatability by targeting English speakers to acquire visibility for Taiwan via its coloniality, the cultural distance is yet to be conquered.

Figure 2. The Euro-American viewers are confused by the appearance of Nogi Maresuke (left) and Kudō Shin'ichi (right). Courtesy of Taiwan Bar Studio.

In Taiwan, anime is well-received and children have grown up with *Case Closed* (1994–).[32] Confusing Kudō Shin'ichi, the protagonist of *Case Closed*, with the colonizer Goto Shinpei is understood by Taiwanese viewers as a satire deconstructing the "heroism" of historical figures in a way that helps Taiwanese to reimagine history outside of the history-textbook context. However, this is not the case for the Western audience. The comment from the viewer is, "I don't know, you just have a grownup version of Conan the detective? Foreigners don't know who he is."[33] Even if the studio had access to separate sound tracks and unlimited freedom to remake some parts of the animation, the "joke" and the power reversion fail to be communicated to the English speakers. Watching English speakers watching the remake, I question how Taiwan Bar sells Taiwan: is the studio drawing parallels between imperial Japan and Taiwan's eagerness to be seen as a "cool kid" by the West?

Coda

In the pilot episode "Taiwan for Sale," the term "*mai tai*" is translated into "selling out Taiwan," while in the English remake, it is translated into "BETRAYAL." The pun of selling (out) Taiwan clearly betrays Taiwanese national identity by selling out Taiwan. However, "*mai tai*" could generate a positive nuance in this context: promoting Taiwanese national identity. The timing of publishing "Taiwan For Sale" right after the Sunflower Movement encourages a dialogue on the current political issues and historical incidents. Instead of "selling out Taiwan" to a powerful regime, the studio has the self-awareness of "selling Taiwan" to Taiwanese by annotating the history of Taiwan with the animation. The issue of "*mai tai*" could thus refer to at least three layers: (1) a critical moment of the beginning of colonial Taiwan, which is not mentioned in history textbooks; (2) a usage that Taiwanese nowadays are familiar with; that is, the political implication of politicians who betray their national identity and surrender to powerful regimes, especially Mainland China; and (3) a "justified" way to "sell" Taiwan to the world; in other words, exactly what Taiwan Bar Studio is doing with the media mix practice.

Earning domestic support via digital social media channels, Taiwan Bar is an example of capturing and representing the current Taiwanese political situation via popular culture heavily influenced by Japan. With the fame of animated IP characters, the studio manages to cooperate with local enterprises by making advertisements for companies. Adapting the Japanese media-mix model with IP characters of Formosan rare animals, the studio successfully created its brand: Taiwan Bar. The animated YouTube shorts and advertisements for Taishin bank, the HSR (high speed railway) public transportation company, and other Taiwanese companies transform the *iyashi* characters into the envoys of "Made in Taiwan" cultural products. In early 2023, the studio started to sell online courses of this series targeting schoolteachers. The success of the episode, "Taiwan for Sale," reflects not only the rapid development of media convergence culture, but changing asymmetrical power dynamics in the East Asia region. The phenomenon entangles the complexity between the capitalist media-mix model, coloniality in Taiwan, and the (trans-)formation of national discourse.

Invited by Taipei Financial Center Corporation to design the animation for the New Year firework display, Taiwan Bar grabbed the chance to put the *iyashi* IP characters on the wall of the landmark skyscraper Taipei 101 as envoys of Taiwan greeting people around the world at the dawn of 2020. By further analyzing the ongoing projects of the studio, the targeted audience, and the fan reaction in the media mix world, I demonstrate how the pilot episode "Taiwan for Sale" tries hard to lead a decolonial turn by indulging in and encouraging a national discourse of coloniality with the animated short. Yet despite the shift of power dynamics in East Asia, Taiwan remains trapped in the hegemonic project forced to seek support for its sovereignty from the West and Japan.

Ai-Ting Chung is a PhD candidate in East Asian Literature and Linguistics at University of Oregon. She is interested in (trans-)formation of subjectivity and identity, especially in the contemporary society, in which people form new hybridized identities in virtual worlds. She has been a member of Society for Animation Studies since 2016. Learning Taiwan Bar Studio from YouTube, she presented the topic in *Society for Cinema and Media Studies*, and reshaped the ideas for the publication in *Mechademia*. Her current project "Decoding Anime: National Discourses and Identities in Japan and Taiwan" historicizes the transnational animation industry in Japan and its former colony Taiwan, and analyzes identity transformation in animation texts in the two countries from the late 1980s to the 2010s to question what is obscured by the global dominance of anime. As a Taiwanese Fulbright Scholar specializing in Japanese studies in the US, she is dedicated to cross-cultural and transmedial research.

Notes

1. Taiwan Bar, "Taiwan Bar EP0 Taiwan for Sale?" (2014), https://youtu.be/eHTV_Xdrkp8, accessed June 20, 2022.
2. Peng Zi Shan, "About Taiwan Bar," *Common Wealth Magazine*, 2014, https://www.cw.com.tw/article/5062426, accessed June 29, 2022.
3. Hauer Hsieh, "How Do I Create A New-media Company Which Is 'Entertaining' and 'Educational'?" (TEDxTaipei, 2015), https://youtu.be/2b8xdieRK4I, accessed June 9, 2022.
4. Marc Steinberg, *Anime's Media Mix: Franchising Toys and Characters in Japan* (Minneapolis: Minnesota University Press, 2012), 196–98.
5. Steinberg, *Anime's Media Mix*.
6. Robert Boyer and Toshio Yamada, eds., *Japanese Capitalism in Crisis: A Regulationist Interpretation* (London: Routledge, 2000), 1–17.
7. Paul D. Barclay, *Outcasts of the Empire: Japan's Rule on Taiwan's "Savage Border," 1874–1945* (Oakland: University of California Press, 2018), 44–48.

8. Hsin-I Sydney Yueh, *Identity Politics and Popular Culture in Taiwan: A Sajiao Generation* (Lanham, MD: Lexington Books, 2017).

9. Zhao Xin-Fu, "The Envoy of Taiwan's Tourism: Oh! Bear," https://www.mjib.gov.tw/FileUploads/eBooks/56089fdb1ae74777a1fec51b3e709ffe/Section_file/b264b7d3783b41c6967752c57c1d35a9.pdf, accessed June 10, 2022.

10. Zhao, "The Envoy of Taiwan's Tourism."

11. Zhao, "The Envoy of Taiwan's Tourism."

12. Kan Huai-Chen, "The Comparison between History Textbooks in Taiwan and Japan," *History Education* 14 (June 2009): 151–70.

13. Kan, "The Comparison between History Textbooks in Taiwan and Japan," 163.

14. Kan, "The Comparison between History Textbooks in Taiwan and Japan," 164.

15. Kan, "The Comparison between History Textbooks in Taiwan and Japan," 168.

16. "Taiwan Bar EP0 Taiwan for Sale?" (2014).

17. "Taiwan Bar EP0 Taiwan for Sale?" (2014).

18. Shyh-Chang Chen, "About Hong Guang," http://anibox-toon.blogspot.com/2011/06/blog-post_13.html, accessed June 10, 2022.

19. James Hevia, *English Lessons: The Pedagogy of Imperialism in Nineteenth-Century China* (Durham: Duke UP, 2003), 4, 18.

20. Taiwan Bar, "Taiwan for Sale? History of Taiwan: EP0" (2018), https://youtu.be/6i5XNwfyHG8, accessed June 20, 2022.

21. Yves Gambier and Henrik Gottlieb, *(Multi) Media Translation: Concepts, Practices, and Research* (Amsterdam: John Benjamins B.V., 2001), x–xii.

22. Markus Nornes, *Cinema Babel: Translating Global Cinema* (Minneapolis: University of Minnesota Press, 2007), 158.

23. Nornes, *Cinema Babel,* 187.

24. "Taiwan Bar EP0 Taiwan for Sale?" (2014).

25. Nornes, *Cinema Babel,* 159.

26. "Taiwan Bar EP0 Taiwan for Sale?" (2014).

27. The order of the subtitles: English, Chinese, Japanese; "Taiwan Bar EP0 Taiwan for Sale?" (2014).

28. The order of the subtitles: English, Chinese, Japanese; "Taiwan Bar EP0 Taiwan for Sale?" (2014).

29. "Taiwan for Sale? History of Taiwan: EP0" (2018).

30. Nornes, *Cinema Babel,* 193.

31. "Taiwan for Sale? History of Taiwan: EP0" (2018), 1:15.

32. Aoyama Gōshō, *Meitantei Konan (Case Closed),* 101 vols. (Tokyo: Shogakukan, 1994–).

33. Taiwan Bar, "Foreigners Watching History of Taiwan / Crowdfunding Project" (2018), 0:48, https://youtu.be/liJAoeM8VG8, accessed June 20, 2022.

Unfinished *Go* Game

Mediatized Memory and the Transnational Travels of Hikaru no Go *in China*

MUYANG ZHUANG

It is no longer surprising news that a Japanese manga or anime is adapted into an audiovisual work in countries outside Japan, especially in East Asia. The case of *Hana yori dango* (1992–2004, Boys over flowers) reflects how manga can be adapted into well-received, transmedial forms in the region, while TV animation series, such as *Pokémon,* have constituted the transgenerational collective memory of many local audiences. Since the normalization of the Sino-Japanese relationship in 1972, frequent cultural communications can be easily tracked between the two neighboring countries. From TV adaptations of *Astro Boy* (*Tetsuwan Atom,* 1980–81) and *Doraemon* (1979–) in the early stage of China's reform era to *Detective Conan* (TV series, 1996–) and more recently Makoto Shinkai's blockbuster *Your Name* (*Kimi no na wa,* 2016) in the twenty-first century, manga and anime have been motivating the booming ACG (Animation, Comics, and Games) culture in China, which in essence promotes manga and anime's transnational media mix. Japanese anime in China, too, has been adapted into various media forms, circulated on changing media platforms, and thereby resulting in discussions of fandom culture as well as IP (intellectual property) issues.[1] These variations bring manga and anime's media mix in China, together with its relationship with today's media platforms, into a complicated phenomenon that requires further investigation.

Reception of Japanese anime and manga in China has a lot to do with the interplays between media and memory. For example, the TV anime of *Doraemon* is tied to childhood memories due to its popularity among Chinese audiences born in the 1980s and early 1990s. As television culture prospered, Japanese animation on Chinese screens reveals not only the foundations of Chinese reception of Japanese pop culture but also the deep entanglements between media and cultural memory. However, as Andrew Hoskins points out, the way memory is shaped in the digital era is rather different from the way collective narratives are made, as the rupture between media and memory is more diffused.[2] In the Chinese context, the rise of the internet does offer a certain space where state-owned media could not (at least have not) fully control, resulting in some alternatives of memory-making apart from what is decided by official, collective spaces. As told by Andreas Hepp, mediatization "seeks to capture the nature of the interrelationship between historical changes in media communication and other transformational processes."[3] Hepp further points out that mediatization "deals with the process in which these diverse types of media communication are established in varying contextual fields and the degree to which these fields are saturated with such types."[4] Citing Hoskins's and Hepp's arguments, Alexander Zahlten extends these discussions to the field of anime studies, proposing "mediatized memory," a combination of mediatization and Hoskins's theory of connective memory, acts as "a departure from the model of collective memory," which witnesses the interplays among East Asian countries driven by Japanese anime such as *Doraemon* and *Your Name*.[5] What the mediatization of anime (and manga) culture in East Asia offers is not only a possible approach to reviewing the media mix in its traditional sense but also a renewed path to the mediation mix and more: not only materialized convergence but also the mixture of media, memory, and the sociohistorical changes of the countries.

Regarding the thriving media culture of online streaming and viewing in China, the way people watch anime has changed. With a connected but not necessarily simultaneous mode of viewing, the shaping of Chinese audiences' cultural memory of Japanese pop culture has a great deal to do with the mediatization of sociocultural changes in China, from the golden age of television and cinema to the flourishing of online streaming platforms. Moreover, from the perspectives of anime and manga's media mix and platform studies, it is also indispensable to study their transnational travels in China by analyzing their transmedial variations or localized accommodations, such as the trends of live-action adaptations of comics or animated works on online streaming platforms. Such adapted audiovisual products may allow us to inspect the intertwined relationship between anime and mediatized memory by mapping the transnational, transmedial, and transgenerational issues. In other words, we can investigate cases like *Doraemon*, an existing cultural icon among Chinese audience, and the phenomenal success of *Your Name* in China through locating the mediatized memory of Chinese viewers shaped through their distribution and projection. Examining the mediatization of cultural memory amid the evolution of Chinese media ecology could also lead to new understandings of anime's media mix in China by capturing transnational and transmedial circuits.

Furthering Zahlten's discussion of the connective turn toward transnational anime culture in East Asia, I examine the mediatized memory of Chinese viewers by studying the adaptation of the Japanese TV animation *Hikaru no Go* (*Hikaru's Go,* 2001–2003) in China. Adapted from Hotta Yumi and Obata Takeshi's popular manga published in *Shonen Jump* magazine of the same title (1999–2003), the anime first aired on TV Tokyo. It was subsequently distributed in Mainland China, Taiwan, and Hong Kong and had achieved great success. Initially boycotted by some local fans of the original anime, the Chinese adaptation of *Hikaru no Go,* or in its Chinese pinyin title *Qihun* (2020), is a live-action drama produced and distributed by the media platform iQiyi two decades after the broadcast of the Japanese TV animation. Surprisingly, *Qihun* has not only satisfied anime fans upon its streaming but also gradually attracted audiences without any knowledge about the original anime and manga through local networks. *Qihun* was broadcast online and on TV in Japan in 2022, offering a particular perspective to analyze the adaptation of *Hikaru no Go* by locating its transnational circuits. Although the adaptation was supposed to capitalize on the shared memory evoked by the original anime and manga works, it became a controversial topic among fans in different states due to the mode of connective viewing online. The Chinese adaptation, of which the plot is based on China in the late twentieth and early twenty-first century, caused controversies among viewers in Mainland China, Hong Kong, and Taiwan over the issue of the handover of Hong Kong in 1997. In one of the episodes that aired shortly after the 2019 social unrest in Hong Kong and still haunted the memories of people of different political stances, the little male protagonist declares that Hong Kong was always part of China when introducing the handover ceremony. The live-action version implies in-depth connections among historical changes, mediatized memory, and media mix.

Referring to scholarly discussions on anime culture, mediatized memory, and media mix, I will first examine the suspension and endurance of the cultural memory of Chinese audiences, which generated from the popularity of *Hikaru no Go* in China during the last two decades.[6] Inspired by Thomas Lamarre's analysis of regional TV, I explain how the regional intimacy and transmedial adaptation of *Hikaru no Go* engage with the mediatized memory and political climate in contemporary China.[7] Contextualizing the success of *Qihun* through local networks, I argue that the cultural memory originally motivated by the anime-manga culture can be reactivated and extended by transnational fandom, regional intimacy, and productive distribution and mediatization.

Through studying such mediatized memories of Chinese audiences, we can also approach the sociohistorical changes of Chinese media ecology. By doing so, this article seeks to shed new light on East Asian pop culture studies and media mix research from transcultural and transmedial perspectives.

Hikaru no Go's Media Mix in China

Hikaru no Go tells the story of a teenager, Shindō Hikaru, who meets the ghost of the ancient *go* (or *igo*) master Fujiwara Sai and learns how to play *go* from him. In the manga, Hikaru becomes a talented professional *go* player after numerous games against his lifetime rival Akira Tatsuya and many other adolescent *go* players. Japanese professional *go* player Umezawa Yukari also participated in the publication of the manga series. The TV series was later awarded the Tezuka Osamu Cultural Prize in 2003. In addition, it spurred a frenzy of *go* in Japan.[8] Like other successful manga, *Hikaru no Go* was then adapted into other media forms, including TV animation, video games, and fiction.

Both the manga and the seventy-five-episode TV animation of *Hikaru no Go* entered Japan's neighboring countries in East Asia in the early twenty-first century. In the Chinese-language world, *Hikaru no Go* has been welcomed by local readers and viewers since 2001. In Hong Kong, the TVB purchased the anime series and broadcast it in 2003. Due to the intimate relationship in terms of media circuits between China and Hong Kong in the early twenty-first century, after the Cantonese dubbed version was released, Chinese audiences, at least those living in Guangdong province next to Hong Kong, were also able to watch the anime through a shared cable TV signal. Additionally, comic books of *Hikaru no Go* were translated into Chinese in the early twenty-first century and had attracted many fans who were interested in *go* but unable to watch the TV animation at that time.

Without violent, sexually explicit, or teenage romance content, *Hikaru no Go* passed censorship in other East Asian states rather easily despite its depiction of the competitive relationship between Japan, China, and South Korea via *go*. Cherished by the three East Asian countries, *go* was highly recognized as a symbolic traditional culture. Also known as *weiqi/weichi* in Chinese and *baduk* in Korean, the game bears a history of more than two thousand years. Originating in ancient China, *go* was listed as one of the four basic skills for Chinese traditional literati. It spread to Korea and Japan in the fifth to seventh centuries CE and has been a well-received game among local players.[9] Today, *go* still serves as a significant mediated vehicle that connects the three East Asian countries in the Confucianist cultural sphere. In the Japanese TV animation, Umezawa showed up frequently after the conclusion of episodes to teach basic knowledge about the *go* game in the short educational series called *Umezawa no GOGO Igo* (Umezawa's GOGO Go). In Taiwan, the Chinese Television System Inc. (CTS) also invited professional *go* players to teach teenage audiences about *go* game after the daily screening of the anime on TV.

Likewise, the popularity of *Hikaru no Go* in Mainland China introduced readers and audiences to the fantastic world of *go* game. Yu Ping, a professional Chinese *go* player, wrote a nostalgic article remembering his days in the Chinese *Go* Academy and his experience of reading the manga *Hikaru no Go*. Yu says that the manga invited readers not only to a world of sportive competition but also to a philosophical space that could inspire many teenagers in China. His article also suggests how China and Japan communicated with each other through *go* and the making of the anime.[10] Yu suggests that the first transnational travel of *Hikaru no Go* in China signified the official cultural communication between the two countries and that manga-anime culture successfully entered mainstream culture. Considering *go*'s educational role in East Asian societies and the subproducts created due to *Hikaru no Go*'s success in the area, it is also arguable that *Hikaru no Go*'s transnational reception expanded the mode of media convergence by reaching out to mainstream and educational forms. As such, the transnational travel of *Hikaru no Go* has shown its potential to be involved in the cultural and historical (ex)changes in the early twenty-first century.

Like most Japanese manga and anime, *Hikaru no Go* also attracted numerous local Chinese fans who gathered via different media platforms, of which the most prosperous ones were and still are online communities such as Baidu Tieba and Douban. On Baidu Tieba, one of the largest online communities in China that features the slogan "born for your interest," the *Hikaru no Go* forum has nearly ninety thousand followers as of this writing. More than two million posts addressing various issues about the manga, anime, and comparisons between the animated series and the live-action adaptation can be viewed on the website.[11] On Douban, which allows registered users to record and leave a comment on films and other audiovisual works, the content page of the anime *Hikaru no Go* shows that there are more than sixty thousand users who have watched the animation and given the anime an overall score of 9.1 (out of 10).[12] Additional proof of its mainstream reception can be found in the subcultural media mix triggered by *Hikaru no Go*, which created a boom during the first decade of the twenty-first century. The internet enriched the manga and anime's transnational media mix, localizing various transmedial practices of the original IP and reshaping viewers' memory of certain works.

As told by Sandra Annett, anime fan communities can be "possible due to the movement of cartoon content through different media platforms introduced across the world throughout the twentieth and early twenty-first centuries, from film to television to the Internet."[13] Such communities could come into life because of the "productive friction" occurring during transnational and transmedial processing.[14] However, during anime and manga's border-crossing travels, offline commercial circulation and online sharing culture may be divided into two directions. Unlike offline products, such as books, magazines, or discs, which have to be circulated by strictly obeying copyright regulations, online sharing materials are usually pirated, especially in early twenty-first-century China. Despite the overlap between online and offline reproduction and the content-driven similarities between mainstream endorsement and subcultural communication, Hikaru no Go, by the essence of "copying culture" in animation and cartoon industries, witnessed the growth of a group of fans who were fascinated with dōjinshi, or amateur creations.[15] The transfigured "CP" (short for "couple") illustrations and fiction featuring LGBT or "Boy's Love" (BL) topics remained the most welcomed online yet underground adaptations of Hikaru no Go. Today, many of these creations can still be obtained via Baidu Tieba's Hikaru no Go forum in a relatively stealthy way of private sharing so that fans can bypass strict online censorship. Such an underground craze for Hikaru no Go on the Chinese internet enabled the enduring yet self-restricted existence of the manga and anime fandom.

In 2003, both the manga and anime series of Hikaru no Go came to an end. No more new plots were added to the officially created go world. Particularly, the experience of watching the TV series of Hikaru no Go was sealed as the shared memory of a group of audiences in China, whereas the localized underground adaptations, especially dōjinshi creations, continued animating the series. Thanks to the internet and the convenient essence of copying culture, fan memories of Hikaru no Go were restored in the archive-like online communities. However, with a number of new anime and manga hitting the Chinese market either officially or underground, and with old-fashioned animated series celebrated by spectators nationwide (like Doraemon returning to Chinese screens), Hikaru no Go and many other once-popular anime (and manga) alike disappeared from mainstream vision. Only a few fans would remember and review the manga or anime works of the series. Together with those underground "co-products," the memory of *Hikaru no Go* was not totally erased but at least suspended and preserved in the internet archives. What reactivated this cultural memory of the original manga and anime is the live-action adaptation two decades later, which first bore witness to debates between the original fans and supporters of the online drama, and then presented the mediatization of cultural memory of local Chinese audiences.

Regional Circuits: From *Hikaru no Go* to *Qihun*

In 1982, when the PRC and Japan celebrated the tenth anniversary of the normalization of Sino-Japanese diplomatic relations, a film called *The Go Masters* was co-produced by the two countries to value their companionship. Also known as *An Unfinished Go Game* in Chinese (*Yipan meiyou xiawan de qi*) and Japanese (*Mikan no taikyoku*), the film delineates the friendship between a Chinese *go* master and his Japanese rival before, during, and after the Second Sino-Japanese War (1931–45). The story of this film may remind people of the famous Chinese-born Japanese *go* master, Go Seigen (Wu Qingyuan, 1914–2014), who is widely recognized as the greatest *go* player in the twentieth century and whose life and career was strongly influenced by wartime and postwar Sino-Japanese relations. In fact, the history of *go* in China and Japan showcases the mediatization of its historical changes. Be it game-like or warlike, national or transnational, *go* stands for this shared value and history, as well as the rivalry between the two neighboring countries. In 2020, another unfinished *go* game in the fantastic manga-anime world was brought back to Chinese screens. However, when the news came that *Hikaru no Go* was going to be adapted into a live-action online drama with localized Chinese characters and plots, negative comments on the project subsequently emerged.

Adapting Japanese anime, manga, or TV drama into localized versions, live-action drama in particular, has been trendy in China in recent decades, but only a few of these adapted works succeeded commercially or were well received and recognized by local audiences. When fans of *Hikaru no Go* heard about the adaptation project launched by iQiyi in 2020, many were doubtful that the online streaming company could adapt it successfully. When the costumed photos of localized characters were released online, the anime and manga enthusiasts flooded internet forums stating that the Chinese adaptation of *Qihun* was doomed to become a failure.[16] The most controversial point was how one of the main characters, Chu Ying, the Chinese version of Sai,

Figure 1. Screenshot of Chu Ying, whose costume design is directly borrowed from his Japanese anime counterpart Sai. *Qihun*, dir. Liu Chang (2020).

wore the same outfit as the anime character but appeared bizarre in the live-action version (Figure 1). This appearance annoyed many fans of the charming anime character and caused other viewers to question whether the costume of a Japanese Heian (794–1192) *go* player could be put on an ancient Chinese *go* master from the Northern and Southern dynasties (420–589).[17] The result was that at the beginning of its online streaming, *Qihun* was rated only 7.2 points out of 10 by users on Douban, while criticism continued saying that the adapted show would be disastrous.

Surprisingly, *Qihun* gradually earned more and more positive feedback from Chinese audiences. Though they disliked the costume of Chu Ying, many fans found that the adapted version represented the original plot very faithfully. Meanwhile, most of the characters were well depicted with various attractive personalities and matched their prototypes as well as being vividly realist figures. One of the producers, Zhu Zhenhua, admits in an interview that their Japanese collaborators insisted on a faithful adapted version; even the melody of the theme song remained the same. Zhu argued that *Qihun's* production team downplayed the campus romantic relationships common to other adapted works in favor of paying more attention to the growth of each character, especially the young *go* players.[18] In this way, the Chinese online drama presents a more realist story, according to director Liu Chang.[19] Liu is known for directing romcoms, but this preference changed when he worked on *Qihun*. He believes that there exists a kind of everyday experience shared by a great number of Chinese audiences, which does not have to be limited to romantic relationships but is more about the memory of growing up in the country.[20]

Of course, what enabled a truthful adaptation is the shared culture of *go* game in China and Japan. Chinese producers did not have to transform the topic into a more localized one. Given the intimacy between China and Japan in terms of cherishing *go* culture, such a cultural sphere in East Asia promotes the mediatization of media regionalism as shown in the case of *Hikaru no Go*. Moreover, the production team spent tons of effort in representing what they think is a realistic representation of China's social development at the turn of the millennium: from the once-popular Personal Handy-phone System, to the thriving internet café, to the anxiety and pressure caused by the examination culture, especially the College Entrance Examination. The adaptation not only reset the Japanese story on the Chinese stage but also navigated Chinese viewers back to the country's urban life two decades ago. Investigating *Hana yori dango*'s transnational, transmedial, and transgenerational adaptations, Thomas Lamarre aptly points out the "media regionalism" generated in "Digital Asia."[21] Lamarre then indicates that the "production of distribution holds together transmedial and transnational processes, and also at what it produces—a feeling of something coming into common, of a region in common."[22] In its reactivation on the Chinese network, the original series of *Hikaru no Go* was adapted in the method of productive distribution. It created a temporal-spatial gap between the manga and anime fans and a new group of audiences influenced by online streaming culture, as well as between admirers of Japanese pop culture and a new generation of viewers who pay less attention to its original cultural background. It expanded the pattern of media mix initiated by the manga and anime series and piloted the convergence into a connective space based on local networks. As such, the suspended memories of *Hikaru no Go* and the anime-manga culture in early twenty-first-century China revived amid what Andrew Hoskins calls the "connective turn."[23]

When *Qihun*'s scores on Douban gradually lifted from 7.2 to 8.6 out of 10, most of the previous controversies were quelled. The show was then considered a splendid Chinese online drama with vivid representation of urban life in China at the turn of the twentieth-first century rather than a clumsy imitation of the Japan-based animated fantasy. Intrigued by the live-action drama, there emerged similar media-mix subproducts and discussions that portrayed the BL or CP features implied in the show. The parallel online fandoms of the original series and the live-action adaptation appeared due to the popularity of the latter, which in turn reactivated anime and manga fans' suspended memory of *Hikaru no Go*. Unlike the cultural memory in the collective form, this time memories of the IP tended to be more unruly due to the intervention of online streaming culture. As Alexander Zahlten points out, local viewers' memory evoked by pop culture, as shown in the transnational reception of anime in other East Asian countries during and after the connective turn, is "increasingly mediatized."[24] The topic of *go* game, the transnational circulation, the underground or subcultural media mix, the transmedial production and distribution, and the newly shaped impression and fandom of the online drama finally intertwined with each other amid the mediatized processing and the memory of *Hikaru no Go* in China. In addition, the case of *Qihun* suggests that the mediatization of connective memory could lead to a more complicated and particularly politicized end, where the mode of media mix will also be reshaped into the mixture of mediations.

Mediatized *Qihun:* Connected Viewing and Connective Memory

Hikaru no Go's transnational travels in China shows that such transcultural communication "is not vertical and linear, taking place solely as transactions between the 'top level' of national governments, industries, and major film studios and the 'bottom level' of radical creators and viewers"; rather, it's "lateral and rhizomatic, as various media platforms allow for the circulation or blockage of visual texts and human desires."[25] In the age of connected viewing, the unexpected success of *Qihun* showcases the mediatization of audiovisual works that run beyond the process of productive distribution. Jennifer Holt and Kevin Sanson contend that connected viewing is the "broader ecosystem in which digital distribution is rendered possible and new forms of user engagement take shape,"[26] Here I argue that such "possible and new forms" could refresh the shaping of the media mix driven by the mediatized memory of local audiences evoked by anime and manga's transnational reception and adaptation, as shown in the case of *Qihun*.

The mediatized memory of the original anime and manga series, which was multilayered, was generated from and reanimated by *Qihun*. On the one hand, the live-action adaptation depicts a nostalgic world of China at its high-speed development at the turn of millennials. Setting the temporal gap between today's China during the pandemic and the reminiscent images of China in the early twenty-first century, *Qihun* invited Chinese viewers of different generations to situate themselves in the world-making on screen. Thus, it brought back the imaginative and resonant lifestyle shared by everyday people of different ages. In other words, *Qihun* encouraged part of its audiences to remember the good old days. Meanwhile, by representing China's urban life two decades ago, the live-action show also resembles the viewers' memory and thus, is intertwined with not only the return but also the reshaping of such memory, stimulating the increasing process of mediatization of cultural memory. One thing that needs special attention is that the period between the popularity of the original manga and anime of *Hikaru no Go* and the making of this live-action adaptation witnessed the most rapid development of the economy of modern China: undergoing the handover of Hong Kong in 1997 and Macau in 1999, joining the WTO in 2001, holding the Beijing Olympics in 2008, and growing into the second largest economy in the world. The return of *Hikaru no Go* on Chinese screens then reminded local audiences of the differences between the decades, either through nostalgic representation, i.e., scenes that usually appear in memories, or through the revoked memory of how people watched *Hikaru no Go* two decades ago. In this way, *Qihun* also kept encouraging viewers to think about what changes the society had undergone over the twenty years of high-speed economic development.

Simultaneously, *Qihun* recalled the fashion of anime-manga culture, especially the manner of *dōjinshi* creations, by reactivating anime-manga fans' memory of the work, while the emerging fandom is being shaped by new forms of online viewing and sharing culture. Relatedly, the ACG culture is no longer considered underground, as leading media platforms such as iQiyi, Tencent, and Bilibili are all trying their utmost to attract the younger generation by creating more influential animated works. Where Japanese anime fans in China may have needed to illegally download episodes to watch *Hikaru no Go* in the past, they can now easily access all episodes via official online streaming. The mode of sharing has also changed and thus the shaping of mediated memory has also been modified and mediatized. Viewers, be they true fans of *Hikaru no Go* or audiences who accidentally click into one of the episodes, can have immediate exchange of feeling when watching the drama by typing on bullet screens or joining tagged discussions on social media (e.g., the influential Sina Weibo). As such, these affects triggered by *Qihun* intertwine with each other and implicate the sociohistorical changes of the country as well as the frame of mind of various groups of audiences.

On the other hand, the interconnection between mediatization and memory was deepened when another controversy over *Qihun* was fermented during its release in Hong Kong and Taiwan. At the beginning of the show, the kid Shi Guang, the Chinese version of the protagonist Hikaru, talked to

Chu Ying in a nationalist tone when they were watching the Hong Kong hand-over ceremony in 1997, which was actually broadcast nationwide on TV. Shi Guang claims in an episode that every Chinese is happy because of the return of Hong Kong to China.[27] Analyzing the political use of Japanese pop culture in Hong Kong, Chun-wah Chin notices that there are also other scenes highlighting the handover in 1997 and asserts that the reappearance of Hong Kong's handover in *Qihun* is a strategy of political propaganda on purpose.[28] Many viewers in Hong Kong and Taiwan also reckoned that these scenes addressing the Hong Kong issue were inserted deliberately, especially after the social movements in Hong Kong in 2019, though iQiyi's representative denied this in an interview.[29] Emily Ying Dai, the online streaming company's vice president, argues that representing Hong Kong's return is one of the strategic ways to adapt the original *Hikaru no Go* from its Japanese context to a more reasonable atmosphere of China at the turn of twenty-first century, because the handover ceremony was a memorable event to many Chinese people.[30]

I do not mean to make any judgments here, but as a matter of fact, Dai's response is true to a certain extent, whether the scenes on Hong Kong were deliberately added or not. The representation of the handover ceremony, together with the controversies, provides us with a perspective to inspect the deepened mediatization of connected viewing and connective memory in analyzing *Qihun*. The handover ceremony was broadcast on TV and was shaped as part of the collective, nationalist memory due to the freshness created by live events on TV screens in late 1990s and early 2000s China. However, the memory reproduced in the online drama in 2020 has to do with sociohistorical changes in both the mainland and Hong Kong, as well as the changing media culture. By transforming a fantastic anime staged in Japan into an online live-action drama in China with a nostalgic vibe, the collective memory of watching the handover ceremony in 1997 on TV was reactivated and consumed through the process of connected viewing. In fact, either the whole show of Qihun or that episode addressing the 1997 handover has been scattered by the viewers' various attitudes and emotions, and by forms through which the controversial scene spread. The scene was simplified as a short video that can be easily accessed and "finished" on social media, or as screenshot(s) that can be transformed into memes. It was then distributed in productive forms and triggered a new wave of politicized debates. This led to various feedback that drove the original collective memory of mainland Chinese people into a kaleidoscopic and connective form, in which people (more than audiences) from the mainland and Hong Kong (and Taiwan) inscribed their own understandings and political stances in their newly shaped and mediatized memory. It was no longer shared by a certain group of people in a certain state. Instead, it encouraged controversies over certain reproduced historical events in the form of consumption mediatized within the reshaping of the connective viewing experience. Whether championed by most of the audience in the PRC or booed by fans in Hong Kong and Taiwan, *Qihun* had become the vehicle carrying numerous newly shaped memories, which in turn had become part of the mediated mix.

Ironically, the anime series of *Hikaru no Go* first reached the Chinese world on Hong Kong and Taiwan TV screens. The remaking of *Hikaru no Go* was supposed to reactivate the shared memory of fans across the three states, as it did in other countries, whereas it bore witness to an explosion of political debates that sparked into the connective form of memory of other historical events. It is also in this way that *Qihun* suggests the possibility of a new mode of media mix. First, it showcases how anime's identity could be further mixed by localized and transmedial adaptation. Stevie Suan has already indicated that anime in the form of animation "is no longer isolated to Japan; there is potential for it to be released from national boundaries and allowed to roam."[31] Indeed, the case of *Hikaru no Go*'s transnational travels in China inspires us to shift our understanding of anime's (and manga's) media mix from its original, national, and media roots to the soils that fertilized its transitional and transmedial adaptation and process of mediatization. The actual representation in *Qihun* that resulted in its success opened the gates of media mix to many other social factors, including highly politicized ones. In this way, anime is no more just Japanese animation but a flexible media ready to be localized.

Second, if transnational communication and underground circulation of manga and anime are used to spur the prosperity of ACG culture and the cultural memory of a certain group of people in China, given the highly mixed internet and media culture today, such types of memory can be guided and (re-)shaped into a new form that would be situated in contemporary media and memory ecologies. Moreover, the adaptation of *Hikaru no Go* suggests how the collective memory about the Hong Kong handover ceremony was reactivated in the age of connected viewing and was, therefore, involved in the process of mediatization. The memory of the original anime and manga was no more specific; the (re)making of memories, be they about life two decades ago or political events happening now, was connectively generated from the original versions, the adaptations, the comparison between them, and the politicized debates. In turn, the media mix of *Hikaru no Go* in China, points to the mediatized memory crouching behind entertainment, transmedia, and politics.

Conclusion

In May 2022, *Qihun* was broadcast on Japanese screens and revived the Japanese manga and anime fans' suspended passion. This time, the regional circuit of the IP was about not only the return of the adaptation of an anime and manga in Japan but the arrival of a Chinese online drama with characteristics that could be shared and championed by Japanese contemporary audiences, such as the culture of *go*, the pressure and anxiety caused by the educational system, and the potentiality of BL *dōjinshi* creation implied in *Qihun* and the fandom. However, unlike the overseas strategy adopted by Netflix, which sees the rapid expansion of the platform in foreign countries, iQiyi is still a company rooted in the local Chinese market. Hence, they did not invest too much to ensure the success of *Qihun* in Japan. Compared with addressing audiences overseas, iQiyi seems to prefer maintaining its status in Mainland China and thus, streaming their products on Japanese screens may just be a way of branding.

Worth noting in *Qihun*'s reception are the comments, both positive and negative, by Chinese audiences that are relatively different from those of the original anime fans. As mentioned above, the case of *Qihun* reveals its mixed identity toward anime, as it is branded as a Chinese online drama instead of an adaptation of the anime and manga. Although the comparison between the anime, manga, and the live-action drama is inevitable, more attention is called to the adaptation itself as it had already created a different and relatively realistic world from the fantastic animated one. In other words, *Qihun* is not *Hikaru no Go* anymore, and what it brings to the Japanese audience is an exotic feeling of China.

What may also appear during *Qihun*'s transnational travel in Japan is the extension of mediatized memory produced through enriched patterns of media mix created by the connected viewing. The controversy over Hong Kong's handover ceremony may continue, while the Chinese adaptation's productive distribution in the Japanese media ecology can also entail other discussions. Still, as an audiovisual work initially produced for Chinese audiences, *Qihun* was welcomed by local viewers and highly praised by the official media.[32] All these comments are shaped into part of the media-mixed product in the title of *Qihun*. The mediatized *Qihun* implicates a complicated cultural and media phenomenon that inspires us to rethink the transnational media mix of Japanese pop culture in China from the perspective of the interplays between mediatization and the shaping of cultural memory.

....

Muyang Zhuang is Assistant Professor in College of Arts and Media at Tongji University. He received his PhD from the Hong Kong University of Science and Technology and obtained a BA in literature and an MA in art theory from Peking University. His research centers on East Asian cinema, media, and visual culture, specializing in animation and cartoons. He is now working on a book project on the historical and medial interplays between Chinese cartoons (*manhua*) and animated films. His publications can be found in *Twentieth-Century China*, Cultural and Social History, Animation: An Interdisciplinary Journal, and *Encyclopedia of Animation Studies Volume 1: Histories and Geographies* (Bloomsbury Reference, forthcoming in 2024).

....

Notes

1. Anthony Fung, Boris Pun, and Yoshitaka Mori, "Reading Border-Crossing Japanese Comics/Anime in China: Cultural Consumption, Fandom, and Imagination," *Global Media and China*, 4, no. 1 (2019): 125–37.

2. Andrew Hoskins, "Media, Memory, Metaphor: Remembering and the Connective Turn," *Parallax* 17, no. 4 (2011): 19–31.

3. Andreas Hepp, *Cultures of Mediatization*, trans. Keith Tribe (Cambridge: Polity Press, 2013), 38.

4. Hepp, *Cultures of Mediatization*, 68.

5. Alexander Zahlten, "*Doraemon* and *Your Name* in China: The Complicated Business of Mediatized Memory in East Asia," *Scree*, 60, no. 2 (Summer 2019): 311–21.

6. Marc Steinberg, *Anime's Media Mix: Franchising Toys and Characters in Japan* (Minneapolis: University of Minnesota Press, 2012), 135–69. Marc Steinberg, "Managing the Media Mix: Industrial Reflexivity in the Anime System," in *Transmedia Storytelling in East Asia: The Age of Digital Media*, ed. Dal Yong Jin (London: Routledge, 2020), 159–82.

7. Thomas Lamarre, "Regional TV: Affective Media Geographies," *Asiascape: Digital Asia* 2 (2015): 93–126.

8. Asahi Shimbun, "Tezuka Osamu Bunkashō," https://www.asahi.com/corporate/award/tezuka/, accessed 4 June 2022.

9. Marc L. Moskowitz, "*Weiqi* Legends, Then and Now: Cultural Paradigms in the Game of Go," in *Asian Popular Culture: New, Hybrid, and Alternate Media*, ed. John A. Lent and Lorna Fitzsimmons (Lanham, MD: Lexington Books), 3–8.

10. Yu, "*Qihun he women de gushi*," 105–6.

11. "*Qihun ba*," https://tieba.baidu.com/f?kw=%C6%E5%BB%EA&fr=ala0&tpl=5&dyTabStr=MCw2LDIsMyw0LDEsNSw4LDcsOQ%3D%3D, accessed 4 June 2022.

12. "*Qihun/Hikaru no Go*," https://movie.douban.com/subject/1474243/, accessed 4 June 2022.

13. Sandra Annett, *Anime Fan Communities: Transcultural Flows and Frictions* (New York: Palgrave Macmillan, 2014), 1.

14. Annett, *Anime Fan Communities*, 5.

15. Laikwan Pang, *Creativity and Its Discontents: China's Creative Industries and Intellectual Property Rights Offenses* (Durham: Duke University Press, 2012), 171–82.

16. Sina Sports, "Hu Xianxu zhuyan zhenrenju *Qihun* kaibo: Zuowei banxiang layanjing?," https://sports.sina.com.cn/go/2020-10-27/doc-iiznezxr8301555.shtml, accessed 4 June 2022.

17. Sina Sports, "Hu Xianxu zhuyan zhenrenju *Qihun* kaibo."

18. Vlinkage, "Zhuanfang zhipianren Zhu Zhenhua: Douban 8 fen koubei zhizuo *Qihun*," https://mp.weixin.qq.com/s/q-1GjqeUD4ScXlga2_vBdQ, accessed 4 June 2022.

19. iQiyi hangye sudi, "*Qihun* daoyan Liu Chang: Wo zhenzheng shanchang de shi xianshizhuyi ticai," https://mp.weixin.qq.com/s/29AlDVhKDqMBh6a8GJEDrg, accessed 4 June 2022.

20. iQiyi hangye sudi. "*Qihun* daoyan Liu Chang."

21. Lamarre, "Regional TV," 93–94.

22. Lamarre, "Regional TV," 94.

23. Hoskins, "Media, Memory, Metaphor," 20.

24. Zahlten, "*Doraemon* and *Your Name* in China," 311.

25. Annett, *Anime Fan Communities*, 5.

26. Jennifer Holt and Kevin Sanson, "Introduction: Mapping Connections," in *Connected Viewing: Selling, Streaming, and Sharing Media in the Digital Era*, ed. Jennifer Holt and Kevin Sanson (New York: Routledge, 2014), 1.

27. *Qihun*, dir. Liu Chang, (2020); available on iQiyi: https://www.youtube.com/watch?v=ZfblSbvhdSk&list=PLlCrV9TCfzMaIDYlwykvUEnji83s_Jm8G.

28. Chun-wah Chin, "The Political Uses of Japanese Pop Culture in Hong Kong," in *Japan and Asia: Business, Political and Cultural Interactions*, ed. Mariko Tanigaki (Singapore: Springer, 2022), 262–73.

29. HK01, "Qihun neidi zhenrenban diyiji jiang huigui: Yiju duibai bei wangmin zhiyi shi zhengzhi xuanchuan," https://www.hk01.com, accessed 4 June 2022.

30. Chin, "The Political Uses of Japanese Pop Culture in Hong Kong," 271.

31. Stevie Suan, *Anime's Identity: Performativity and Form beyond Japan* (Minneapolis: University of Minnesota Press, 2021), 6.

32. Wang Kaihao, "Series Makes a Master Move with Go Drama Adapted from Comics," *China Daily*, https://www.chinadaily.com.cn/a/202012/02/WS5fc6f240a31024ad0ba9946c.html, accessed 4 June 2022.

Anime's Knowledge Cultures
Geek, Otaku, Zhai
Jinying Li

"[This is] one of the most compelling recent interventions into anime studies and global digital media studies. A must-read book that is as informative as it is brilliant."
—**Marc Steinberg**, author of *The Platform Economy: How Japan Transformed the Consumer Internet*

$30.00 paperback | 372 pages

Godzilla and Godzilla Raids Again
Shigeru Kayama
Translated and with an afterword by Jeffrey Angles

"With an informative afterword by Angles, [this book] finally allows English readers to better understand the important context behind the monster." —*The Japan Times*

$19.95 paperback | 248 pages

Asians on Demand
Mediating Race in Video Art and Activism
Feng-Mei Heberer

"Rich with acerbic critique . . . an essential resource." —**Steven Chung**, author of *Split Screen Korea*

$25.00 paperback | 194 pages

The Flesh of Animation
Bodily Sensations in Film and Digital Media
Sandra Annett

"A timely and important intervention into the burgeoning conversation about embodiment in animation and digital media." —**Deborah Levitt**, author of *The Animatic Apparatus*

$29.00 paperback | 284 pages

The New Real
Media and Mimesis in Japan from Stereographs to Emoji
Jonathan E. Abel

"Reimagines Japanese media genealogies to vastly expand our sense of Japan and its media cultures." —**Akira Mizuta Lippit**, author of *Cinema without Reflection*

$30.00 paperback | 344 pages